MAPPING THE ATARI

Ian Chadwick
Introduction by Bill Wilkinson

Published by **COMPUTE! Books**,
A Division of Small System Services, Inc.,
Greensboro, North Carolina,
In Conjunction With Irata Press, Ltd.

A
Small System
Services, Inc.
Publication

The authors wish to thank Cheryl Belkin of McCarthy and McCarthy and David Langdon of Irwin Electronics, Canadian Distributors for Atari Products, for their assistance.

Other than as an independent publisher of quality products regarding the Atari personal computer systems, Small System Services, Inc., is in no way affiliated with Atari, Inc.

We do not accept any responsibility for any damage done to the reader's programs through use or misuse of the information presented here. Readers are advised to read the warning in the introduction with regard to saving critical programs and removing important disks or cassettes before attempting to use this manual.

Printed and published in the United States of America by **COMPUTE! Books**, A Division of Small System Services, Inc. Robert C. Lock, President and Publisher

ISBN 0-942386-09-4

10 9 8 7 6 5 4 3 2 1

AUTHOR'S PREFACE

What exactly is a memory map? It is a guide to the memory locations in your computer. A memory location is one of 65536 storage places called bytes in which a number is stored. Each of these bytes holds a number for programs, data, color, sound, system operation, or is empty (i.e., has a zero in it), waiting for you to fill it with your own program.

Each byte is composed of eight bits, each of which can be either a one (on) or a zero (off). The alterable area of memory you use for your programs is called the Random Access Memory (RAM), while the area used by the Atari to run things is called the Read Only Memory (ROM). Although some of the memory locations in the special Atari chips were designed to be written to like the RAM, the rest of the ROM, including the Operating System ROM, cannot be altered by you since it contains routines such as the floating point mathematics package and the input/output routines.

I hope that the reader is familiar enough with his or her Atari to understand some of these rudimentary uses of a memory map. It is not the scope of this manual to fully explain how to use PEEK and POKE statements; refer to your BASIC manual. Briefly, however, PEEK allows you to look at the value stored in any one memory location. If you want that value to be printed to the screen, you must preface the PEEK statement with a PRINT statement such as:

PRINT PEEK (708)

If you haven't changed your color registers, this will return the number 40 to your screen. All bytes in the Atari can hold a number between zero and 255. POKE allows you to place a value into a byte, such as:

POKE 755,4

By doing this you will have turned your text upside down! You can return it to normal by:

POKE 755,2

Similarly, POKE 710,80 will turn your screen dark purple! As with PEEK, POKE can only involve numbers between zero and 255. You will not be able to POKE into most of the ROM locations since the numbers in many of them are "hard-wired," "burned" into the chip, and cannot be changed in this manner.

So how does the Atari (or other eight-bit microcomputers, for that matter) store a number larger than 255? By breaking it down into two parts; the Most Significant Byte (MSB), which is the number divided by 256 and rounded down to the nearest whole number, and the Least Significant Byte (LSB), which is the original number minus the MSB. The Atari knows to multiply the MSB by 256 and add the LSB to get the number. For example, the number 45290 is stored as two parts: 234

(LSB) and 176 (MSB). 176 times 256 equals 45056, plus 234 equals 45290.

LEAST-MOST STORAGE

The Atari uses the convention of storing addresses in the LSB/MSB manner in memory (i.e., the smaller part is in the first memory location). For example, locations 88 and 89 store the lowest address of the screen memory. Let's say the numbers found there are 22 and 56, respectively. To get the decimal address, you take the MSB (stored in 89) and multiply it by 256, then you add it to the LSB at 88. In our case that's 56 * 256 equals 14336, plus 22 equals 14358. This is the address of the upper left corner of the screen. A simple way to do this in BASIC is:

BYTE = PEEK (88) + PEEK (89) * 256

The reverse (to break up a decimal location into MSB and LSB) is done by:

MSB = INT (BYTE/256):LSB = BYTE − MSB * 256

This process is easier for assembly language programmers who use hexadecimal numbers, since the right two digits are always the LSB and the two left of them are the MSB. For example:

$D016 (hexadecimal for 53270) equals 16 (LSB) and D0 (MSB)

$16 equals 22 in decimal, and $D0 equals 208 decimal. Multiply the MSB by 256 and add 22 and you get 53270. Throughout the map portion of this book I have provided both decimal and hexadecimal numbers together for ease of reference. In 8K BASIC, you can use decimal numbers only with POKE, and PEEK will return only decimal values to you.

Hexadecimal is a base 16 used instead of the normal base ten system because it is more suited to the eight-bit structure of the computer. So, when we say 2175 in decimal, what we really mean is:

10000	1000	100	10	1
0	2	1	7	5

In hex, the same number is $87F. That breaks down to:

4096	256	16	1
0	8	7	F

Rather than multiply each next step up by ten, we multiply by 16. Okay, but where do we get "F" from? Well, if base ten has the numbers zero to nine, base 16 will have to have some letters added to the end to make up for the extra numbers:

Decimal	0	1	2	3	4	5	6	7	8	9	10	11	12	13	14	15
Hex	0	1	2	3	4	5	6	7	8	9	A	B	C	D	E	F

So $F equals 15 in decimal. Now here's how it all relates to binary math and bits:

Each byte can be broken up into two parts (nybbles), like this:

0000 0000

If each nybble is considered a separate number, in decimal, the value of each would range from zero to 15, or zero to $F. Aha! So if all the bits in each group are on (one, or set), then you have:

1111	1111	Binary
15	15	Decimal
F	F	Hex

You join the two hex numbers together and you get $F (255 in decimal), the largest number a byte can hold. So you can see how we translate bytes from binary to hex, by translating each nybble. For example:

1001	1101	Binary
9	13	Decimal
9	D	Hex

$9D equals nine times 16 plus 13, or 157 in decimal.

0100	0110	Binary
4	6	Decimal
4	6	Hex

$46 equals four times 16 plus six, or 70 in decimal.

1111	1010	Binary
15	10	Decimal
F	A	Hex

$FA equals 15 times 16 plus ten, or 250 in decimal.

Obviously, it is easier to do this with a translation program or a calculator!

Since I will often be discussing setting bits and explaining a small amount of bit architecture, you should be aware of the simple procedures by which you can turn on and off specific bits in any location (that is, how to manipulate one of the eight individual bits within a byte). Each byte is a collection of eight bits: numbers are represented by turning on the particular bits that add up to the number stored in that byte. Bits can be either zero (0 equals off) or one (1 equals on, or SET). The bits are numbered zero to seven and represent the following decimal numbers:

Bit	7	6	5	4	3	2	1	0
Value	128	64	32	16	8	4	2	1

The relationship between the bits and the powers of two should be obvious. Adding up all the numbers (all the bits are set) gives us 255. So each byte can hold a number between zero (no bits are set) and 255 (all bits are set).

Sometimes, instead of zero, no bits set is intended to mean 256. That will be noted in the relevant locations. So how do you set a bit? Simple: POKE it with the appropriate number. For example, to set Bit 5, POKE the location with 32. To set Bits 7, 5 and 4, add up their values, 128 + 32 + 16, and POKE the location with the total: 176.

Sometimes you need to set a bit without changing other bits already set, so you:

POKE number, PEEK (number) + decimal value for the bit to be set. (i.e., POKE 50418, PEEK (50418) + 32)

To turn off a bit, instead of adding the value you would subtract it with POKE number, PEEK (number), minus the decimal value for the bit to be turned off. Binary math is simple and easy to learn; if you don't understand it now, you should do further reading on machine language before attempting any serious use of this guide.

AND, OR, And EOR

It is useful for the reader to know how to perform Boolean logic on bits. There are three functions used in assembly code for bit manipulation in this manner: AND, OR and EOR (exclusive OR). Each requires you to use two numbers, the one being acted upon and the one used to perform the function. Here is a brief explanation of how these logical functions work:

AND is usually used as a mask — to zero out unwanted bits. You compare two binary numbers using AND; if both bits in the same location are one, then the result is one. If either bit is zero, then the result is zero. For example:

```
        51 = 00110011
AND     15 = 00001111
Result     = 00000011 = 3
```

OR is frequently used to force setting of a bit. If either bit in the original or the mask is one, then the result is one. For example:

```
        65 = 01000001
OR     128 = 10000000
Result     = 11000001 = 193
```

In this case, 65 is the ATASCII "A". By ORing it with 128, we get 193, the ATASCII inverse "A".

EOR "flips" bits in the original if the mask has a one in the same location. For example:

```
          193 = 11000001
EOR       128 = 10000000
Result        = 01000001 = 65
```

In this case, we have returned the inverse "A" to the normal ATASCII value. An EOR with 255 (all ones) will produce the complement of the number:

```
          171 = 10101011
EOR       255 = 11111111
Result        = 01010100 = 84
```

In brief:

Original:	Mask:	AND:	OR:	EOR:
0	0	0	0	0
0	1	0	1	1
1	0	0	1	1
1	1	1	1	0

Atari BASIC supports AND, OR and NOT; NOT is the logical complement where NOT1 equals zero and NOT0 equals one. If the expression is true, you get a zero; if NOT true, a one is returned — for example, NOT ((3 + 4) > = 6) results in zero. See **COMPUTE!**, May 1981 for a machine language routine to allow you to perform Boolean bit logic using a USR call from BASIC.

In general, I have attempted to avoid using 6502 assembly language mnemonics, but *have* included them where I felt their use described the action to be taken better than a lengthy explanation. Most common are JMP (jump to location), JSR (jump to subroutine), RTS (return from subroutine), and RTI (return from interrupt). Readers should be minimally familiar with machine language in order to understand any machine language subroutines used here.

I also suggest that if the reader doesn't already have one, he or she obtain a program to translate hex to decimal and decimal to hex (possibly even one with binary translations as well). The ROM cartridge from Eastern House Software, *Monkey Wrench*, is useful for this purpose. Perhaps the easiest to use is the TI Programmer calculator from Texas Instruments.

The examples in this book were all written using Atari 8K BASIC. They are intended to demonstrate the use or the effect of a particular memory location. They are not intended as the best examples of BASIC programming; they were written for simplicity, not sophistication.

As a final note, any question or doubt as to either a particular location or explanation has been noted. It can't hurt to play around yourself, POKEing in the memory to see what other effects you can discover. If you find something I didn't, good! Please write and let me know.

You can't hurt the machine by POKEing about in memory, although you may crash any program in memory, so SAVE your program first. Usually you can salvage it by pushing RESET, but you may have to turn off the machine and reboot on occasion. You can learn a lot about your machine by simply playing around with it.

ABOUT LANGUAGES

The majority of the information here concerns language-independent locations and can be used regardless of the language you use for your programming. When the location is language-dependent, such as the BASIC or DOS areas, I have noted it in the proper section. You may exert the same control over your Atari in FORTH, Pascal, LISP, or whatever language you chose. You will obviously have to change the commands PEEK and POKE to the proper commands of your language.

BASIC is a good language to start with: you can use it to learn programming, to explore your computer, to experiment with, and to have fun with. However, when you are ready to go on, you will have to learn a more efficient, faster language if you really want to make the best use of your Atari. Many people choose 6502 machine language because of its speed.

If you want to stay with a high-level language, I suggest you learn FORTH. It has some of the speed of machine language code with the ease of "higher level language" programming.

Computer languages, whichever you use, are quite exact in their meaning, especially compared to English. Consider that in English, a *fat* chance and a *slim* chance both mean the same thing. Yet POKE, PUT, and PUSH have very different meanings in computerese.

TEXT KEY
Example: 912-927 390-39F IOCB5

The main memory map shows you the decimal and then the hexadecimal location, the label (assigned by Atari and used by OS, DOS or DUP routines), and then comments and description. The label has no real function; it is merely a mnemonic convenience. Readers are referred to Stan Kelly-Bootle's delightful book, *The Devil's DP Dictionary* (McGraw-Hill Ryerson, 1981), for a full definition of the word "label". The following abbreviations are also noted in the comments:

(R)   Read
(W)   Write

Sometimes the functions are different in a particular location, so each is noted.

(D:)   Disk Drive
(E:)   Screen Editor
(S:)   Display
(K:)   Keyboard
(P:)   Printer
(C:)   Cassette
(R:)   RS-232 interface. (Don't confuse this with (R) for Read.) The
        context should be obvious.

(number) e.g. (708) Shadow Register. This is a RAM register which
corresponds to a ROM register in one of the special Atari chips such as
GTIA or POKEY. The shadow location is the address you use to PEEK
and POKE values. These shadow locations are polled by the hardware
addresses 30 times a second at every stage two VBLANK interval, and
the values used are transferred to the hardware locations for use. In
order to effect any "permanent" change to the hardware location, you
have to use the shadow register in BASIC (of course, every change is
negated when you turn the machine off!). Only machine language is
fast enough to use the hardware addresses directly.

For example, location 54273 is for character control. It polls location
755 to see if the screen characters are to be normal, inverse, or upside-
down. To change the characters, you POKE location 755 — the shadow
— not 54273. If you POKE 54273, you will get the desired effect — for
1/60 of a second! As mentioned above, you *can* use the hardware
addresses directly in machine language, but not in BASIC. It's just too
slow.

Sometimes, where most appropriate, a hexadecimal number will be
displayed and the decimal number put in parentheses. The context
should be obvious concerning which is a shadow or a decimal number.

(* letter) refers to a source in the case of a conflicting location
        or explanation. See the source below.

($number) refers to a hexadecimal (also called hex) number
        (i.e.: $D40E). I also refer to "pages" in memory. Pages are
        sections of 256 bytes ($100) of memory which end with 00 (i.e.:
        $E200, $C000, $600). Four pages ($400) equals 1024 bytes or 1K
        (kilobyte) of memory.

GLOSSARY
ANTIC, CTIA AND GTIA, PIA, POKEY: Special Atari
        chips controlling the 400/800's graphics, color and screen
        resolution, controller jacks and sound, respectively. Located in
        ROM, locations 53248 to 54783. ANTIC also processes the Non-
        Maskable Interrupts and POKEY processes the Interrupt Requests.
        These chips, along with the 6502 microprocessor which runs the
        rest of the Atari, are housed inside your computer, protected by

AUTHOR'S PREFACE

the metal shielding underneath the plastic cover.

BIT, BYTE: A bit is the smallest size division of memory in your computer. It is so small that it can hold only one value in it: off (zero) or on (one). Eight bits together form a byte; this is the size of the memory locations discussed in this book. You will sometimes hear programmers talk about a half-byte called a "nybble."

CIO: Central Input/Output routines located in ROM. Controls Input/Output Control Block operations. Briefly, CIO handles the data input and output through the device driver(s) (also known as device handlers), then passes control to those drivers. It's a single interface with which to access all peripherals in a device-independent manner (i.e., uniform handling of data with no regard to the device being accessed). As an example: writing data to a disk file is treated in an identical manner as writing data to the screen; commas insert blanks between elements and both semi-colons and commas suppress the End-Of-Line character (EOL).

DCB: Device Control Block, used by Serial Input/Output.

DL: Display List. This is a set of instructions which tell the ANTIC chip where to find the screen display data and how that data is to be placed on the TV screen.

DLI: Display List Interrupt. A DLI causes the display to stop processing to temporarily run a user-written routine.

DOS: Disk Operating System. The software loaded from disk file DOS.SYS that controls all disk I/O. The latest edition of DOS is called DOS 2.0S (S for single density).

DUP: Disk Utilities Package. The software loaded from disk file DUP.SYS that handles the DOS menu functions such as Copy.

FMS (or sometimes **DFMS**): File Management System portion of DOS; a dedicated device driver that controls all I/O operations for device "D:".

FP: Floating Point mathematical package in ROM.

I/O: Input/Output.

IOCB: Input/Output Control Block. Area of RAM (locations 832 to 959) used by CIO to define operations to devices such as the disk drive (D:), printer (P:), screen display (S:), keyboard (K:) and screen editor (E:). ZIOCB is the page zero IOCB.

IRQ: Interrupt Request used for serial port communication, peripheral devices, timing and keyboard input. IRQ's are processed by the POKEY chip.

NMI: Non-Maskable Interrupt; used for video display and RESET. NMIs are processed by the ANTIC chip.

OS: Operating System. The resident system that runs the Atari. The OS resides in the 10K front cartridge slot under the hood in your Atari 800. It's not visible in the 400 without taking the cover apart (not recommended). The OS is the same for both the 400 and 800. There are two versions of the OS currently in circulation: the older "A" ROMs and the newer "B" ROMs, released around January 1982. The new OS is almost identical to the old OS except that it corrects a few bugs and changes some addresses. Not all of your old software will run with the new OS. The differences between the two are better explained in Appendix Four.

Although people often refer to the entire ROM area as the OS, this is not correct. The OS ROM is that portion of memory which holds the floating point package, the Atari character set, the device handlers, and both CIO and SIO. The actual operating system itself is the portion of the OS ROM which handles the I/O.

PMG, PM Graphics: Player/missile graphics. Players and missiles are special moveable, user-defined, colored screen objects. They are often used for games, animation, or special cursors. PM graphics are unique in that you can establish the manner (priority) in which they interact with the rest of the screen display and each other.

RAM: Random Access Memory. All memory below the OS area (0 to 49151) which is used for storage, programs, buffers, cartridges, DOS, IOCB, shadow registers, and registers for the special Atari chips. Random Access means you can get to and from these locations at random, not that they store information randomly!

ROM: Read Only Memory. That part of high memory (locations 49152 to 65535) in which the special hardware chips and the OS reside. ROM is also used to describe cartridge memory such as the 8K BASIC ROM, which cannot be user-altered (the cartridge ROM supersedes the RAM). You cannot alter most of the ROM, although some of the locations in the special Atari chips may be temporarily set to a new value.

With both RAM and ROM, we refer to areas with lesser values as being in "low" memory and locations with larger values as being in "high" memory.

SIO: Serial Input/Output routines located in ROM. Controls serial operations including the 850 interface (R:) and cassette recorder (C:). Briefly, SIO controls the Atari peripherals as per the request placed in its Device Control Block (DCB) by the proper device driver. It is also accessed by FMS for data transfer.

VBI: VBLANK interrupt. A VBI is an interrupt that occurs during the VBLANK interval, causing the computer to jump to a user-specified location to process a short user-written routine during the VBLANK process.

VBLANK: Vertical Blank. The interval between the time the TV electron beam turns off after reaching the bottom right corner of the screen and returns to the top left corner and turns back on again. This small time period may be used by machine language programmers for short routines without interrupting the display by writing a VBI (above). There are two VBLANK stages. Stage one is performed every VBLANK cycle (1/60 second). Stage two is performed either every 1/30 second or every 1/60 second when it doesn't interrupt time-critical code being executed. See the end of the memory map for the processes executed in each stage.

SOURCES

Letters in brackets are used in this guide to identify the source.

(*M) *Master Memory Map* Ver. 2, Santa Cruz Educational Software, 1981. A memory guide by the same people who brought us the TRICKY TUTORIAL series. The latter are both tutorials and applications utilities. The map does contain some annoying errata.

(*Y) *Your Atari Computer,* by Lon Poole with Martin McNiff & Steven Cook, Osborne/McGraw-Hill, 1982. The best guide to date on general use of the Atari. Very highly recommended.

(*C) *COMPUTE!'s First Book of Atari,* by the Editors of **COMPUTE!** Magazine, Small System Services Inc., 1981. A good collection of early articles that appeared in the magazine.

At the time of this writing, *COMPUTE!'s Second Book of Atari* had just been released. It is therefore not used as a reference source here, but it is a must for serious programmers. It contains a wealth of information on an enormous range of topics, including advanced graphics, forced-read modes, page flipping, Atari BASIC and many valuable utilities. It should be a staple in most Atari owners' libraries.

(*I) *Inside Atari DOS,* compiled by Bill Wilkinson, published by **COMPUTE! Books**, Small System Services, Inc., 1982. An explanation and copyrighted source code for the FMS portion of DOS 2.0.

Atari BASIC: Learning by Using, by Thomas Rowley, Hofhacker Press, 1981. A lot of information packed into a surprisingly good little book.

The following publications are all from Atari, Inc. I recommend them to all truly interested in understanding their Atari computers:

(*D): *De Re Atari:* an arcane, but indispensable reference to the Atari's operations and come of its most impressive aspects, by Chris

Crawford et al. Serialized in BYTE magazine, late 1981 to mid 1982. Earlier editions have some errata, so make sure you obtain the latest edition.

(*O) *Operating System User's Manual* and

(*H) *Hardware Manual.* The famous "technical manuals" pair. Indispensable for serious users, albeit heavy going and not generally very professional in their presentation of material.

(*8) *850 Interface Module Operator's Manual.* The 850 manual gives many examples in BASIC of how to use the RS232 serial interface ports for both printer control and telecommunications. A very good terminal program called Jonesterm, in BASIC with machine language subroutines, is in the public domain and is available on many electronic bulletin board systems, including CompuServe. Modem users will find many useful programs available in CompuServe.

(*L) *Operating Systems Listing* and

(*U) *Disk Utilities Listings* are the commented, copyrighted source code listings for the OS and the DUP.SYS portion of DOS.

(*B) *Atari BASIC Reference Manual.*

(*S) *Disk Operating System II Reference Manual.*

(*A) *Atari Microsoft BASIC Instruction Manual.* Microsoft BASIC makes excellent use of PEEKs and POKEs to accomplish many tasks. It also has many powerful commands not available in the 8K BASIC.

MAGAZINES

ANTIC Magazine had an extensive memory map, written by James Capparell, which continued over a number of issues. When it was used as a source, I labelled these references with (AM). It has a few minor errata in it.

I found a number of other magazine articles useful, particularly those in **COMPUTE!** and *Creative Computing.* I also found *Softside, BYTE, ANALOG* and *Micro* magazines to be useful in the preparation of this book. These are all referred to throughout the book by month or issue.

We owe a vote of thanks to the folks at Atari who published the technical manuals and the source listings of the operating system and the DOS. We owe another vote of thanks to Bill Wilkinson, of Optimized Systems Software Inc., who created the DUP portion of DOS and decided to publish the source code in his *Inside Atari DOS.* No other computer manufacturer has, to my knowledge, ever provided users with such in-depth material or the details of its own operating systems. Without it, none of this would have been possible: a lot of the information here was gleaned from those sources.

This book is arranged in four sections: a numerical listing of the main

AUTHOR'S PREFACE

Atari memory locations, their labels and their use; a general map diagram to show how the memory is broken down; an appendix of utility material with charts and tables, and an index/cross-reference guide.

There is an awful lot of information contained here; tedious as it might appear, I suggest that you read this manual through at least once. Some of the information which is not clear in one area may be elaborated on and made clearer in another area. Wherever another location is referred to in one description, you should turn to the reference and read it after you have read through the first location. You should also refer to the locations used in any sample program. The more familiar you are with the memory, the more you will get out of your Atari. When you read the description in any memory location, make sure you refer to either the shadow or the hardware register mentioned, for more information.

CAVEAT EMPTOR

This map is meant to complement, not to replace, your other source books. For full details and explanation of the material in this book, please refer to the sources listed above. This is particularly important for information regarding FMS, DOS, and DUP. The information contained here was found accurate for an Atari purchased in early 1982. I cannot vouchsafe for later modifications to either the OS or DOS nor for any typographical errors that might have entered into the text to make any information less than accurate.

It is the intention of both the author and the publisher to keep this map up to date with every upgrade Atari makes to its computers. We have already begun this by cataloging the differences between the old and new OS ROMs in the appendix and throughout the book. While every attempt has been made to verify this information, we cannot guarantee it nor take responsibility for any damage done by your use of this information. PEEKing and POKEing will not harm your system, although you may destroy any program residing in memory. Caution should be exercised when using the IOCB areas so that you first experiment with non-valuable information and disks that have no indispensable material which might accidentally get erased.

My thanks to everyone who encouraged and supported me in this project; especially Michael Reichmann, my co-publisher, who was as enthusiastic about it as I was. There are too many people whose interest helped keep this alive to thank properly, but I'd like to express special gratitude to Hilary Hannigan, Debra Phillips, David Humphreys, editor of *InfoAge Magazine*, Valerie Reid, Stan and Joyce Jantos, Dawn Kalebaba, and Tom Blood for their support. Many thanks as well to Debra Goody, who helped me with many of my writing projects in the past. Finally, a special thanks to Susan Nolte for "being there."

Ian Chadwick
Toronto, 1982
CompuServe 70001,1002

ATARI is a registered trademark of Atari, Inc.

POWERUP AND RESET

COLD STARTS

On powerup (when you turn on the computer) the Atari OS performs a number of functions, some of which are noted as defaults in the memory locations to follow. Among these functions are:

Determine the highest RAM address and clear all RAM to zeroes (except locations zero to 15; $0 to $F).

Erase and format the device table.

S:, E:, K:, P:, C: handlers, SIO, CIO and interrupt processor are all initialized.

Set the screen to GRAPHICS mode zero, 24 lines by 40 columns; set screen margins.

Initialize the cartridge(s) if present; test for the B (right), then for the A (left) cartridge.

Check the cartridge slots for disk boot instructions and, if they are present, boot disk.

Transfer control to the cartridge or booted program.

Initialize the RAM interrupt vectors at 512 to 548 ($200 to $224).

Store zero in the following hardware registers: 53248 to 53503, 53760 to 54527 ($D000 - $D0FF, $D200 - $D4FF).

The START key flag is tested and, if set (the START key is held down), CKEY (74; $4A) requests a cassette boot.

HATABS (794; $31A) is initialized to point to the ROM-resident device handlers.

IOCB zero is OPENed to device E:.

Coldstart (powerup) essentially wipes the computer clean and should only be used for such. It's rather drastic.

WARM STARTS

When the RESET key is pushed, the OS performs some of the same functions as in powerup as well as some unique functions, including:

Set the warmstart flag (location 8) to true (255; $FF).

Clear the OS portion of RAM from locations 16 to 127 ($10 - $7F) and

512 to 1023 ($200 - $3FF).

Reset all RAM interrupt vectors.

Reformat the device handler table (HATABS); added vectors are lost.

Re-initialize the cartridge(s).

Return to GRAPHICS mode zero.

Transfer control to the cartridge or booted program.

Restore the default values in RAM.

Note that a RESET does not wipe RAM, but leaves it intact. Usually your program and variables will be secure when you press RESET. This is considerably less drastic than powerup as above.

There are two vectors for initialization so that these processes may be user initiated: 58484 ($E474) for RESET and 58487 ($E477) for powerup.

See the *OS User's Manual,* pages 109 to 112, and *De Re Atari* for a flowchart of the process.

TABLE OF CONTENTS ▬▬

INTRODUCTION

Bill Wilkinson

When I was asked by the editors at **COMPUTE!** to write this introduction, I was at first a little hesitant. How does one introduce what is essentially a map of the significant locations on the Atari other than by saying "This is a map of . . ."?

And, yet, there is something about this book which makes it more than "simply a map." After all, if this were "simply" a memory map, I might "simply" use it to learn that "SSKCTL" is the "serial port control" and that it is at location $232. But what does that mean? Why would I want to control the serial port? How would I control it?

The value of this book, then, lies not so much in the map itself as it does in the explanations of the various functions and controls and the implications thereof. Even though I consider myself reasonably familiar with the Atari (and its ROM-based operating system), I expect to use this book often.

Until now, if I needed to use an exotic location somewhere in the hardware registers, I would have to first locate the proper listing, then find the right routine within the listing, figure out why and how the routine was accessing the given register, and finally try to make sure that there were no other routines that also accessed this same register. Whew! Now, I will open this book, turn to the right page, find out what I need to know, and start programming.

Okay. So much for this introduction. And if you are comfortable programming your "home" language, the language you know best, and two or three other languages, you don't need any more from me. So good luck and bon voyage.

A Common Problem

What? Still with me? Does that mean that you are not comfortable doing memory mapped access in three or four languages? Well, to tell the truth, neither am I. And so the one thing I decided would be of most value in this introduction would be a summary of how to do memory access from no less than seven different languages. (Or is it eight? Well . . . .)

The title of this section is perhaps a little misleading (on purpose, of course, as those of you who read my column "Insight: Atari" in **COMPUTE!** Magazine can attest). The "common problem" we will discuss here is not a bug-type problem. Rather, it is a task-type problem which occurs in many common programs. Or perhaps we could approach it as a quiz. Why not?

Quiz: Devise a set of routines which will (1) alter the current cursor position (in any standard OS graphics mode) to that horizontal and vertical position specified by the variables "H" and "V" and (2) retrieve the current cursor position in a like manner. To receive full credit for this problem, implement the routine in at least seven different computer languages.

INTRODUCTION

Well, our first task will be to decide what seven languages we will use. First step in the solution: find out what languages are available on the Atari computers. Here's my list:

Atari BASIC
BASIC A +
Atari Microsoft BASIC
Forth
C
Pascal
PILOT
LISP
Assembler/Machine Language

Does it match yours? You don't get credit for more than one assembler or more than one Forth. And, actually, you shouldn't get credit for Microsoft BASIC, since it uses exactly the same method as Atari BASIC. And I will tell you right now that I will *not* attempt this task in LISP. If you are a LISP fanatic, more power to you; but I don't have any idea of how to approach the problem with Datasoft's LISP (the only LISP currently available on the Atari).

Anyway, let's tackle these languages one at a time.

Atari BASIC And Microsoft BASIC

Well, how about two at a time this one time? The implementation really is the same for these two languages.

Actually, the first part of this problem set is done for you in Atari BASIC: the POSITION statement indeed does exactly what we want (POSITION H,V will do the assigned task). But that's cheating, since the object of these problems is to discover how to do machine level access without such aids.

Step 1 is to look at the memory map and discover that COLCRS, at locations 85 and 86, is supposed to be the current graphics cursor column (COLumn of CuRSor). Also, ROWCRS (ROW of CuRSor) at location 84 is the current graphics cursor row.

Let's tackle the row first. Assuming that the row number is in the variable "V" (as specified above), then we may set the row cursor via "POKE 84,V". And, in a like manner, we may say "V = PEEK(84)" to assign the current position to "V". Now that's fairly straightforward: to change a single memory location, use "POKE address,value"; to retrieve the contents of a single memory location, use "PEEK(address)". Virtually anyone who has programmed in BASIC on an Atari is at least familiar with the existence of PEEK and POKE, since that is the only method of accessing certain functions of the machine (and since the game programs published in magazines are loaded with PEEKs and POKEs).

But now let's look at the cursor column, specified as being

INTRODUCTION

locations 85 and 86, a "two byte" value. What does that mean? How can something occupy two locations? Actually, it all stems from the fact that a single location (byte, memory cell, character, etc.) in an Atari computer can store only 256 different values (usually numbered 0 to 255). If you need to store a bigger number, you have to use more bytes. For example, two contiguous bytes can be used to store 65536 different values, three bytes can store 16,777,216 different values, etc.

Since the Atari graphics mode can have as many as 320 columns, we can't use a single one-byte location to store the column number. Great! We'll simply use two bytes and tell BASIC that we want to talk to a bigger memory cell. What's that? You can't tell BASIC to use a bigger memory cell? Oops.

Ah, but have no fear. We can still perform the task; it just takes a little more work in BASIC. The first sub-problem is to break the column number (variable "H") into two "pieces," one for the first byte and one for the second. The clearest way to accomplish this is with the following code:

```
H1 = INT( H/256)
H2 = H -256 * H1
```

Because of the nature of machine language "arithmetic," numbers designed to be two-byte integers must usually be divided as shown: the "high order byte" must be obtained by dividing the number by 256, and any fractional part of the quotient must be discarded. The "low order byte" is actually the remainder after all units of 256 have been extracted (often designated as "the number modulo 256").

So, if we have obtained "H1" and "H2" as above, we can change the cursor row as follows:

```
POKE 85,H2
POKE 86,H1
```

Notice the reversal of the order of the bytes! For the Atari (and many other microcomputers), the low order (or least significant) byte comes first in memory, followed by the high order (or most significant) byte.

Now, suppose we wish to avoid the use of the temporary variables "H1" and "H2" and further suppose that we would now like to write the entire solution to the first problem here. Voilà!

```
POKE 84,V
POKE 86,INT( H/256 )
POKE 85,H -256 * INT( H/256 )
```

And we wrote those last two lines in "reverse" order so that we could offer a substitute last line, which will not be explained here but which should become clear a few paragraphs hence:

```
POKE 85,H -256*PEEK( 86 )
```

INTRODUCTION

Whew! All that to solve just that first problem! Cheer up, it does get easier. In fact, we already mentioned above that you can retrieve the current row via "PEEK(84)". But how about the column?

Again, we must remember that the column number might be big enough to require two adjacent bytes (locations, memory cells, etc.). Again, we could construct the larger number via the following:

    H2 = PEEK(85)
    H1 = PEEK(86)
    H = H2 + 256 * H1

Do you see the relationship between this and the POKEs? To "put it back together," we must multiply the "high order byte" by 256 (because, remember, it is actually the number of 256's we could obtain from the larger number) before adding it to the "low order byte."

Again, let us summarize and simplify. The following code will satisfy the second problem requirement for BASIC:

    V = PEEK(84)
    H = PEEK(85) + 256 * PEEK(86)

Okay. We did it. For two languages. And if you are only interested in BASIC, you can quit now. But if you are even a little bit curious, stick with us. It gets better.

BASIC A +

There might be a little bit of prejudice on my part here, but I do feel that this is the easiest language to explain to beginners. In fact, rather than start with text, let's show the solutions:

    Problem 1.
      POKE 84,V
      DPOKE 85,H
    Problem 2.
      V = PEEK(84)
      H = DPEEK(85)

As you can see, for the single memory cell situations, BASIC A + functions exactly the same as the Atari and Microsoft BASICs. But for the double-byte problems, BASIC A + has an extra statement and an extra function, designed specifically to interface to the double-byte "words" of the Atari's 6502 processor.

DPOKE (Double POKE) performs exactly the equivalent of the two POKEs required by Atari BASIC. DPEEK (Double PEEK) similarly combines the functions of both the Atari BASIC PEEKs. And that's it. Simple and straightforward.

Forth

I think the ease of performing the required problems in Forth will show how tightly and neatly Forth is tied to the machine level of the computer. In fact, we don't really have to "invent" a way to solve these problems; the solutions are within the normal specifications, expectations, and capabilities of virtually all Forth implementations.

Again, I think I will show the solutions before explaining:

Problem 1.
  V @ 84 c!
  H @ 85 !
Problem 2.
  84 c@ H !
  85 @ V !

Now, if you are not a Forth user, that may all look rather cryptic (looks like a secret code to me), but let's translate it into pseudo-English. The first line of the first problem might be read like this:

V   means the location (or variable) called "V"
@   means fetch the contents of that location
84 means use the number 84
c! means store the character (byte) that we fetched first into the location that we fetched second

or, in shorter form,
"V is to be fetched as the data and 84 is to be used as the address of a byte-sized memory store."

The second line, then, would read essentially the same except that the "!" used (instead of "c!") implies a full word (double byte) store, as does DPOKE in BASIC A+.

The similarity and symmetry of the solutions of Problems 1 and 2 are striking. Let us "read" the first line of the second problem:

84 means use the number 84 (in this case, as a location)
c@ means fetch the byte (character) at that location
V   means fetch the location (variable) called "V"
!   means store the data fetched first into the location fetched second

And, again, the only difference between this and the next line is that "@" (instead of "c@") implies a double-byte fetch (again, as does DPEEK of BASIC A+).

Neither is there space here nor it is appropriate now to discuss the foibles of Forth's reverse Polish notation and its stacking mechanism, but even dyed-in-the-wool algorithmic language freaks (like me) can appreciate its advantages in situations such as those demonstrated here.

C

No, that does not mean "Section C." Believe it or not, "C" is the name of a computer language. In fact, it is one of the more popular computer

INTRODUCTION

languages among systems programmers. It is "the" language used on and by the UNIX operating system, which appears to have the inside track on being the replacement for CP/M on the largest microcomputers (e.g., those based on 68000 and other more advanced processors).

C, somewhat like Forth, is fairly intimately tied to the machine level. For example, there are operators in C which will increment or decrement a memory location, just as there are such instructions in the assembly language of most modern microprocessors.

Unlike Forth, however, C requires the user to declare that he/she is going beyond the scope of the language structures in order to "cheat" and access the machine level directly. In standard C (i.e., as found on UNIX), we could change the current cursor row via something like this:

```
* ( (char *) 84 ) = V;
```

Which, I suppose, is just as cryptic as Forth to the uninitiated. If you remember that parentheses imply precedence, just as in BASIC, you could read the above as "Use the expression '84' as a pointer to a character (i.e., the address of a byte — specified by 'char*') and store V (' = ') indirectly (the first '*') into that location." Whew! Even experienced C users (well, some of us) often find themselves putting in extra parentheses to be sure the expression means what they want it to.

Anyway, that '(char *)' is called "type casting" and is a feature of more advanced C compilers than those available for the Atari. But, to be fair, it is really a poor way of doing the job, anyway. So let's do it "right":

```
Problem 1.
    char *pc ; /* pc is a pointer to a byte */
    int *pi ; /* pi is a pointer to a double byte */
    pc = 84 ; pi = 85 ;
    . . .
    *pc = V ; *pi = H ;
Problem 2.
    char *pc ;
    int *pi ;
    pc = 84 ; pi = 85 ;
    . . .
    V = *pc ; H = *pi ;
```

As with the Pascal solutions, in the following section, we must declare the "type" of a variable, rather than simply assuming its existence (as in BASIC) or declaring its existence (as in Forth). The theory is that this will let the compiler detect more logic errors, since you aren't supposed to do the wrong thing with the wrong variable type. (In practice, the C compilers available for the Atari, including our own C/65, are "loose" enough to allow you to cheat most of the time.)

Here, the declarations establish that "pc" (program counter) will always point to (i.e., contain the address of) a byte-sized item. But "pi" will always point to a word-sized (double byte) item. Now, actually, these variables point to nothing until we put an address into them, which we proceed to do via "pc = 84" and "pi = 85".

And, finally, the actual "assignments" to or from memory are handled by the last line in each problem solution. Now, all this looks very complicated and hardly worthwhile, but the advantage of C is, once we have made all our declarations, that we can use the variables and structures wherever we need them in a program module, secure in the knowledge that our code is at least partially self-documented.

Pascal

Actually, standard Pascal has *no* methods whatsoever available to solve these problems. Remember, Pascal is a "school" language, and access to the machine level was definitely *not* a desirable feature in such an environment. In fact, most of the Pascal compilers in use today have invented some way to circumvent the restrictions of "standard" Pascal, and it is largely because of such "inventions" that the various versions of the language are incompatible.

Anyway, Atari Pascal does provide a method to access individual memory cells. I am not sure that the method I will show here is the best or easiest way, but it appears to work. Again, the solution is presented first:

> *Note:* the code in this first part is common to both problems, both for **H** and **V**.
> (* in the "type" declarations section *)
> charaddr = record
>   row : char ;
>   end ;
> wordaddr = record
>   col : integer ;
>   end ;
> (* in the "var" declarations section *)
> pc : ^charaddr ;
> pw : ^wordaddr ;
> rowcrs : absolute [84] ^charaddr ;
> colcrs : absolute [85] ^wordaddr ;
> Problem 1.
> (includes the above common code)
> (* execution code in the procedure *)
> pc : = rowcrs ;
> pw : = colcrs ;

```
pc^.row : = V ;
pw^.col : = H ;
```
Problem 2.
```
(includes the above common code)
(* again, procedure execution code *)
pc : = rowcrs ;
pw : = colcrs ;
V : = pc^.row ;
H : = pw^.col ;
```

Did you get lost? Don't feel bad. I really felt that this could be written in a simpler fashion, but I wanted to present a version which I felt reasonably sure would work under most circumstances.

The type declarations are necessary simply to establish record formats which can be pointed to (and it was these record formats which I felt to be redundant). Then the variables which indeed point to these record formats are declared. Most importantly, the "absolute" type allows us to inform the Pascal compiler that we have a constant which really is (honest, really, please let it be) the address of one of those record formats we wanted to point to. (And it is this "absolute" type which is the extension of Pascal which is not in the standard.)

Once we have made all our declarations, the code looks surprisingly like the C code: assign the absolute address to the pointer and then fetch or store via the pointer. The overhead of the record element reference (the ".row" and ".col") is the only real difference (and perhaps unneeded, as I stated).

PILOT

And here we are at last at the simplest of the Atari languages. Again, standard PILOT has no defined way of accessing individual memory cells. And, again, the reason for this is that PILOT was (and is) a language designed for use in schools, where the last thing you want is poking around in memory and crashing the 100 megabyte disk with next year's budget on it.

However, when using PILOT on an Atari computer, the worst anyone can do is to crunch their own copy of their own disk or cassette. So Atari has thoughtfully provided a way to access memory cells from PILOT; and they have done it in a fashion that is remarkably reminiscent of BASIC. Once more, the solution is given first:

Problem 1.
```
C:@B84 = #V
C:@B86 = #H/256
C:@B85 = #H\256
```
Problem 2.
```
C:#V = @B84
C:#H = @B85 + (256 * @B86)
```

INTRODUCTION

The trick to this is that Atari PILOT uses the "@B" operator to indicate a memory reference. When used on the left side of the equals sign in a C: (compute) statement, it implies a store (just as does POKE in BASIC). When used on the right side of an equals sign (or, for that matter, in Jump tests, etc.), it implies a memory fetch (just as does PEEK in BASIC).

If you have already examined the BASIC code, you will probably note a marked similarity between it and this PILOT example. Again, we must take the larger number apart into its two components: the number of units of 256 each (#H/256) and the remainder. Notice that with PILOT we do not need to (nor can we) specify "INT(#H/256)". There is no INT function simply because all arithmetic in Atari PILOT is done with double-byte integers already. Sometimes, as in this instance, that can be an advantage. Other times, the lack of floating point will preclude PILOT being used for several applications.

Notice the last line of the solution to problem 1: the use of the "\" (modulo) operator is essentially just a convenient shorthand available in several languages. In PILOT,

"#H \256"

is exactly equivalent to

"#H – (256 * (# H/256))".

Atari PILOT is much more flexible and usable than the original, so why not take advantage of all its features? Experiment. You will be glad you did.

Assembly And Machine Language

I almost didn't include this section, since anyone working with assembly language (and especially those trying to debug at the machine language level) would presumably know how to manipulate bytes and words. And yet, it might prove interesting to those who do not know assembler to see just how the 6502 processor really does perform its feats.

For the purposes of the example solutions, we will presume that somewhere in our program we have coded something equivalent to the following:

```
V * = * + 1   ; reserve one byte for V
H * = * + 2   ; reserve two bytes for H
```

Those lines do *not* give values to V and H; they simply assign memory space to hold the eventual values (somewhat like DIMensioning an array in Atari BASIC, which does not put any particular values into the array). If we wished not only to reserve space for the "variables" V and H but also to assign an initial value to them, we could code this instead:

INTRODUCTION

```
V .BYTE 3      ; assign initial value of 3 to byte V
H .WORD 290 ; assign initial value of 290 to word H
```

Anyway, given that H and V have been reserved and have had some value(s) placed in them, here are the solutions to the problems:

Problem 1.
```
LDA V       ; get the contents of V
STA 84      ; and store them in ROWCRS
LDA H       ; then get the first byte of H
STA 85      ; and store in first byte of COLCRS
LDA H + 1 ; what's this? the second byte of H !
STA 86      ; into the second byte of COLCRS
```
Problem 2.
```
LDA 84      ; almost, we don't need to comment this . . .
STA V       ; it's just problem 1 in reverse!
LDA 85      ; first byte of COLCRS again
STA H       ; into the least significant byte of H
LDA 86      ; and also the second byte
STA H + 1  ; the high order byte of H
```

Do you wonder why we didn't try to move both bytes of H at one time, as we did in BASIC A + , above? Simple: the 6502 microprocessor has *no way* to move two bytes in a single instruction! Honest! (And this is probably its biggest failing as a CPU.)

Of course, if you have a macro assembler, you could write a macro to perform these operations. Here is an example using one macro assembler available for the Atari, though all macro assemblers will operate in at least a similar fashion. First, we define a pair of macros:

```
.MACRO   MOVEWORD
LDA      %1
STA      %2
LDA      %1 + 1
STA      %2 + 1
.ENDM
.MACRO   MOVEBYTE
LDA      %1
STA      %2
.ENDM
```

Both these macros simply move their first "argument" into their second "argument" (and we won't define here just what "arguments" are and how they work — examine a macro assembler manual for more information). The first macro moves two adjacent bytes (i.e., a "word"), and the second moves a single byte. And now we can write our problem code in a much simpler fashion:

Problem 1.
    MOVEBYTE   V,84
    MOVEWORD   H,85
Problem 2.
    MOVEBYTE   84,V
    MOVEWORD   85,H

And yet another concept before we leave assembly language. One of the most powerful features of an assembler is its ability to handle equated symbols. The real beauty of this, aside from producing more readable code, is that you can change all references to a location or value or whatever by simply changing a single equate in your source code. Thus, if somewhere near the beginning of our source program we had coded the following two lines:

ROWCRS =   84 ; address of ROW CuRSor
COLCRS =   85 ; address of COLumn CuRSor

then we could have "solved" the problems thus:

Problem 1.
    MOVEBYTE   V,ROWCRS
    MOVEWORD   H,COLCRS
Problem 2.
    MOVEBYTE   ROWCRS,V
    MOVEWORD   COLCRS,H

And I believe that this looks as elegant and readable as any of the higher level languages! In fact, it looks more readable than most of the examples given above. To be fair, though, we should note that all of the examples could have been made more readable by substituting variable names instead of the absolute numbers "84" and "85," but the overhead of declaring and assigning variables is sometimes not worth it for languages such as BASIC and PILOT.

Luckily, the remaining languages (Forth, C, and Pascal) all have a means of declaring constants (akin to the assembly language equate) which has little or no consequential overhead. So go ahead — be the oddball on your block and make your code readable and maintainable. It may lose you friends, but it might help you land a job.

Happy Mapping

Well, we made it. I hope you now at least have an idea of what to do to modify and examine various memory locations in all of the languages shown. Virtually all of the many locations mapped in this book will fall into one of the two categories examined: they will involve changing or examining either a single byte or a double byte (word, integer, address, etc.). Follow the models shown here, and you should have little trouble effecting your desires.

For those few locations which do not follow the above patterns

INTRODUCTION

(e.g., the system clock, which is a three-byte location in high-middle-low order), you may be able to accomplish your ends by considering each byte individually. Also, we have made no discussion here of the Atari floating point format, which is truly accessible in any reasonable fashion only from assembly language, and which has little pertinence to this memory map in any case.

I think I would like to add only one more comment, which will be in the form of a caution: If you aren't sure what you are doing when changing or examining memory locations, make sure that your program in memory is backed up (on disk or cassette), and then make sure that you have "popped" (unloaded) your disks and/or tapes. It is unlikely that changing memory will cause problems affecting your saved files, but why take chances. (And, if you make a mistake or are in doubt, re-boot the disk; don't just hit RESET, since that won't necessarily clean up all your errors.)

Good luck and happy mapping.

MEMORY MAP

Locations zero to 255 ($0 to $FF) are called "page zero" and have special importance for assembly language programmers since these locations are accessed faster and easier by the machine.

Locations zero to 127 ($0 to $7F) are reserved as the OS page zero, while 128 to 255 ($80 to $FF) are the BASIC and the user zero page RAM. Locations zero to 1792 ($0 to $700) are all used as the OS and (if the cartridge is present) 8K BASIC RAM (except page six). Locations zero to 8191 ($0 to $1FFF) are the minimum required for operation (8K).

Locations two through seven are not cleared on any start operation.

DECIMAL   HEX   LABEL

0.1   0.1   LINZBS

LINBUG RAM, replaced by the monitor RAM. See the OS Listing, page 31. It seems to be used to store the VBLANK timer value. One user application I've seen for location zero is in a metronome program in *De Re Atari*. Also used in cross-assembling the Atari OS.

2.3   2.3   CASINI

Cassette initialization vector: JSR through here if the cassette boot was successful. This address is extracted from the first six bytes of a cassette boot file. The first byte is ignored. The second contains the number of records, the third and fourth contain the low and high bytes of the load address, and the fifth and sixth contain the low and high bytes of the initialization address. Control upon loading jumps to the load address plus six for a multi-stage load and through CASINI for initialization. JSR through DOSVEC (10 and 11; $A,$B) to transfer control to the application.

4.5   4.5   RAMLO

RAM pointer for the memory test used on powerup. Also used to store the disk boot address — normally 1798 ($706) — for the boot continuation routine.

6   6   TRAMSZ

Temporary Register for RAM size; used during powerup sequence to test RAM availability. This value is then moved to RAMTOP, location 106 ($6A). Reads one when the BASIC or the A (left) cartridge is plugged in.

7   7   TSTDAT

RAM test data register. Reads one when the B or the right cartridge is inserted.

RAMLO, TRAMSZ and TSTDAT are all used in testing the RAM

size on powerup. On DOS boot, RAMLO and TRAMSZ also act as temporary storage for the boot continuation address. TRAMSZ and TSTDAT are used later to flag whether or not the A (left) and/or B (right) cartridges, respectively, are plugged in (non-zero equals cartridge plugged in) and whether the disk is to be booted.

Locations eight through 15 ($8-$F) are cleared on coldstart only.

8   8   WARMST

Warmstart flag. If the location reads zero, then it is in the middle of powerup; 255 is the normal RESET status. Warmstart is similar to pressing RESET, so should not wipe out memory, variables, or programs. WARMST is initialized to zero and will not change values unless POKEd or until the first time the RESET button is pressed. It will then read 255 ($FF).

Warmstart normally vectors to location 58484 ($E474). WARMST is checked by the NMI status register at 54287 ($D40F) when RESET is pressed to see whether or not to re-initialize the software or to re-boot the disk.

9   9   BOOT?

Boot flag success indicator. A value of 255 in this location will cause the system to lockup if RESET is pressed. If BOOT? reads one, then the disk boot was successful; if it reads two, then the cassette boot was successful. If it reads zero, then neither peripheral was booted.

If it is set to two, then the cassette vector at locations two and three will be used on RESET. Set to one, it will use the DOS vector at 10 and 11 ($A and $B). Coldstart attempts both a cassette and a disk boot and flags this location with the success or failure of the boots. BOOT? is checked during both disk and cassette boot.

10,11   A,B   DOSVEC

Start vector for disk (or non-cartridge) software. This is the address BASIC jumps to when you call up DOS. Can be set by user to point to your own routine, but RESET will return DOSVEC to the original address. To prevent this, POKE 5446 with the LSB and 5450 with the MSB of your vector address and re-save DOS using the WRITE DOS FILES option in the menu. Locations 10 and 11 are usually loaded with 159 and 23 ($9F and $17), respectively. This allows the DUP.SYS section of DOS to be loaded when called. It is initially set to blackboard mode vector (58481; $ E471 — called by typing "BYE" or "B." from BASIC); it will also vector to the cassette run address if no DOS vector is loaded in. If you create an AUTORUN.SYS file that doesn't end with an RTS instruction, you should set BOOT? to one and 580 ($244) to zero.

12,13   C,D   DOSINI

Initialization address for the disk boot. Also used to store the cassette-boot RUN address, which is then moved to CASINI (2, 3). When you powerup without either the disk or an autoboot cassette tape, DOSINI will read zero in both locations.

14,15   E,F   APPMHI

Applications memory high limit and pointer to the end of your BASIC program, used by both the OS and BASIC. It contains the lowest address you can use to set up a screen and Display List (which is also the highest address usable for programs and data below which the display RAM may not be placed). The screen handler will not OPEN the "S:" device if it would extend the screen RAM or the Display List below this address; memory above this address may be used for the screen display and other data (PM graphics, etc.).

If an attempted screen mode change would extend the screen memory below APPMHI, then the screen is set up for GRAPHICS mode zero; MEMTOP (locations 741, 742; $2E5, $2E6) is updated and an error is returned to the user. Otherwise, the memory is not too small for the screen editor; the mode change will take effect and MEMTOP will be updated. This is one of five locations used by the OS to keep track of the user and display memory. Initialized to zero by the OS at powerup. Remember, you cannot set up a screen display *below* the location specified here.

If you use the area below the Display List for your character sets, PM graphics or whatever, be sure to set APPMHI above the last address used so that the screen or the DL data will not descend and destroy your own data. See RAMTOP location 106 ($6A), MEMTOP at 741, 742 ($2E5, $2E6), PMBASE at 54279 ($D407) and CHBASE at 54281 ($D409) for more information.

Locations 16 through 127 ($10-$7F) are cleared on either cold- or warmstart.

16   10   POKMSK

POKEY interrupts: the IRQ service uses and alters this location. Shadow for 53774 ($D20E). POKE with 112 ($70; also POKE this same value into 53774) to disable the BREAK key. If the following bits are set (to one), then these interrupts are enabled (bit decimal values are in parentheses):

BIT	DECIMAL	FUNCTION
7	128	The BREAK key is enabled.
6	64	The "other key" interrupt is enabled.

5	32	The serial input data ready interrupt is enabled.
4	16	The serial output data required interrupt is enabled.
3	8	The serial out transmission finished interrupt is enabled.
2	4	The POKEY timer four interrupt is enabled (only in the "B" or later versions of the OS ROMs).
1	2	The POKEY timer two interrupt is enabled.
0	1	The POKEY timer one interrupt is enabled.

Timer interrupt enable means the associated AUDF registers are used as timers and will generate an interrupt request when they have counted down to zero. See locations 528 to 535 ($210 to $217) and the POKEY chip from locations 53760 ($D200) on, for a full explanation. 192 ($C0) is the default on powerup.

You can also disable the BREAK key by POKEing here with 64 ($40; or any number less than 128; $80) and also in location 53774. The problem with simple POKEs is that the BREAK key is re-enabled when RESET is pressed and by the first PRINT statement that displays to the screen, or any OPEN statement that addresses the screen (S: or E:), or the first PRINT statement after such an OPEN and any GRAPHICS command. In order to continually disable the BREAK key if such commands are being used, it's best to use a subroutine that checks the enable bits frequently during input and output operations, and POKEs a value less than 128 into the proper locations, such as:

```
1000   BREAK = PEEK(16)  - 128:  IF BREA
       K < 0 THEN RETURN
1010   POKE 16, BREAK: POKE 53774, BRE
       AK: RETURN
```

The new OS "B" version ROMs have a vector for the BREAK key interrupt, which allows users to write their own routines to process the interrupt in the desired manner. It is located at 566, 567 ($236, $237).

17   11   BRKKEY

Zero means the BREAK key is pressed; any other number means it's not. A BREAK during I/O returns 128 ($80). Monitored by both keyboard, display, cassette and screen handlers. See location 16 ($A) for hints on disabling the BREAK key. The latest editions of OS provide for a proper vector for BREAK interrupts. The BREAK key abort status code is stored in STATUS (48; $30). It is also checked during all I/O and scroll/draw routines. During the keyboard handler routine, the status code is stored in DSTAT

(76; $4C). BRKKEY is turned off at powerup. BREAK key abort status is flagged by setting BIT 7 of 53774 ($D20E). See the note on the BREAK key vector, above.

18,19,20   12,13,14   RTCLOK

Internal realtime clock. Location 20 increments every stage one VBLANK interrupt (1/60 second = one jiffy) until it reaches 255 ($FF); then location 19 is incremented by one and 20 is reset to zero (every 4.27 seconds). When location 19 reaches 255, it and 20 are reset to zero and location 18 is incremented by one (every 18.2 minutes or 65536 TV frames). To use these locations as a timer of seconds, try:

TIME = INT ((PEEK (18) * 65536 + PEEK (19) * 256 + PEEK (20)) / 60)

To see the count in jiffies, eliminate the "/60" at the end. To see the count in minutes, change "/60" to "/360." The maximum value of the RT clock is 16,777,215. When it reaches this value, it will be reset to zero on the next VBLANK increment. This value is the result of cubing 256 (i.e., 256 * 256 * 256), the maximum number of increments in each clock register. The RT clock is always updated every VBLANK regardless of the time-critical nature of the code being processed.

A jiffy is actually a long time to the computer. It can perform upwards of 8000 machine cycles in that time. Think of what can be done in the VBLANK interval (one jiffy). In human terms, a jiffy can be upwards of 20 minutes, as witnessed in the phrase "I'll be ready in a jiffy." Compare this to the oft-quoted phrase, "I'll be there in a minute," used by intent programmers to describe a time frame upwards of one hour.

Users can POKE these clock registers with suitable values for their own use. The realtime clock is always updated during the VBLANK interval. Some of the other timer registers (locations 536 to 544; $218 to $220) are not always updated when the OS is executing time critical code.

Here's one way to use the realtime clock for a delay timer:

```
10   GOSUB 100
  .
  .
  .
100  POKE 20,0: POKE 19,0
110  IF NOT PEEK(19) THEN 110
120  RETURN
```

Line 110 waits to see if location 19 returns to zero and, when it does, passes control to the RETURN statement.

See **COMPUTE!**, August 1982, for a useful program to create a small realtime clock that will continue to display during your BASIC programming. See also *De Re Atari* for another realtime clock application.

21,22   15,16   BUFADR

Indirect buffer address register (page zero). Temporary pointer to the current disk buffer.

23   17   ICCOMT

Command for CIO vector. Stores the CIO command; used to find the offset in the command table for the correct vector to the handler routine.

24,25   18,19   DSKFMS

Disk file manager pointer. Called JMPTBL by DOS; used as vector to FMS.

26,27   1A,1B   DSKUTL

The disk utilities pointer. Called BUFADR by DOS, it points to the area saved for a buffer for the utilities package (data buffer; DBUF) or for the program area (MEMLO; 743, 744; $2E7, $2E8).

28   1C   PTIMOT

Printer timeout, called every printer status request. Initialized to 30, which represents 32 seconds (the value is 64 seconds per 60 increments in this register); typical timeout for the Atari 825 printer is five seconds. The value is set by your printer handler software. It is updated after each printer status rquest operation. It gets the specific timeout status from location 748 ($2EC), which is loaded there by SIO.

The new "B" type OS ROMs have apparently solved the problem of timeout that haunted the "A" ROMs; you saw it when the printer or the disk drive periodically went to sleep (timed out) for a few seconds, causing severe anxiety attacks in the owners who thought their Ataris had just mysteriously died. This is compounded when one removes a disk from the drive, believing the I/O process to be finished — only to have the drive start up again after the timeout and trying to write to or read from a nonexistent disk. Usually both the system and the user crash simultaneously at this point. See the appendix for more information on the new ROMs.

29   1D   PBPNT

Print buffer pointer; points to the current position (byte) in the print buffer. Ranges from zero to the value in location 30.

30   1E   PBUFSZ

Print buffer size of printer record for current mode. Normal buffer size and line size equals 40 bytes; double-width print equals 20 bytes (most printers use their own control codes for expanded print); sideways printing equals 29 bytes (Atari 820 printer only). Printer status request equals four. PBUFSZ is initialized to 40. The printer handler checks to see if the same value is in PBPNT and, if so, sends the contents of the buffer to the printer.

31   1F   PTEMP

Temporary register used by the printer handler for the value of the character being output to the printer.

Locations 32 to 47 ($20 to $2F) are the ZIOCB: Page zero Input-Output Control Block. They use the same structure as the IOCB's at locations 832 to 959 ($340 to $3BF). The ZIOCB is used to communicate I/O control data between CIO and the device handlers. When a CIO operation is initiated, the information stored in the IOCB channel is moved here for use by the CIO routines. When the operation is finished, the updated information is returned to the user area.

32   20   ICHIDZ

Handler index number. Set by the OS as an index to the device name table for the currently open file. If no file is open on this IOCB (IOCB free), then this register is set to 255 ($FF).

33   21   ICDNOZ

Device number or drive number. Called MAXDEV by DOS to indicate the maximum number of devices. Initialized to one.

34   22   ICCOMZ

Command code byte set by the user to define how the rest of the IOCB is formatted, and what I/O action is to be performed.

35   23   ICSTAZ

Status of the last IOCB action returned by the device, set by the OS. May or may not be the same status returned by the STATUS command.

36,37   24,25   ICBALZ/HZ

Buffer address for data transfer or the address of the file name for commands such as OPEN, STATUS, etc.

38,39   26,27   ICPTLZ/HZ

Put byte routine address set by the OS. It is the address minus one byte of the device's "put one byte" routine. It points to CIO's "IOCB not OPEN" on a CLOSE statement.

40,41   28,29   ICBLLZ/HZ

Buffer length byte count used for PUT and GET operations;

decreased by one for each byte transferred.

42   2A   ICAX1Z

Auxiliary information first byte used in OPEN to specify the type of file access needed.

43   2B   ICAX2Z

CIO working variables, also used by some serial port functions. Auxiliary information second byte.

44,45   2C,2D   ICAX3Z/4Z

Used by BASIC NOTE and POINT commands for the transfer of disk sector numbers. These next four bytes to location 47 are also labelled as: ICSPRZ and are defined as spare bytes for local CIO use.

46   2E   ICAX5Z

The byte being accessed within the sector noted in locations 44 and 45. It is also used for the IOCB Number multiplied by 16. Each IOCB block is 16 bytes long. Other sources indicate that the 6502 X register also contains this information.

47   2F   ICAX6Z

Spare byte. Also labelled CIOCHR, it is the temporary storage for the character byte in the current PUT operation.

---

48   30   STATUS

Internal status storage. The SIO routines in ROM use this byte to store the status of the current SIO operation. See page 166 of the *OS User's Manual* for status values. STATUS uses location 793 ($319) as temporary storage. STATUS is also used as a storage register for the timeout, BREAK abort and error values during SIO routines.

49   31   CHKSUM

Data frame checksum used by SIO: single byte sum with carry to the least significant bit. Checksum is the value of the number of bytes transmitted (255; $FF). When the number of transmitted bytes equals the checksum, a checksum sent flag is set at location 59 ($3B). Uses locations 53773 ($D20D) and 56 ($38) for comparison of values (bytes transmitted).

50,51   32,33   BUFRLO/HI

Pointer to the data buffer, the contents of which are transmitted during an I/O operation, used by SIO and the Device Control Block (DCB); points to the byte to send or receive. Bytes are transferred to the eight-bit parallel serial output holding register or from the input holding register at 53773 ($D20D). This register is a one-byte location used to hold the eight bits which will be transmitted one bit at a time (serially) to or from the device. The computer takes the eight bits for processing when the register is full or replaces another byte in it when empty after a transmission.

52,53   34,35   BFENLO/HI

Next byte past the end of the SIO and DCB data buffer described above.

54   36   CRETRY

Number of command frame retries. Default is 13 ($0D). This is the number of times a device will attempt to carry out a command such as read a sector or format a disk.

55   37   DRETRY

Number of device retries. The default is one.

56   38   BUFRFL

Data buffer full flag (255; $FF equals full).

57   39   RECVDN

Receive done flag (255; $FF equals done).

58   3A   XMTDON

Transmission done flag (255; $FF equals done).

59   3B   CHKSNT

Checksum sent flag (255; $FF equals sent).

60   3C   NOCKSM

Flag for "no checksum follows data." Not zero means no checksum follows; zero equals checksum follows transmission data.

61   3D   BPTR

Cassette buffer pointer: record data index into the portion of data being read or written. Ranges from zero to the current value at location 650 ($28A). When these values are equal, the buffer at 1021 ($3FD) is empty if reading or full if writing. Initialized to 128 ($80).

62   3E   FTYPE

Inter-record gap type between cassette records, copied from location 43 ($2B; ICAX2Z) in the ZIOCB, stored there from DAUX2 (779; $30B) by the user. Normal gaps are a non-zero positive number; continuous gaps are zero (negative number).

63   3F   FEOF

Cassette end of file flag. If the value is zero, an end of file (EOF) has not been reached. Any other number means it has been

64

detected. An EOF record has been reached when the command byte of a data record equals 254 ($FE). See location 1021 ($3FD).

64   40   FREQ

Beep count retain register. Counts the number of beeps required by the cassette handler during the OPEN command for play or record operations; one beep for play, two for record.

65   41   SOUNDR

Noisy I/O flag used by SIO to signal the beeping heard during disk and cassette I/O. POKE here with zero for blessed silence during these operations. Other numbers return the beep. Initialized to three. The hardware solution to this problem is to turn your speaker volume down. This can also be used to silence the digital track when playing synchronized voice/data tapes. See location 54018.

66   42   CRITIC

Critical I/O region flag; defines the current operation as a time-critical section when the value here is non-zero. Checked at the NMI process after the stage one VBLANK has been processed. POKEing any number other than zero here will disable the repeat action of the keys and change the sound of the CTRL-2 buzzer.

Zero is normal; setting CRITIC to a non-zero value suspends a number of OS processes including system software timer counting (timers two, three, four and five; see locations 536 to 558; $218 to $22E). It is suggested that you do not set CRITIC for any length of time. When one timer is being set, CRITIC stops the other timers to do so, causing a tiny amount of time to be "lost." When CRITIC is zero, both stage one and stage two VBLANK procedures will be executed. When non-zero, only the stage one VBLANK will be processed.

67-73   43-49   FMZSPG

Disk file manager system (FMS) page zero registers (seven bytes).

67,68   43,44   ZBUFP

Page zero buffer pointer to the user filename for disk I/O.

69,70   45,46   ZDRVA

Page zero drive pointer. Copied to here from DBUFAL and DBUFAH; 4905 and 4913 ($1329, $1331). Also used in FMS "free sector," setup and "get sector" routines.

71,72   47,48   ZSBA

Zero page sector buffer pointer.

73   49   ERRNO

Disk I/O error number. Initialized to 159 ($9F) by FMS.

74 4A CKEY

Cassette boot request flag on coldstart. Checks to see if the
START key is pressed and, if so, CKEY is set. Autoboot cassettes
are loaded by pressing the START console key while turning the
power on. In response to the beep, press the PLAY button on the
recorder.

75 4B CASSBT

Cassette boot flag. The Atari attempts both a disk and a cassette
boot simultaneously. Zero here means no cassette boot was successful. See location 9.

76 4C DSTAT

Display status and keyboard register used by the display handler.
Also used to indicate memory is too small for the screen mode,
cursor out of range error, and the BREAK abort status.

77 4D ATRACT

Attract mode timer and flag. Attract mode rotates colors on your
screen at low luminance levels when the computer is on but no
keyboard input is read for a long time (seven to nine minutes).
This helps to save your TV screen from "burn-out" damage suf-
fered from being left on and not used. It is set to zero by IRQ
whenever a key is pressed, otherwise incremented every four
seconds by VBLANK (see locations 18 - 20; $12 - $14). When the
value in ATRACT reaches 127 ($7F), it is then set to 254 ($FE) until attract mode is terminated. This sets the flag to reduce the
luminance and rotate the colors when the Atari is sitting idle.
POKE with 128 ($80) to see this effect immediately: it normally
takes seven to nine minutes to enable the attract mode. The OS
cannot "attract" color generated by DLI's, although your DLI
routine can, at a loss of time.

Joysticks alone will not reset location 77 to zero. You will have to
add a POKE 77,0 to your program periodically or frequently call
in a subroutine to prevent the Atari from entering attract mode if
you are not using any keyboard input.

78 4E DRKMSK

Dark attract mask; set to 254 ($FE) for normal brightness when
the attract mode is inactive (see location 77). Set to 246 ($F6)
when the attract mode is active to guarantee screen color
luminance will not exceed 50%. Initialized to 254 ($FE).

79 4F COLRSH

Color shift mask; attract color shifter; the color registers are
EORd with locations 78 and 79 at the stage two VBLANK (see
locations 18 - 20; $12 - $14). When set to zero and location 78
equals 246, color luminance is reduced 50%. COLRSH contains

the current value of location 19, therefore is given a new color value every 4.27 seconds.

Bytes 80 to 122 ($50 to $7A) are used by the screen editor and display handler.

80   50   TEMP

Temporary register used by the display handler in moving data to and from screen. Also called TMPCHR.

81   51   HOLD1

Same as location 80. It is used also to hold the number of Display List entries.

82   52   LMARGN

Column of the left margin of text (GR.0 or text window only). Zero is the value for the left edge of the screen; LMARGN is initialized to two. You can POKE the margin locations to set them to your specific program needs, such as POKE 82,10 to make the left margin start ten locations from the edge of the screen.

83   53   RMARGN

Right margin of the text screen, initialized to 39 ($27). Both locations 82 and 83 are user-alterable, but ignored in all GRAPHICS modes except zero and the text window.

Margins work with the text window and blackboard mode and are reset to their default values by pressing RESET. Margins have no effect on scrolling or the printer. However, DELETE LINE and INSERT LINE keys delete or insert 40 character lines (or delete one program line), which always start at the left margin and wrap around the screen edge back to the left margin again. The right margin is ignored in the process. Also, logical lines are always three physical lines no matter how long or short you make those lines.

The beep you hear when you are coming to the end of the logical line works by screen position independent of the margins. Try setting your left margin at 25 (POKE 82,25) and typing a few lines of characters. Although you have just a few characters beyond 60, the buzzer will still sound on the third line of text.

84   54   ROWCRS

Current graphics or text screen cursor row, value ranging from zero to 191 ($BF) depending on the current GRAPHICS mode (maximum number of rows, minus one). This location, together with location 85 below, defines the cursor location for the next element to be read/written to the screen. Rows run horizontally, left to right across the TV screen. Row zero is the topmost line; row 192 is the maximum value for the bottom-most line.

85,86   55,56   COLCRS

Current graphics or text mode cursor column; values range from zero to 319 (high byte, for screen mode eight) depending on current GRAPHICS mode (maximum number of columns minus one). Location 86 will *always* be zero in modes zero through seven. Home position is 0,0 (upper left-hand corner). Columns run vertically from the top to the bottom down the TV screen, the leftmost column being number zero, the rightmost column the maximum value in that mode. The cursor has a complete top to bottom, left to right wraparound on the screen.

ROWCRS and COLCRS define the cursor location for the next element to be read from or written to in the main screen segment of the display. For the text window cursor, values in locations 656 to 667 ($290 to $29B) are exchanged with the current values in locations 84 to 95 ($54 to $5F), and location 123 ($7B) is set to 255 ($FF) to indicate the swap has taken place. ROWCRS and COLCRS are also used in the DRAW and FILL functions to contain the values of the endpoint of the line being drawn. The color of the line is kept in location 763 ($2FB). These values are loaded into locations 96 to 98 ($60 to $62) so that ROWCRS and COLCRS may be altered during the operation.

BASIC's LOCATE statement not only examines the screen, but also moves the cursor one position to the right at the next PRINT or PUT statement. It does this by updating locations 84 and 85, above. You can override the cursor advance by saving the contents of the screen before the LOCATE command, then restoring them after the LOCATE. Try:

```
100   REM: THE SCREEN MUST HAVE BEEN O
      PENED FOR READ OR READ/WRITE PREV
      IOUSLY
110   LOOK = PEEK(84): SEE = PEEK(85)
120   LOCATE X,Y,THIS
130   POKE 84, LOOK: POKE 85, SEE
```

Note that CHR$(253) is a non-printing character — the bell — and doesn't affect the cursor position.

See **COMPUTE!**, August 1981, for an example of using COLCRS for dynamic data restore and updating with the screen editor and the IOCBs.

87   57   DINDEX

Display mode/current screen mode. Labelled CRMODE by (*M). DINDEX contains the number obtained from the low order four bits of most recent open AUX1 byte. It can be used to fool the OS into thinking you are in a different GRAPHICS mode by

POKEing DINDEX with a number from zero to 11. POKE with seven after you have entered GRAPHICS mode eight, and it will give you a split screen with mode seven on top and mode eight below. However, in order to use both halves of the screen, you will have to modify location 89 (below) to point to the area of the screen you wish to DRAW in. (See *Your Atari 400/800*, pp. 280 - 283.)

Watch for the cursor out-of-range errors (number 141) when changing GRAPHICS modes in this manner and either PRINTing or DRAWing to the new mode screen. POKE 87 with the BASIC mode number, not the ANTIC mode number.

Did you know you can use PLOT and DRAWTO in GR.0? Try this:

```
10     GR. 0
20     PLOT 0,0: DRAWTO 10,10: DRAWTO 0
       ,10
30     DRAWTO 39,0: DRAWTO 20,23: DRAWT
       O 0,20
40     GOTO 40
```

You can also set the text window for PRINT and PLOT modes by POKEing 87 with the graphics mode for the window. Then you must POKE the address of the top left corner of the text window into 88 and 89 ($58, $59). The screen mode of the text window is stored at location 659 ($293).

You may have already discovered that you cannot call up the GTIA modes from a direct command. Like the + 16 GRAPHICS modes, they can only be called up during a program, and the screen display will be reset to GR.0 on the first INPUT or PRINT (not PRINT#6) statement executed in these modes.

Since this location only takes BASIC modes, you can't POKE it with the other ANTIC modes such as "E", the famous "seven-and-a-half" mode which offers higher resolution than seven and a four color display (used in Datasoft's *Micropainter* program). If you're not drawing to the screen, simply using it for display purposes, you can always go into the Display List and change the instructions there. But if you try to draw to the screen, you risk an out-of-bounds error (error number 141).

See *Creative Computing*, March 1982, for an excellent look at mode 7½. The short subroutine below can be used to change the Display List to GR. 7½:

```
1000   GRAPHICS 8+16: DLIST = PEEK(560
       ) + PEEK(561) * 256:POKE DLIST +
       3,78
```

```
1010   FOR CHANGE = DLIST + 6 TO DLIST
       + 204: IF PEEK(CHANGE) = 15 THE
       N POKE CHANGE,14
1020   IF PEEK(CHANGE) = 79 THEN POKE
       CHANGE,78:NEXT CHANGE
1030   POKE 87,7:RETURN
```

(Actually, 15 ($F) is the DL number for the maximum memory mode; it also indicates modes eight through eleven. The DL's for these modes are identical.) Fourteen is the ANTIC E mode; GR.7½. This program merely changes GR.8 to mode E in the Display List. The value 79 is 64 + 15; mode eight screen with BIT 6 set for a Load Memory Scan (LMS) instruction (see the DL information in locations 560, 561; $230, $231). It does not check for other DL bits.

You can also POKE 87 with the GTIA values (nine to eleven). To get a pseudo-text window in GTIA modes, POKE the mode number here and then POKE 623 with 64 for mode nine, 128 for mode ten, and 192 for mode eleven, then POKE 703 with four, in program mode. (In command mode, you will be returned to GR.0.) You won't be able to read the text in the window, but you will be able to write to it. However, to get a true text window, you'll need to use a Display List Interrupt (see **COMPUTE!**, September 1982). If you don't have the GTIA chip, it is still possible to simulate those GRAPHICS modes by using DINDEX with changes to the Display List Interrupt. See **COMPUTE!**, July 1981, for an example of simulating GR.10.

88,89   58,59   SAVMSC

The lowest address of the screen memory, corresponding to the upper left corner of the screen (where the value at this address will be displayed). The upper left corner of the text window is stored at locations 660, 661 ($294, $295).

You can verify this for yourself by:

WINDOW = PEEK(88) + PEEK(89) * 256: POKE WINDOW, 33

This will put the letter "A" in the upper left corner in GR.0, 1 and 2. In other GRAPHICS modes, it will print a colored block or bar. To see this effect, try:

```
5    REM FIRST CLEAR SCREEN
10   GRAPHICS Z: IF Z > 59 THEN END
15   SCREEN = PEEK (88) + PEEK (89) *
     256
20   FOR N = 0 TO 255: POKE SCREEN + N
     ,N
25   NEXT N: FOR N = 1 TO 300: NEXT N:
```

```
      Z = Z + 1
30 GOTO 10
```

You will notice that you get the Atari internal character code, not the ATASCII code. See also locations 560, 561 ($230, $231) and 57344 ($E000).

How do you find the entire screen RAM? First, look at the chart below and find your GRAPHICS mode. Then you multiply the number of rows-per-screen type by the number of bytes-per-line. This will tell you how many bytes each screen uses. Add this value, minus one, to the address specified by SAVMSC. However, if you subtract MEMTOP (locations 741, 742; $2E5, $2E6) from RAMTOP (106; $6A * 256 for the number of bytes), you will see that there is more memory reserved than just the screen area. The extra is taken up by the display list or the text window, or is simply not used (see the second chart below).

Mode	0	1	2	3	4	5	6	7	8	9-12
Rows										
Full	24	24	12	24	48	48	96	96	192	192
Split	—	20	10	20	40	40	80	80	160	—
Bytes per										
Line	40	20	20	10	10	20	20	40	40	40
Columns										
per Line	40	20	20	40	80	80	160	160	320	80
Memory (1)	993	513	261	273	537	1017	2025	3945	7900	7900
Memory (2)										
Full	992	672	420	432	696	1176	2184	4200	8138	8138
Split	—	674	424	434	694	1174	2174	4190	8112	—

(1) According to the *Atari BASIC Reference Manual*, p. 45; *OS User's Manual*, p. 172, and *Your Atari 400/800*, p. 360.

(2) According to *Your Atari 400/800*, p. 274, and *Atari Microsoft Basic Manual*, p. 69. This is also the value you get when you subtract MEMTOP from RAMTOP (see above).

For example, to POKE the entire screen RAM in GR.4, you would find the start address of the screen (PEEK(88) + PEEK(89) * 256), then use a FOR-NEXT loop to POKE all the locations specified above:

```
10   GRAPHICS 4: SCRN = PEEK(88) + PE
     EK(89) * 256
20   FOR LOOP = SCRN to SCRN + 479: R
     EM 48 ROWS * 10 BYTES - 1
30   POKE LOOP,35: NEXT LOOP
```

Why the minus one in the calculation? The first byte of the screen is the first byte in the loop. If we add the total size, we will go one byte past the end of the screen, so we subtract one from the total. Here's how to arrive at the value for the total amount of memory located for screen use, display list and text window:

Total memory allocation for the screen

		Screen display			Display List		
GR	Text window	unused always	bytes cond.	screen use	unused bytes	used bytes	Total
0	. . .	none	none	960	none	32	992
1	160	none	80	400	none	34	674
2	160	none	40	200	none	24	424
3	160	none	40	200	none	34	434
4	160	none	80	400	none	54	694
5	160	none	160	800	none	54	1174
6	160	none	320	1600	none	94	2174
7	160	none	640	3200	96	94	4190
8	160	16	1280	6400	80	176	8112

The number of bytes from RAMTOP (location 106; $6A) is counted from the left text window column towards the total column. MEMTOP (741, 742; $2E5, $2E6) points to one byte below RAMTOP * 256 minus the number of bytes in the total column. If 16 is added to the GRAPHICS mode (no text window), then the conditional unused bytes are added to the total. Then the bytes normally added for the text window become unused, and the Display List expands slightly. (See **COMPUTE!**, September 1981.)

When you normally PRINT CHR$(125) (clear screen), Atari sends zeroes to the memory starting at locations 88 and 89. It continues to do this until it reaches one byte less than the contents of RAMTOP (location 106; $6A). Here is a potential source of conflict with your program, however: CHR$(125) — CLEAR SCREEN — and any GRAPHICS command actually continue to clear the first 64 ($40) bytes *above* RAMTOP!

It would have no effect on BASIC since BASIC is a ROM cartridge. The OS Source Listing seems to indicate that it ends at RAMTOP, but Atari assumed that there would be nothing after RAMTOP, so no checks were provided. Don't reserve any data within 64 bytes of RAMTOP or else it will be eaten by the CLEAR SCREEN routine, or avoid using a CLEAR SCREEN or a GRAPHICS command. Scrolling the text window also clears 800 bytes of memory above RAMTOP.

You can use this to clear other areas of memory by POKEing the

LSB and MSB of the area to be cleared into these locations. Your routine should always end on a $FF boundary (RAMTOP indicates the number of pages). Remember to POKE back the proper screen locations or use a GRAPHICS command immediately after doing so to set the screen right. Try this:

```
10   BOTTOM = 30000: TOP = 36863: REM
     LOWEST AND HIGHEST ADDRESS TO CLEA
     R = $7530 & $8FFF
20   RAMTOP = PEEK(106): POKE 106, INT
     (TOP + 1 / 256)
30   TEST = INT(BOTTOM / 256): POKE89,
     TEST
40   POKE 88, BOTTOM - 256 * TEST
50   PRINT CHR$(125): POKE 106, RAMTOP
60   GRAPHICS 0
```

This will clear the specified memory area and update the address of screen memory. If you don't specify TOP, the CLEAR SCREEN will continue merrily cleaning out memory and, most likely, will cause your program to crash. Use it with caution.

Here's a means to SAVE your current GR.7 screen display to disk using BASIC:

```
1000   SCREEN = PEEK(88) + PEEK(89) *
       256
1010   OPEN #2,8,0,"D:picturename"
1020   MODE = PEEK(87): PUT #2, MODE:
       REM SAVE GR. MODE
1030   FOR SCN = 0 TO 4: COL = PEEK(70
       8 + SCN): PUT #2,COL: NEXT SCN:
       REM SAVE COLOR REGISTERS
1040   FOR TV = SCREEN TO SCREEN + 319
       9:BYTE = PEEK(TV): PUT #2, BYTE:
       NEXT TV: CLOSE #2
```

To use this with other screen modes, you will have to change the value of 3199 in line 1040 to suit your screen RAM (see the chart above). For example, GR.7 + 16 would require 3839 bytes (3840 minus one). You can use the same routine with cassette by using device C:. To retrieve your picture, you use GET#2 and POKE commands. You will, however, find both routines *very* slow. Using THE CIO routine at 58454 ($E456) and the IOCBs, try this machine language save routine:

```
10   DIM ML$(10): B$(10): GR.8+16
20   B$ = "your picture name":Q = PEEK
     (559)
30   FOR N = 1 TO 6: READ BYTE: ML$(N,
```

```
    N) = CHR$(BYTE): NEXT N
35  DATA 104,162,16,76,86,228
36  REM PLA,LDX,$10,JMP $E456
40  OPEN #1,4,0,B$
50  POKE 849,1: POKE 850,7: POKE 852,
    PEEK(88): POKE 853,PEEK(89): POKE
    856,70: POKE 857,30: POKE 858,4
55  REM THESE POKES SET UP THE IOCB
60  POKE 559,0: REM TURN OFF THE SCRE
    EN TO SPEED THINGS UP
70  X = USR(ADR(ML$)): CLOSE #1
80  POKE 559,Q: REM TURN IT BACK ON A
    GAIN
```

Note that there is no provision to SAVE the color registers in this program, so I suggest you have them SAVEd after you have SAVEd the picture. It will make it easier to retrieve them if they are at the end of the file. You will have to make suitable adjustments when SAVEing a picture in other than GR.8 + 16 — such as changing the total amount of screen memory to be SAVEd, POKEd into 856 and 857. Also, you will need a line such as 1000 GOTO 1000 to keep a GTIA or + 16 mode screen intact. See the Atari column in *InfoAge Magazine*, July 1982, for more on this idea. See location 54277 ($D405) for some ideas on scrolling the screen RAM.

A SHORT DIGRESSION

There are two techniques used in this book for calling a machine language program from BASIC with the USR command. One method is to POKE the values into a specific address — say, page six — and use the starting address for the USR call, such as X = USR(1536). For an example of this technique, see location 632 ($278).

The other technique, used above, is to make a string (ML$) out of the routine by assigning to the elements of the string the decimal equivalents of the machine language code by using a FOR-NEXT and READ-DATA loop. To call this routine, you would use X = USR(ADR(ML$)). This tells the Atari to call the machine language routine located at the address where ML$ is stored. This address will change with program size and memory use. The string method won't be overwritten by another routine or data since it floats around safely in memory. The address of the string itself is stored by the string/array table at location 140 ($8C).

---

90   **5A**   **OLDROW**

Previous graphics cursor row. Updated from location 84 ($54) before every operation. Used to determine the starting row for the DRAWTO and XIO 18 (FILL command).

91,92   5B,5C   OLDCOL

Previous graphics cursor column. Updated from locations 85 and 86 ($55, $56) before every operation. These locations are used by the DRAWTO and XIO 18 (FILL) commands to determine the starting column of the DRAW or FILL.

93   5D   OLDCHR

Retains the value of the character under the cursor, used to restore that character when the cursor moves.

94,95   5E,5F   OLDADR

Retains the memory location of the current cursor location. Used with location 93 (above) to restore the character under the cursor when the cursor moves.

96   60   NEWROW

Point (row) to which DRAWTO and XIO 18 (FILL) will go.

97,98   61,62   NEWCOL

Point (column) to which DRAWTO and XIO 18 (FILL) will go. NEWROW and NEWCOL are initialized to the values in ROWCRS and COLCRS (84 to 86; $54 to $56) above, which represent the destination end point of the DRAW and FILL functions. This is done so that ROWCRS and COLCRS can be altered during these routines.

99   63   LOGCOL

Position of the cursor at the column in a logical line. A logical line can contain up to three physical lines, so LOGCOL can range between zero and 119. Used by the display handler.

100,101   64,65   ADRESS

Temporary storage used by the display handler for the Display List address, line buffer (583 to 622; $247 to $26E), new MEMTOP value after DL entry, row column address, DMASK value, data to the right of cursor, scroll, delete, the clear screen routine and for the screen address memory (locations 88, 89; $58, $59).

102,103   66,67   MLTTMP

Also called OPNTMP and TOADR; first byte used in OPEN as temporary storage. Also used by the display handler as temporary storage.

104,105   68,69   SAVADR

Also called FRMADR. Temporary storage, used with ADRESS above for the data under the cursor and in moving line data on the screen.

106   6A   RAMTOP

RAM size, defined by powerup as passed from TRAMSZ (location 6), given in the total number of available pages (one page equals 256 bytes, so PEEK(106) * 256 will tell you where the Atari thinks the last usable address — byte — of RAM is). MEMTOP (741, 742; $2E5, $2E6) may not extend below this value. In a 48K Atari, RAMTOP is initialized to 160 ($A0), which points to location 40960 ($A000). The user's highest address will be one byte less than this value.

This is initially the same value as in location 740. PEEK(740) / 4 or PEEK(106) / 4 gives the number of 1K blocks. You can fool the computer into thinking you have less memory than you actually have, thus reserving a relatively safe area for data (for your new character set or player/missile characters, for example) or machine language subroutines by:

POKE(106), PEEK(106) – # of pages you want to reserve.

The value here is the number of memory pages (256-byte blocks) present. This is useful to know when changing GR.7 and GR.8 screen RAM. If you are reserving memory for PM graphics, POKE 54279, PEEK(106) – # of pages you are reserving before you actually POKE 106 with that value. To test to see if you have exceeded your memory by reserving too much memory space, you can use:

```
10    SIZE = (PEEK(106) - # of pages)
   * 256
20    IF SIZE < = PEEK(144) + PEEK(145
   ) * 256 THEN PRINT "TOO MUCH MEMOR
   Y USED"
```

If you move RAMTOP to reserve memory, always issue a GRAPHICS command (even issuing one to the same GRAPHICS mode you are in will work) immediately so that the display list and data are moved beneath the new RAMTOP.

You should note that a GRAPHICS command and a CLEAR command (or PRINT CHR$ (125)) actually clear the first 64 bytes above RAMTOP (see location 88; $58 for further discussion). Scrolling the text window of a GRAPHICS mode clears up to 800 ($320) bytes above RAMTOP (the text window scroll actually scrolls an entire GR.0 screen-worth of data, so the unseen 20 lines * 40 bytes equals 800 bytes). PM graphics may be safe (unless you scroll the text window) since the first 384 or 768 bytes (double or single line resolution, respectively) are unused. However, you should take both of these effects into account when writing your programs.

To discover the *exact* end of memory, use this routine (it's a tad slow):

```
10  RAMTOP = 106: TOP = PEEK(RAMTOP)
20  BYTE = TOP * 256: TEST = 255 - PE
    EK(BYTE): POKE BYTE,TEST
30  IF PEEK(BYTE) = TEST THEN TOP = T
    OP +1: POKE BYTE, 255 - TEST
40  GOTO 20
50  PRINT "MEMORY ENDS AT ": BYTE
```

One caution: BASIC cannot always handle setting up a display list and display memory for GRAPHICS 7 and GRAPHICS 8 when you modify this location by less than 4K (16 pages; 4096 bytes). Some bizarre results may occur if you use PEEK(106) – 8 in these modes, for example. Use a minimum of 4K (PEEK(106) - 16) to avoid trouble. This may explain why some people have difficulties with player/missile graphics in the hi-res (high resolution; GR.7 and GR.8) modes. See location 54279 ($D407).

Another alternative to reserving memory in high RAM is to save an area below MEMLO, location 743 ($2E7: below your BASIC program). See also MEMTOP, locations 741, 742 ($2E5, $2E6).

107　　　6B　　　BUFCNT

Buffer count: the screen editor current logical line size counter.

108,109　　　6C,6D　　　BUFSTR

Editor low byte (AM). Display editor GETCH routine pointer (location 62867 for entry; $F593). Temporary storage; returns the character pointed to by BUFCNT above.

110　　　6E　　　BITMSK

Bit mask used in bit mapping routines by the OS display handler at locations 64235 to 64305 ($FAEB to $FB31). Also used as a display handler temporary storage register.

111　　　6F　　　SHFAMT

Pixel justification: the amount to shift the right justified pixel data on output or the amount to shift the input data to right justify it. Prior to the justification process, this value is always the same as that in 672 ($2A0).

112,113　　　70,71　　　ROWAC

ROWAC and COLAC (below) are both working accumulators for the control of row and column point plotting and the increment and decrement functions.

114,115　　　72,73　　　COLAC

Controls column point plotting.

116,117   74,75   ENDPT

End point of the line to be drawn. Contains the larger value of either DELTAR or DELTAC (locations 118 and 119, below) to be used in conjunction with ROWAC/COLAC (locations 112 and 114, above) to control the plotting of line points.

118   76   DELTAR

Delta row; contains the absolute value of NEWROW (location 96; $60) minus ROWCRS (location 84; $54).

119,120   77,78   DELTAC

Delta column; contains the absolute value of NEWCOL (location 97; $61) minus the value in COLCRS (location 85; $55). These delta register values, along with locations 121 and 122 below, are used to define the slope of the line to be drawn.

121   79   ROWINC

The row increment or decrement value (plus or minus one).

122   7A   COLINC

The column increment or decrement value (plus or minus one). ROWINC and COLINC control the direction of the line drawing routine. The values represent the signs derived from the value in NEWROW (location 96; $60) minus the value in ROWCRS (location 84; $54) and the value in NEWCOL (locations 97, 98; $61, $62) minus the value in COLCRS (locations 85, 86; $55, $56).

123   7B   SWPFLG

Split-screen cursor control. Equal to 255 ($FF) if the text window RAM and regular RAM are swapped; otherwise, it is equal to zero. In split-screen modes, the graphics cursor data and the text window data are frequently swapped in order to get the values associated with the area being accessed into the OS data base locations 84 to 95 ($54 to $5F). SWPFLG helps to keep track of which data set is in these locations.

124   7C   HOLDCH

A character value is moved here before the control and shift logic are processed for it.

125   7D   INSDAT

Temporary storage byte used by the display handler for the character under the cursor and end of line detection.

126,127   7E,7F   COUNTR

Starts out containing the larger value of either DELTAR (location 118; $76) or DELTAC (location 119; $77). This is the number of iterations required to draw a line. As each point on a line is drawn, this value is decremented. When the byte equals zero, the line is complete (drawn).

User and/or BASIC page zero RAM begins here. Locations 128 to 145 ($80 to $91) are for BASIC program pointers; 146 to 202 ($92 to $CA) are for miscellaneous BASIC RAM; 203 to 209 ($CB to $D1) are unused by BASIC, and 210 to 255 ($D2 to $FF) are the floating point routine work area. The Assembler Editor cartridge uses locations 128 to 176 ($80 to $B0) for its page zero RAM. Since the OS doesn't use this area, you are free to use it in any non-BASIC or non-cartridge environment. If you are using another language such as FORTH, check that program's memory map to see if any conflict will occur.

See *COMPUTE!'s First Book of Atari*, pages 26 to 53, for a discussion of Atari BASIC structure, especially that using locations 130 to 137 ($82 to $89). Included in the tutorials are a memory analysis, a line dump, and a renumber utility. See also *De Re Atari*, *BYTE*, February 1982, and the locations for the BASIC ROM 40960 to 49151 ($A000 to $BFFF).

128,129   80,81   LOMEM

Pointer to BASIC's low memory (at the high end of OS RAM space). The first 256 bytes of the memory pointed to are the token output buffer, which is used by BASIC to convert BASIC statements into numeric representation (tokens; see locations 136, 137; $88, $89). This value is loaded from MEMLO (locations 743, 744; $2E7, $2E8) on initialization or the execution of a NEW command (not on RESET!). Remember to update this value when changing MEMLO to reserve space for drivers or buffers.

When a BASIC SAVE is made, two blocks of information are written: the first block is the seven pointers from LOMEM to STARP (128 to 141; $80 to $8D). The value of LOMEM is subtracted from each of these two-byte pointers in the process, so the first two bytes written will both be zero. The second block contains the following: the variable name table, the variable value table, the tokenized program, and the immediate mode line.

When a BASIC LOAD is made, BASIC adds the value at MEMLO (743, 744; $2E7, $2E8) to each of the two-byte pointers SAVEd as above. The pointers are placed back in page zero, and the values of RUNSTK (142, 143; $8E, $8F) and MEMTOP (144, 145; $90, $91) are set to the value in STARP. Then 256 bytes are reserved above the value in MEMLO for the token output buffer, and the program is read in immediately following this buffer.

When you don't have DOS or any other application program using low memory loaded, LOMEM points to 1792 ($700). When

DOS 2.0 is present, it points to 7420 ($1CFC). When you change your drive and data buffer defaults (see 1801, 1802; $709, $70A), you will raise or lower this figure by 128 bytes for each buffer added or deleted, respectively. When you boot up the RS-232 handler, add another 1728 ($6C0) bytes used.

LOMEM is also called ARGOPS by BASIC when used in expression evaluation. When BASIC encounters any kind of expression, it puts the immediate results into a stack. ARGOPS points to the same 256 byte area; for this operation it is reserved for both the argument and operator stack. It is also called OUTBUFF for another operation, pointing to the same 256 byte buffer as ARGOPS points to. Used by BASIC when checking a line for syntax and converting it to tokens. This buffer temporarily stores the tokens before moving them to the program.

130,131   82,83   VNTP

Beginning address of the variable name table. Variable names are stored in the order input into your program, in ATASCII format. You can have up to 128 variable names. These are stored as tokens representing the variable number in the tokenized BASIC program, numbered from 128 to 255 ($80 to $FF).

The table continues to store variable names, even those no longer used in your program and those used in direct mode entry. It is not cleared by SAVEing your program. LOADing a new program replaces the current VNT with the one it retrieves from the file. You must LIST the program to tape or disk to save your program without these unwanted variables from the table. LIST does not SAVE the variable name or variable value tables with your program. It stores the program in ATASCII, not tokenized form, and requires an ENTER command to retrieve it. You would use a NEW statement to clear the VNT in memory once you have LISTed your program.

Each variable name is stored in the order it was entered, not the ATASCII order. With numeric (scalar) variables, the MSB is set on the last character in a name. With string variables, the last character is a "$" with the MSB (BIT 7) set. With array variables, the last character is a "(" with the MSB set. Setting the MSB turns the character into its inverse representation so it can be easily recognized.

You can use variable names for GOSUB and GOTO routines, such as:

```
10   CALCULATE = 1000
 .
 .
```

```
100 GOSUB CALCULATE
```

This can save a lot of bytes for a frequently called routine. But remember, each variable used for a GOSUB or GOTO address uses one of the 128 possible variable names. A disadvantage of using variable names for GOTO and GOSUB references is when you try to use a line renumbering program. Line renumbering programs will *not* change references to lines with variable names, only to lines with numbered references.

Here's a small routine you can add to the start of your BASIC program (or the end if you change the line numbers) to print out the variable names used in your program. You call it up with a GOTO statement in direct mode:

```
1    POKE 1664, PEEK(130): POKE 1665,
     PEEK(131)
2    IF PEEK(1664) = PEEK(132) THEN IF
     PEEK(1665) = PEEK(133) THEN STOP
3    PRINT CHR$(PEEK(PEEK(1664) + PEEK
     (1665) * 256)));
4    IF PEEK(PEEK(1664) + PEEK(1665) *
     256)) > 127 THEN PRINT"";
5    IF PEEK(1664) = 255 THEN POKE 166
     4, 0: POKE 1665, PEEK(1665) + 1: GO
     TO 2
6    POKE 1664, PEEK(1664) + 1: GOTO 2
```

See **COMPUTE!**, October 1981.

132,133   84,85   VNTD

Pointer to the ending address of the variable name table plus one byte. When fewer than 128 variables are present, it points to a dummy zero byte. When 128 variables are present, this points to the last byte of the last variable name, plus one.

It is often useful to be able to list your program variables; using locations 130 to 133, you can do that by:

```
10   VARI = PEEK(130) + PEEK(131) * 2
     56 :REM This gives you the start o
     f the table.
20   FOR VARI = VARI TO PEEK(132) + P
     EEK(133) * 256 - 1: PRINT CHR$(PEE
     K(VARI) - 128 * PEEK(VARI > 127));
     CHR$(27 + 128 * PEEK(VARI) > 127)
     );:NEXT VARI
25   REM this finds the end of the va
     riable name table (remember table
     is end + 1), then PRINTs ASCII cha
```

```
    racters < 128
30    NUM = 0: FOR VARI = PEEK(130) +
   PEEK(313) * 256 TO PEEK(132) + PEE
   K(131) * 256 - 1:NUM = NUM + (PEEK
   (VARI) < 127):NEXT VARI: PRINT   NU
   M;"Variables in use"
```

Or try this, for a possibly less opaque example of the same routine:

```
1000   NUM = 0: FOR LOOP = PEEK(130) +
   PEEK(131) * 256 TO PEEK(132) +
   PEEK(133) * 256 - 1
1010   IF PEEK(LOOP) < 128 THEN PRINT
   CHR$(PEEK(LOOP));: GOTO 1030
1020   PRINT CHR$(PEEK(LOOP) - 128): N
   UM = NUM + 1
1030   NEXT LOOP: PRINT: PRINT NUM; "
   VARIABLES IN USE": END
```

134,135   86,87   VVTP

Address for the variable value table. Eight bytes are allocated for each variable in the name table as follows:

Byte	1	2	3 4 5	6 7	8
Variable					
Scalar	00	var #	six byte BCD constant		
Array;DIMed	65	var #	offset	first	second
unDIMed	64		from STARP	DIM + 1	DIM + 1
String;DIMed	129	var #	offset	length	DIM
unDIMed	128		from STARP		

In scalar (undimensioned numeric) variables, bytes three to eight are the FP number; byte three is the exponent; byte four contains the least significant two decimal digits, and byte eight contains the most significant two decimal digits.

In array variables, bytes five and six contain the size plus one of the first dimension of the array (DIM + 1; LSB/MSB), and bytes seven and eight contain the size plus one of the second dimension (the second DIM + 1; LSB/MSB).

In string variables, bytes five and six contain the current length of the variable (LSB/MSB), and bytes seven and eight contain the actual dimension (up to 32767). There is an undocumented BASIC statement, "COM," mentioned only in the *BASIC Reference Manual*'s index, which executes exactly the same as the "DIM" statement (see *Your Atari 400/800,* p. 346). Originally, it was to be used to implement "common" variables.

In all cases, the first byte is always one of the number listed on the chart above (you will seldom, if ever, see the undimensioned values in a program). This number defines what type of variable information will follow. The next byte, var # (variable number), is in the range from zero to 127. Offset is the number of bytes from the beginning of STARP at locations 140 and 141 ($8C, $8D). Since each variable is assigned eight bytes, you could find the values for each variable by:

```
1000  VVTP = PEEK(134) + PEEK(135) *
      256: INPUT VAR: REM VARIABLE NUM
      BER
1010  FOR LOOP = 0 TO 7: PRINT PEEK(V
      VTP + LOOP + 8 * VAR): NEXT LOOP
```

where VAR is the variable number from zero to 127.

If you wish to assign the same value to every element in a DIMed string variable, use this simple technique:

```
10    DIM TEST$(100)
20    TEST$ = "*": REM or use TEST$(1)
30    TEST$(100) = TEST$
40    TEST$(2) = TEST$: PRINT TEST$
```

By assigning the first, last, and second variables in the array, in that order, your Atari will then assign the same value to the rest of the array. Make sure you make the second and last elements equal to the string, not the character value (i.e., don't use TEXT$(2) = "*").

See *De Re Atari* for an example of SAVEing the six-byte BCD numbers to a disk file — very useful when dealing with fixed record lengths.

136,137   88,89   STMTAB

The address of the statement table (which is the beginning of the user's BASIC program), containing all the tokenized lines of code plus the immediate mode lines entered by the user. Line numbers are stored as two-byte integers, and immediate mode lines are given the default value of line 32768 ($8000). The first two bytes of a tokenized line are the line number, and the next is a dummy byte reserved for the byte count (or offset) from the start of this line to the start of the next line.

Following that is another count byte for the start of this line to the start of the next statement. These count values are set only when tokenization for the line and statement are complete.

Tokenization takes place in a 256 byte ($100) buffer that resides at the end of the reserved OS RAM (pointed to by locations 128, 129; $80, $81).

To see the starting address of your BASIC line numbers, use this routine:

```
10    STMTAB = PEEK(136) + PEEK(137)*2
56
20    NUM = PEEK(STMTAB) + PEEK(STMTAB
+1)*256
30    IF NUM = 32768 THEN END
40    PRINT"LINE NUMBER: ";NUM;" ADDRE
SS: ";STMTAB
50    STMTAB = STMTAB + PEEK(STMTAB+2)
60    GOTO 20
```

The August 1982 issue of *ANTIC* provided a useful program to delete a range of BASIC line numbers. The routine can be appended to your program and even be used to delete itself.

138,139   8A,8B   STMCUR

Current BASIC statement pointer, used to access the tokens being currently processed within a line of the statement table. When BASIC is awaiting input, this pointer is set to the beginning of the immediate mode (line 32768).

Using the address of the variable name table, the length, and the current statement (locations 130 to 133, 138, 139), here is a way to protect your programs from being LISTed or LOADed: they can only be RUN! Remember, that restricts you too, *so make sure you have SAVEd an unchanged version before you do this:*

```
32000    FOR VARI = PEEK(130) + PEEK(1
31) * 256 TO PEEK(132) + PEEK(1
33) * 256:POKE VARI,155:NEXT VA
RI
32100    POKE PEEK(138) + PEEK(139) *
256 + 2,0: SAVE "D:filename": N
EW
```

This will cause all variable names to be replaced with a RETURN character. Other characters may be used: simply change 155 for the appropriate ATASCII code for the character desired. Make sure that these are the last two lines of your program and that NEW is the last statement. CLOAD will not work, but a filename with C: will.

140,141   8C,8D   STARP

The address for the string and array table and a pointer to the end of your BASIC program. Arrays are stored as six-byte binary coded decimal numbers (BCD) while string characters use one bye each. The address of the strings in the table are the same as those returned by the BASIC ADR function. Always use this function under program control, since the addresses in the table change according to your program size. Try:

```
10    DIM A$(10),B$(10)
20    A$ = "*": A$(10) = A$: A$(2) = A
      $
30    B$ = "&": B$(10) = B$: B$(2) = B
      $
40    PRINT ADR(A$), ADR(B$)
50    PRINT PEEK(140) + PEEK(141) * 25
      6: REM ADDRESS OF A$
60    PRINT PEEK(140) + PEEK(141) * 25
      6 + 10: REM ADRESS OF A$ + 10 BYTE
      S = ADDRESS OF B$
```

This table is expanded as each dimension is processed by BASIC, reducing available memory. A ten-element numeric array will require 60 bytes for storage. An array variable such as DIM A(100) will cost the program 600 bytes (100 * six per dimensioned number equals 600). On the other hand, a string array such as DIM A$(100) will only cost 100 bytes! It would save a lot of memory to write your arrays as strings and retrieve the array values using the VAL statement. For example:

```
10    DIM A$(10): A$ = "1234567890"
20    PRINT VAL(A$)
30    PRINT VAL(A$(4,4))
40    PRINT VAL(A$(3,3))+VAL(A$(8,9))
```

See **COMPUTE!**, June 1982, for a discussion of STARP and VVTP. See *De Re Atari* for a means to SAVE the string/array area with your program.

142,143   8E,8F   RUNSTK

Address of the runtime stack which holds the GOSUB entries (four bytes each) and the FOR-NEXT entries (16 bytes each). The POP command in BASIC affects this stack, pulling entries off it one at a time for each POP executed. The stack expands and contracts as necessary while the program is running.

Each GOSUB entry consists of four bytes in this order: a zero to indicate a GOSUB, a two-byte integer line number on which the call occurred, and an offset into that line so the RETURN can come back and execute the next statement.

Each FOR-NEXT entry contains 16 bytes in this order: first, the limit the counter variable can reach; second, the step or counter increment. These two are allocated six bytes each in BCD format (12 bytes total). The 13th byte is the counter variable number with the MSB set; the 14th and 15th are the line number and the 16th is the line offset to the FOR statement.

RUNSTK is also called ENDSTAR; it is used by BASIC to point to the end of the string/array space pointed to by STARP above.

144,145   90,91   MEMTOP

Pointer to the top of BASIC memory, the end of the space the program takes up. There may still be space between this address and the display list, the size of which may be retrieved by the FRE(0) command (which actually subtracts the MEMTOP value that is at locations 741 and 742; $2E5, $2E6). Not to be confused with locations 741 and 742, which have the same name but are an OS variable. MEMTOP is also called TOPSTK; it points to the top of the stack space pointed to by RUNSTK above.

When reserving memory using location 106 ($6A) and MEMTOP, here's a short error-trapping routine you can add:

```
10    SIZE = (PEEK(106)- # of pages yo
u are reserving) * 256
20    IF SIZE < = PEEK(144) + PEEK(145
) * 256 THEN PRINT " PROGRAM TOO L
ARGE": END
```

Locations 146 to 202 ($92 to $CA) are reserved for use by the 8K BASIC ROM.

Locations 176 to 207 ($B0 to $CF) are reserved by the Assembler Editor cartridge for the user's page zero use. The Assembler debug routine also reserves 30 bytes in page zero, scattered from location 164 ($A4) to 255 ($FF), but they cannot be used outside the debug process. (See *De Re Atari*, Rev. 1, Appendix A for a list of these available bytes.)

186,187   BA,BB   STOPLN

The line where a program was stopped either due to an error or the use of the BREAK key, or a STOP or a TRAP statement occurred. You can use PEEK (186) + PEEK (187) * 256 in a GOTO or GOSUB statement.

195   C3   ERRSAVE

The number of the error code that caused the stop or the TRAP. You can use this location in a program in a line such as:

```
10 IF PEEK(195) <> 144 THEN 100
```

201   C9   PTABW

This location specifies the number of columns between TAB stops. The first tab will be at PEEK(201). The default is ten. This is the value between items separated in a PRINT statement by commas — such as PRINT A$, LOOP, C(12) — not by the TAB key spacing.

The minimum number of spaces between TABS is three. If you POKE 201,2, it will be treated as four spaces, and POKE 201,1 is treated as three spaces. POKE 201,0 will cause the system to hang when it encounters a PRINT statement with commas. To change the TAB key settings, see TABMAP (locations 675 to 689; $2A3 - $2B1). PTABW is *not* reset to the default value by pressing RESET or changing GRAPHICS modes (unlike TABMAP).

PTABW works in all GRAPHICS modes, not merely in text modes. The size of the spaces between items depends on the pixel size in the GRAPHICS mode in use. For example, in GR.0, each space is one character wide, while in GR.8 each space is one-half color clock (one dot) wide.

203-207   CB-CF   ....
Unused by either the BASIC or the Assembler cartridges.

208-209   D0-D1   ....
Unused by BASIC. The only time I have seen any of these unused locations in use is in **COMPUTE!** (March 1982 and October 1981), when they were used for user sort routines, and in *ANTIC* (June 1982), where they were used as flags in a graphic demonstration. The bytes from 203 to 209 ($CB to $D1) are the only page zero bytes uncontestably left free by BASIC.

210-211   D2-D3   ....
Reserved for BASIC or other cartridge use.

Locations 212 to 255 ($D4 to $FF) are reserved for the floating point package use. The FP routines are in ROM, from locations 55296 to 57393 ($D800 to $E031). These page zero locations may be used if the FP package is not called by the user's program. However, do not use any of these locations for an interrupt routine, since such routines might occur during an FP routine called by BASIC, causing the system to crash.

Floating Point uses a six-byte precision. The first byte of the Binary Coded Decimal (BCD) number is the exponent (where if BIT 7 equals zero, then the number is positive; if one, then it is negative). The next five bytes are the mantissa. If only that were all there was to it. The BCD format is rather complex and is best explained in chapter eight of *De Re Atari*.

212-217   D4-D9   FR0
Floating point register zero; holds a six-byte internal form of the FP number. The value at locations 212 and 213 are used to return a two-byte hexadecimal value in the range of zero to 65536

($FFFF) to the BASIC program (low byte in 212, high byte in 213). The floating point package, if used, requires all locations from 212 to 255. All six bytes of FR0 can be used by a machine language routine, provided FR0 isn't used and no FP functions are used by that routine. To use 16 bit values in FP, you would place the two bytes of the number into the least two bytes of FR0 (212, 213; $D4, $D5), and then do a JSR to $D9AA (55722), which will convert the integer to its FP representation, leaving the result in FR0. To reverse this operation, do a JSR to $D9D2 (55762).

218-223   DA-DF   FRE
FP extra register (?)

224-229   E0-E5   FR1
Floating point register one; holds a six-byte internal form of the FP number as does FR0. The FP package frequently transfers data between these two registers and uses both for two-number arithmetic operations.

230-235   E6-EB   FR2
FP register two.

236   EC   FRX
FP spare register.

237   ED   EEXP
The value of E (the exponent).

238   EE   NSIGN
The sign of the FP number.

239   EF   ESIGN
The sign of the exponent.

240   F0   FCHRFLG
The first character flag.

241   F1   DIGRT
The number of digits to the right of the decimal.

242   F2   CIX
Character (current input) index. Used as an offset to the input text buffer pointed to by INBUFF below.

243,244   F3,F4   INBUFF
Input ASCII text buffer pointer; the user's program line input buffer, used in the translation of ATASCII code to FP values. The result output buffer is at locations 1408 to 1535 ($580 to $5FF).

245,246   F5,F6   ZTEMP1
Temporary register.

247,248 **F7,F8** **ZTEMP4**
Temporary register.

249,250 **F9,FA** **ZTEMP3**
Temporary register.

251 **FB** **RADFLG**
Also called DEGFLG. When set to zero, all of the trigonometric functions are performed in radians; when set to six, they are done in degrees. BASIC's NEW command and RESET both restore RADFLG to radians.

252,253 **FC,FD** **FLPTR**
Points to the user's FP number.

254,255 **FE,FF** **FPTR2**
Pointer to the user's second FP number to be used in an operation.
End of the page zero RAM.

PAGE ONE: THE STACK

Locations 256 to 511 ($100 to $1FF) are the stack area for the OS, DOS and BASIC. This area is page one. Machine language JSR,PHA and interrupts all cause data to be written to page one, and RTS, PLA and RTI instructions all read data from page one. On powerup or RESET, the stack pointer is initialized to point to location 511 ($1FF). The stack then pushes downward with each entry to 256 ($100). In case of overflow, the stack will wrap around from 256 back to 511 again.

PAGES TWO TO FOUR

Locations 512 to 1151 ($200 to $47F) are used by the OS for working variables, tables and data buffers. In this area, locations 512 to 553 ($200 to $229) are used for interrupt vectors, and locations 554 to 623 ($22A to $26F) are for miscellaneous use. Much of pages two through five cannot be used except by the OS unless specifically noted. A number of bytes are marked as "spare", i.e., not in use currently. The status of these bytes may change with an Atari upgrade, so their use is not recommended.

There are two types of interrupts: Non-Maskable Interrupts (NMI) processed by the ANTIC chip and Interrupt Requests (IRQ) processed by the POKEY and the PIA chips. NMI's are for the VBLANK interrupts (VBI's; 546 to 549, $222 to $225), display list interrupts (DLI) and RESET key interrupts. They initiate the stage one and stage two VBLANK procedures; usually vectored through an OS service routine, they can be vectored to point to a user routine. IRQ's are for the timer interrupts, peripheral and serial bus interrupts, BREAK and other key interrupts, and 6502 BRK instruction interrupts. They can usually be used to vector to user routines. See NMIST 54287 ($D40F) and IRQEN 53774 ($D20E) for more information. NMI interrupt vectors are marked NMI; IRQ interrupt vectors are marked IRQ.

Refer to the chart below location 534 for a list of the interrupt vectors in the new OS "B" version ROMs.

512,513   200,201   VDSLST

The vector for NMI Display List Interrupts (DLI): containing the address of the instructions to be executed during a DLI (DLI's are used to interrupt the processor flow for a few microseconds at the particular screen display line where the bit was set, allowing you to do another short routine such as music, changing graphics modes, etc.). The OS doesn't use DLI's; they must be user-enabled, written and vectored through here. The NMI status register at 54287 ($D40F) first tests to see if an interrupt was caused by a DLI and, if so, jumps through VDSLST to the routine written by the user. DLI's are disabled on powerup, but VBI's are enabled (see 546 to 549; $222 to $225).

VDSLST is initialized to point to 59315 ($E7B3), which is merely an RTI instruction. To enable DLI's, you must first POKE 54286 ($D40E) with 192 ($C0); otherwise, ANTIC will ignore your request. You then POKE 512 and 513 with the address (LSB/MSB) of the first assembly language routine to execute during the DLI. You must then set BIT 7 of the Display List instruction(s) where the DLI is to occur. You have only between 14 and 61 machine cycles available for your DLI, depending on your GRAPHICS mode. You must first push any 6502 registers onto the stack, and you must end your DLI with an RTI instruction. Because you are dealing with machine language for your DLI, you can POKE directly into the hardware registers you plan to change, rather than using the shadow registers that BASIC uses.

There is, unfortunately, only one DLI vector address. If you use more than one DLI and they are to perform different activities, then changing the vectoring to point to a different routine must be done by the previous DLI's themselves.

Another way to accomplish interrupts is during the VBLANK interval with a VBI. One small problem with using DLI's is that the keyboard "click" routine interferes with the DLI by throwing off the timing, since the click is provided by several calls to the WSYNC register at 54282 ($D40A). Chris Crawford discusses several solutions in *De Re Atari*, but the easiest of them is not to allow input from the keyboard! See *Micro*, December 1981, *Creative Computing*, July 1981 and December 1981.

Here's a short example of a DLI. It will print the lower half of your
text screen upside down:
```
10    START = PEEK(560) + PEEK(561) *
      256: POKE START + 16,130
20    PAGE = 1536: FOR PGM = PAGE TO P
AGE + 7: READ BYTE: POKE PGM, BYTE
      : NEXT PGM
30    DATA 72,169,4,141,1,212,104,64
40    POKE 512,0: POKE 513,6: POKE 542
      86,192
50    FOR TEST = 1 TO 240: PRINT"SEE  "
      ;: NEXT TEST
60    GOTO 60
```
Another example of a DLI changes the color of the bottom half of
the screen. To use it, simply change the PAGE + 7 to PAGE + 10
in the program above and replace line 30 with:
```
30    DATA 72,169,222,141,10,212,141,2
      4,208,104,64
```
Finally, delete lines 50 and 60. See also location 54282 ($D40A).

514,515   202,203   VPRCED

Serial (peripheral) proceed line vector, initialized to 59314
($E7B2), which is merely a PLA, RTI instruction sequence. It is
used when an IRQ interrupt occurs due to the serial I/O bus
proceed line which is available for peripheral use. According to
De Re Atari, this interrupt is not used and points to a PLA, RTI
instruction sequence. This interrupt is handled by the PIA chip
and can be used to provide more control over external devices.
See the OS Listing, page 33.

516,517   204,205   VINTER

Serial (peripheral) interrupt vector, initialized to 59314 ($E7B2).
Used for the IRQ interrupt due to a serial bus I/O interrupt.
According to *De Re Atari*, this interrupt is not used and points to
a PLA, RTI sequence. This interrupt is processed by PIA. See the
OS Listing, page 33.

518,519   206,207   VBREAK

Software break instruction vector for the 6502 BRK ($00)
command (not the BREAK key, which is at location 17; $11),
initialized to 59314 ($E7B2). This vector is normally used for
setting break points in an assembly language debug operation.
IRQ.

520,521   208,209   VKEYBD

POKEY keyboard interrupt vector, used for an interrupt
generated when any keyboard key is pressed other than BREAK

or the console buttons. Console buttons never generate an interrupt unless one is specifically user-written. VKEYBD can be used to process the key code before it undergoes conversion to ATASCII form. Initialized to 65470 ($FFBE), which is the OS keyboard IRQ routine.

522,523   20A,20B   VSERIN

POKEY serial I/O bus receive data ready interrupt vector, initialized to 60177 ($EB11), which is the OS code to place a byte from the serial input port into a buffer. Called INTRVEC by DOS, it is used as an interrupt vector location for an SIO patch. DOS changes this vector to 6691 ($1A23), the start of the DOS interrupt ready service routine. IRQ.

524,525   20C,20D   VSEROR

POKEY serial I/O transmit ready interrupt vector, initialized to 60048 (EA90), which is the OS code to provide the next byte in a buffer to the serial output port. DOS changes this vector to 6630 ($19E6), the start of the DOS output needed interrupt routine. IRQ.

526,527   20E,20F   VSEROC

POKEY serial bus transmit complete interrupt vector, initialized to 60113 ($EAD1), which sets a transmission done flag after the checksum byte is sent. IRQ.

SIO uses the three last interrupts to control serial bus communication with the serial bus devices. During serial bus communication, all program execution is halted. The actual serial I/O is interrupt driven; POKEY waits and watches for a flag to be set when the requested I/O operation is completed. During this wait, POKEY is sending or receiving bits along the serial bus. When the entire byte has been transmitted (or received), the output needed (VSEROR) or the input ready (VSERIN) IRQ is generated according to the direction of the data flow. This causes the next byte to be processed until the entire buffer has been sent or is full, and a flag for "transmission done" is set. At this point, SIO exits back to the calling routine. You can see that SIO wastes time waiting for POKEY to send or receive the information on the bus.

528,529   210,211   VTIMR1

POKEY timer one interrupt vector, initialized to 59314 ($E7B2), which is a PLA, RTI instruction sequence. Timer interrupts are established when the POKEY timer AUDF1 (53760; $D200) counts down to zero. Values in the AUDF registers are loaded into STIMER at 53769 ($D209). IRQ.

530,531   212,213   VTIMR2
POKEY timer two vector for AUDF2 (53762, $D202), initialized to 59314 ($E7B2). IRQ.

532,533   214,215   VTIMR4
POKEY timer four vector for AUDF4 (53766, $D206), initialized to 59314 ($E7B2). This IRQ is only vectored in the "B" version of the OS ROMs.

534,535   216,217   VIMIRQ
The IRQ immediate vector (general). Initialized to 59126 ($E6F6). JMP through here to determine cause of the IRQ interrupt. Note that with the new ("B") OS ROMs, there is a BREAK key interrupt vector at locations 566, 567 ($236, $237).

See 53774 ($D20E) for more information on IRQ interrupts.

The new "B" version OS ROMs change the vectors above as follows:

VDSLST	59280 ($E790)
VPRCED	59279 ($E78F)
VINTER	59279 ($E78F)
VBREAK	59279 ($E78F)
VKEYBD	NO CHANGE
VSERIN	60175 ($EB0F)
VSEROR	NO CHANGE
VSEROC	60111 ($EACF)
VTIMR 1-4	59279 ($E78F)
VIMIRQ	59142 ($E706)
VVBLKI	59310 ($E7AE)
VVBLKD	59653 ($E905)

The locations from 536 to 558 ($218 to $22E) are used for the system software timers. Hardware timers are located in the POKEY chip and use the AUDF registers. These timers count backwards every 1/60 second (stage one VBLANK) or 1/30 second (stage two VBLANK) interval until they reach zero. If the VBLANK process is disabled or intercepted, the timers will not be updated. See *De Re Atari* for information regarding setting these timers in an assembly routine using the SETVBV register (58460; $E45C). These locations are user-accessible and can be made to count time for music duration, game I/O, game clock and other functions.

Software timers are used for durations greater than one VBLANK interval (1/60 second). For periods of shorter duration, use the hardware registers.

536,537   218,219   CDTMV1
System timer one value. Counts backwards from 255. This SIO

timer is decremented every stage one VBLANK. When it reaches zero, it sets a flag to jump (JSR) through the address stored in locations 550, 551 ($226, $227). Only the realtime clock (locations 18-20; $12-14), timer one, and the attract mode register (77; $4D) are updated when the VBLANK routine is cut short because time-critical code (location 66; $42 set to non-zero for critical code) is executed by the OS. Since the OS uses timer one for its I/O routines and for timing serial bus operations (setting it to different values for timeout routines), you should use another timer to avoid conflicts or interference with the operation of the system.

538,539   21A,21B   CDTMV2

System timer two. Decremented at the stage two VBLANK. Can be decremented every stage one VBLANK, subject to critical section test as defined by setting of CRITIC flag (location 66; $42). This timer may miss (skip) a count when time-critical code (CRITIC equals non-zero) is being executed. It performs a JSR through location 552, 553 ($228, $229) when the value counts down to zero.

540,541   21C,21D   CDTMV3

System timer three. Same as 538. Timers three, four, and five are stopped when the OS sets the CRITIC flag to non-zero as well. The OS uses timer three to OPEN the cassette recorder and to set the length of time to read and write tape headers. Any prior value in the register during this function will be lost.

542,543   21E,21F   CDTMV4

System timer four. Same as 538 ($21A).

544,545   220,221   CDTMV5

System timer five. Same as 538 ($21A). Timers three, four, and five all set flags at 554, 556 and 558 ($22A, $22C, $22E), respectively, when they decrement to zero.

546,547   222,223   VVBLKI

VBLANK immediate register. Normally jumps to the stage one VBLANK vector NMI interrupt processor at location 59345 ($E7D1); in the new OS "B" ROMs; 59310, $E7AE). The NMI status register tests to see if the interrupt was due to a VBI (after testing for a DLI) and, if so, vectors through here to the VBI routine, which may be user-written. On powerup, VBI's are enabled and DLI's are disabled. See location 512; $200.

548,549   224,225   VVBLKD

VBLANK deferred register; system return from interrupt, initialized to 59710 ($E93E, in the new OS "B" ROMs; 59653;

$E905), the exit for the VBLANK routine. NMI.

These two VBLANK vectors point to interrupt routines that occur at the beginning of the VBLANK time interval. The stage one VBLANK routine is executed; then location 66 ($42) is tested for the time-critical nature of the interrupt and, if a critical code section has been interrupted, the stage two VBLANK routine is not executed with a JMP made through the immediate vector VVBLKI. If not critical, the deferred interrupt VVBLKD is used. Normally the VBLANK interrupt bits are enabled (BIT 6 at location 54286; $D40E is set to one). To disable them, clear BIT 6 (set to zero).

The normal sequence for VBLANK interrupt events is: after the OS test, JMP to the user immediate VBLANK interrupt routine through the vector at 546, 547 (above), then through SYSVBV at 58463 ($E45F). This is directed by the OS through the VBLANK interrupt service routine at 59345 ($E7D1) and then on to the user-deferred VBLANK interrupt routine vectored at 548, 549. It then exits the VBLANK interrupt routine through 58466 ($E462) and an RTI instruction.

If you are changing the VBLANK vectors during the interrupt routine, use the SETVBV routine at 58460 ($E45C). An immediate VBI has about 3800 machine cycles of time to use; a deferred VBI has about 20,000 cycles. Since many of these cycles are executed while the electron beam is being drawn, it is suggested that you do not execute graphics routines in deferred VBI's. See the table of VBLANK processes at the end of the map area.

If you create your own VBI's, terminate an immediate VBI with a JMP to 58463 ($E45F) and a deferred VBI with a JMP to 58466 ($E462). To bypass the OS VBI routine at 59345 ($E7D1) entirely, terminate your immediate VBI with a JMP to 58466 ($E462).

Here's an example of using a VBI to create a flashing cursor. It will also blink any text you display in inverse mode.

```
10    FOR BLINK = 1664 TO 1680: READ B
YTE: POKE BLINK, BYTE: NEXT BLINK
20    POKE 548,128: POKE 549,6
30    DATA 8,72,165,20,41,16,74,74,74,
141
40    DATA 243,2,104,40,76,62,233
```

To restore the normal cursor and display, POKE 548,62 and POKE 549,233.

550,551   226,227   CDTMA1

System timer one jump address, initialized to 60400 ($EBF0).

When locations 536, 537 ($218, $219) reach (count down to) zero, the OS vectors through here (jumps to the location specified by these two addresses). You can set your machine code routine address here for execution when timer one reaches (counts down to) zero. Your code should end with the RTS instruction. Problems may occur when timer values are set greater than 255, since the 6502 cannot manipulate 16-bit values directly (a number in the range of zero to 255 is an eight-bit value; if a value requires two bytes to store, such as a memory location, it is a 16-bit value). Technically, a VBLANK interrupt could occur when one timer byte is being initialized and the other not yet set. To avoid this, keep timer values less than 255. See the *Atari OS User's Manual,* page 106, for details.

Since the OS uses timer one, it is recommended that you use timer two instead, to avoid conflicts with the operation of the Atari. Initialized to 60396 ($EBEA) in the old ROMs, 60400 ($EBF0) in the new ROMs. NMI

552,553   228,229   CDTMA2

System timer two jump address. Not used by the OS, available to user to enter the address of his or her own routine to JMP to when the timer two (538, 539; $21A, $21B) count reaches zero. Initialized to zero; the address must be user specified. NMI

554   22A   CDTMF3

System timer three flag, set when location 540, 541 ($21C, $21D) reaches zero. This register is also used by DOS as a timeout flag.

555   22B   SRTIMR

Software repeat timer, controlled by the IRQ device routine. It establishes the initial ½ second delay before a key will repeat. Stage two VBLANK establishes the 1/10 second repeat rate, decrements the timer and implements the auto repeat logic. Every time a key is pressed, STIMER is set to 48 ($30). Whenever SRTIMR is equal to zero and a key is being continuously pressed, the value of that key is continually stored in CH, location 764 ($2FC).

556   22C   CDTMF4

System timer four flag. Set when location 542, 543 ($21E, $21F) counts down to zero.

557   22D   INTEMP

Temporary register used by the SETVBL routine at 58460 ($E45C).

558   22E   CDTMF5

System timer five flag. Set when location 558, 559 ($22E, $22F) counts down to zero.

559 22F SDMCTL

Direct Memory Access (DMA) enable. POKEing with zero allows
you to turn off ANTIC and speed up processing by 30%. Of
course, it also means the screen goes blank when ANTIC is
turned off! This is useful to speed things up when you are doing a
calculation that would take a long time. It is also handy to turn off
the screen when loading a drawing, then turning it on when the
screen is loaded so that it appears instantly, complete on the
screen. To use it you must first PEEK(559) and save the result in
order to return your screen to you. Then POKE 559,0 to turn off
ANTIC. When you are ready to bring the screen back to life,
POKE 559 with the number saved earlier.

This location is the shadow register for 54272 ($D400), and the
number you PEEKed above defines the playfield size, whether or
not the missiles and players are enabled, and the player size
resolution. To enable your options by using POKE 559, simply
add up the values below to obtain the correct number to POKE
into SDMCTL. Note that you must choose only one of the four
playfield options appearing at the beginning of the list:

Option	Decimal	Bit
No playfield	0	0
Narrow playfield	1	0
Standard playfield	2	0,1
Wide playfield	3	0,1
Enable missle DMA	4	2
Enable player DMA	8	3
Enable player and missile DMA	12	2,3
One line player resolution	16	4
Enable instructions to fetch DMA	32	5 (see below)

Note that two-line player resolution is the default and that it is not
necessary to add a value to 559 to obtain it. I have included the
appropriate bits affected in the table above. The default is 34
($22).

The playfield is the area of the TV screen you will use for display,
text, and graphics. Narrow playfield is 128 color clocks (32
characters wide in GR.0), standard playfield is 160 color clocks
(40 characters), and wide playfield is 192 color clocks wide (48
characters). A color clock is a physical measure of horizontal
distance on the TV screen. There are a total of 228 color clocks on
a line, but only some of these (usually 176 maximum) will be
visible due to screen limitations. A pixel, on the other hand, is a

logical unit which varies in size with the GRAPHICS mode. Due to the limitations of most TV sets, you will not be able to see all of the wide playfield unless you scroll into the offscreen portions. BIT 5 must be set to enable ANTIC operation; it enables DMA for fetching the display list instructions.

560,561 230,231 SDLSTL

Starting address of the display list. The display list is an instruction set to tell ANTIC where the screen data is and how to display it. These locations are the shadow for 54274 and 54275 ($D402, $D403). You can also find the address of the DL by PEEKing one byte above the top of free memory:

PRINT PEEK(741) + PEEK(742) * 256 + 1.

However, 560 and 561 are more reliable pointers since custom DL's can be elsewhere in memory. Atari standard display lists simply instruct the ANTIC chip as to which types of mode lines to use for a screen and where the screen data may be found in memory. Normally, a DL is between 24 and 256 bytes long (most are less than 100 bytes, however), depending on your GRAPHICS mode (see location 88,89 for a chart of DL sizes and screen display use).

By altering the DL, you can mix graphics modes on the same screen; enable fine scrolling; change the location of the screen data; and force interrupts (DLI's) in order to perform short machine language routines.

DL bytes five and six are the addresses of the screen memory data, the same as in locations 88 and 89 ($58, $59). Bytes four, five, and six are the first Load Memory Scan (LMS) instruction. Byte four tells ANTIC what mode to use; the next two bytes are the location of the first byte of the screen RAM (LSB/MSB). Knowing this location allows you to write directly to the screen by using POKE commands (you POKE the internal character codes, not the ATASCII codes — see the *BASIC Reference Manual*, p. 55).

For example, the program below will POKE the internal codes to the various screen modes. You can see not only how each screen mode handles the codes, but also roughly where the text window is in relation to the display screen (the 160 bytes below RAMTOP). Note that the GTIA modes have no text window. If you don't have the GTIA chip, your Atari will default to GRAPHICS 8, but with GTIA formatting.

```
1    TRAP 10: GRAPHICS Z
5    SCREEN = PEEK(560) + PEEK(561) *
     256
```

```
6    TV = SCREEN + 4: TELE = SCREEN + 5
8    DISPLAY = PEEK(TV) + PEEK(TELE) *
     256
10   FOR N = 0 TO 255: POKE DISPLAY +
     N,N: NEXT N
20   DISPLAY = DISPLAY + N
30   IF DISPLAY > 40959 THEN Z = Z + 1
     : GOTO 1
40   GOTO 10
50   Z = Z + 1:IF Z > 60 THEN END
60   GOTO 1
```

Here's another short program which will allow you to examine the DL in any GRAPHICS mode:

```
10   REM CLEAR SCREEN FIRST
20   PRINT"ENTER GRAPHICS MODE": REM A
     DD 16 TO THE MODE TO SUPPRESS THE
     TEXT WINDOW
30   INPUT A: GRAPHICS A
40   DLIST = PEEK(560) + PEEK(561) * 2
     56
50   LOOK = PEEK(DLIST): PRINT LOOK;"
     ";
60   IF LOOK <> 65 THEN DLIST = DLIST
     + 1: GOTO 50
70   LPRINT PEEK(DLIST + 1);" ";PEEK(D
     LIST + 2)
80   END
```

The value 65 in the DL is the last instruction encountered. It tells ANTIC to jump to the address in the next two bytes to re-execute the DL, and wait for the next VBLANK. If you don't have a printer, change the LPRINT commands to PRINT and modify the routine to save the data in an array and PRINT it to the screen after (in GR.0).

If you would like to examine the locations of the start of the Display List, screen, and text window, try:

```
5    REM CLEAR SCREEN FIRST
6    INPUT A: GRAPHICS A
10   DIM DLIST$(10), SAVMSC$(10), TXT$
     (10)
15   DLIST$ = "DLIST": SAVMSC$ = "SAVM
     SC": TXT$ = "TEXT"
20   DLIST = PEEK(560) + PEEK(561) * 2
     56
30   SAV = PEEK(88) + PEEK(89) * 256:
```

```
    TXT = PEEK(660) + PEEK(661) * 256
40   PRINT DLIST$;" ";DLIST,SAVMSC$;"
     ";SAV
50   PRINT TXT$;" ";TEXT
60   INPUT A: GRAPHICS A: GOTO 20
```

Since an LMS is simply a map mode (graphics) or character mode (text) instruction with BIT six set, you can make any or all of these instructions into LMS instructions quite easily, pointing each line to a different RAM area if necessary. This is discussed in *De Re Atari* on implementing horizontal scrolling.

DL's can be used to help generate some of the ANTIC screen modes that aren't supported by BASIC, such as 7.5 (ANTIC mode E) or ANTIC mode three, the lowercase with descenders mode (very interesting; ten scan lines in height which allow true descenders on lowercase letters).

If you create your own custom DL, you POKE its address here. Hitting RESET or changing GRAPHICS modes will restore the OS DL address, however. The display list instruction is loaded into a special register called the Display Instruction Register (IR) which processes the three DL instructions (blank, jump, or display). It cannot be accessed directly by the programmer in either BASIC or machine language. A DL cannot cross a 1K boundary unless a jump instruction is used.

There are only four display list instructions: blank line (uses BAK color), map mode, text mode, and jump. Text (character mode) instructions and map mode (graphics) instructions range from two to 15 ($2 to $F) and are the same as the ANTIC GRAPHICS modes. A DL instruction byte uses the following conventions (functions are enabled when the bit is set to one):

Bit	Decimal	Function
7	128	Display List Interrupt when set (enabled equals one)
6	64	Load Memory Scan. Next two bytes are the LSB/MSB of the data to load.
5	32	Enable vertical fine scrolling.
4	16	Enable horizontal fine scrolling.
3-0	8-1	Mode

```
          0  0  1  0   Character
             to         Modes
          0  1  1  1

          . . . . . .
          1  0  0  0   Map
             to         Modes
          1  1  1  1
```

The above bits may be combined (i.e., DLI, scrolling and LMS together) if the user wishes.

Special DL instructions (with decimal values):

Blank 1 line =   0   5 lines =   64
     2 lines = 16   6 lines =   80
     3 lines = 32   7 lines =   96
     4 lines = 48   8 lines = 112

Jump instruction (JMP) = zero (three-byte instruction).

Jump and wait for Vertical Blank (JVP) = 65 (three-byte instruction).

Special instructions may be combined only with DL interrupt instructions.

A Display List Interrupt is a special form of interrupt that takes place during the screen display when the ANTIC encounters a DL instruction with the interrupt BIT 7 set. See location 512 ($200) for DLI information.

Since DL's are too large a topic to cover properly in this manual, I suggest you look in the many magazines (i.e., *Creative Computing*, July 1981, August 1981; *Micro*, December 1981; *Softside*, #30 to 32, and *BYTE*, December 1981) for a more detailed explanation.

562   **232**   **SSKCTL**

Serial port control register, shadow for 53775 ($D20F). Setting the bits in this register to one has the following effect:

Bit	Decimal	Function
0	1	Enable the keyboard debounce circuit.
1	2	Enable the keyboard scanning circuit.
2	4	The pot counter completes a read within two scan lines instead of one frame time.
3	8	Serial output transmitted as two-tone instead of logic true/false (**POKEY** two-tone mode).
4-6	16-64	Serial port mode control.
7	128	Force break; serial output to zero.

Initialized to 19 ($13), which sets bits zero, one and four.

563   **233**   **SPARE**

No OS use. See the note at location 651 regarding spare bytes.

564   **234**   **LPENH**

Light pen horizontal value: shadow for 54284 ($D40C). Values range from zero to 227.

565   **235**   **LPENV**

Light pen vertical value: shadow for 54285 ($D40D). Value is the same as VCOUNT register for two-line resolution (see 54283; $D40B). Both light pen values are modified when the trigger is pressed (pulled low). The light pen positions are not the same as the normal screen row and column positions. There are 96 vertical positions, numbered from 16 at the top to 111 at the bottom, each one equivalent to a scan line. Horizontal positions are marked in color clocks. There are 228 horizontal positions, numbered from 67 at the left. When the LPENH value reaches 255, it is reset to zero and begins counting again by one to the rightmost edge, which has a value of seven.

Obviously, because of the number of positions readable and the small size of each, a certain leeway must be given by the programmer when using light pen readouts on a program. At the time of this writing, Atari had not yet released its light pen onto the market, although other companies have.

566,567   236,237   BRKKY

BREAK key interrupt vector. This vector is available only with the version "B" OS ROMs, not the earlier version. You can use this vector to write your own BREAK key interrupt routine. Initialized to 59220 ($E754).

568,569   238,239   ....

Two spare bytes.

570   23A   CDEVIC

Four-byte command frame buffer (CFB) address for a device — used by SIO while performing serial I/O, not for user access. CDEVIC is used for the SIO bus ID number. The other three CFB bytes are:

571   23B   CCOMND

The SIO bus command code.

572   23C   CAUX1

Command auxiliary byte one, loaded from location 778 ($30A) by SIO.

573   23D   CAUX2

Command auxiliary byte two, loaded from location 779 ($30B) by SIO.

574   23E   TEMP

Temporary RAM register for SIO.

575   23F   ERRFLG

SIO error flag; any device error except the timeout error (time equals zero).

576	**240**	**DFLAGS**

Disk flags read from the first byte of the boot file (sector one) of the disk.

577	**241**	**DBSECT**

The number of disk boot sectors read from the first disk record.

578,579	**242,243**	**BOOTAD**

The address for where the disk boot loader will be put. The record just read will be moved to the address specified here, followed by the remaining records to be read. Normally, with DOS, this address is 1792 ($700), the value also stored temporarily in RAMLO at 4, 5. Address 62189 ($F2ED) is the OS disk boot routine entry point (DOBOOT).

580	**244**	**COLDST**

Coldstart flag. Zero is normal; if zero, then pressing RESET will not result in reboot. If POKEd with one (powerup in progress flag), the computer will reboot whenever the RESET key is pressed. Any non-zero number indicates the initial powerup routine is in progress.

If you create an AUTORUN.SYS file, it should end with an RTS instruction. If not, it should POKE 580 with zero and POKE 9 with one. You can turn any binary file that boots when loaded with DOS menu selection "L" into an auto-boot file simply by renaming it "AUTORUN.SYS". Be careful not to use the same name for any two files on the same disk.

When this is combined with the disabling of the BREAK key discussed in location 16 ($10) and the program protection scheme discussed in location 138 ($8A), you have the means to protect your BASIC software fairly effectively from being LISTed or examined, although not from being copied.

581	**245**	**. . . .**

Spare byte.

582	**246**	**DSKTIM**

Disk time-out register (the address of the OS worst case disk time-out). It is said by many sources to be set to 160 at initialization, which represents a 171 second time-out, but my system shows a value of 224 on initialization. Timer values are 64 seconds for each 60 units of measurement expressed.

It is updated after each disk status request to contain the value of the third byte of the status frame (location 748; $2EC). All disk operations have a seven second time-out (except FORMAT), established by the disk handler (you had noticed that irritating little delay, hadn't you?). The "sleeping disk syndrome" (the printer suffers from this malady as well) happens when your drive times out, or the timer value reaches zero. This has been cured by the new OS "B" version ROMs.

583-622   247-26E   LINBUF

Forty-byte character line buffer, used to temporarily buffer one physical line of text when the screen editor is moving screen data. The pointer to this buffer is stored in 100, 101 ($64, $65) during the routine.

623   26F   GPRIOR

Priority selection register, shadow for 53275 ($D01B). Priority options select which screen objects will be "in front" of others. It also enables you to use all four missiles as a fifth player and allows certain overlapping players to have different colors in the areas of overlap. You add your options up as in location 559, prior to POKEing the total into 623. In this case, choose only *one* of the four priorities stated at the beginning. BAK is the background or border. You can also use this location to select one of GTIA GRAPHICS modes nine, ten, or eleven.

Priority options in order	Decimal	Bit
Player 0 - 3, playfield 0 - 3, BAK (background)	1	0
Player 0 - 1, playfield 0 - 3, player 2 - 3, BAK	2	1
Playfield 0 - 3, player 0 - 3, BAK	4	2
Playfield 0 - 1, player 0 - 3, playfield 2 -3, BAK	8	3
Other options		
Four missiles = fifth player	16	4
Overlaps of players have 3rd color	32	5
GRAPHICS 9 (GTIA mode)	64	6
GRAPHICS 10 (GTIA mode)	128	7
GRAPHICS 11 (GTIA mode)	192	6, 7

It is quite easy to set conflicting priorities for players and playfields. In such a case, areas where both overlap when a conflict occurs will turn black. The same happens if the overlap option is not chosen.

With the color/overlap enable, you can get a multicolor player by combining players. The Atari performs a logical OR to colors of players 0/1 and 2/3 when they overlap. Only the 0/1, 2/3 combinations are allowed; you will not get a third color when players 1 and 3 overlap, for example (you will get black instead). If player one is pink and player 0 is blue, the overlap is green. If you don't enable the overlap option, the area of overlap for all

623

players will be black.

In GTIA mode nine, you have 16 different luminances of the same hue. In BASIC, you would use SETCOLOR 4,HUE,0. To see an example of GTIA mode nine, try:

```
10    GRAPHICS 9: SETCOLOR 4,9,0
20    FOR LOOP = 1 TO 15: COLOR LOOP
30    FOR LINE = 1 TO 2
40    FOR TEST = 1 TO 25: PLOT 4 + TES
   T, LOOP + LINE +  SPACE: NEXT TEST
45    NEXT LINE
50    SPACE = SPACE + 4
60    NEXT LOOP
70    GOTO 70: REM WITHOUT THIS LINE,
   SCREEN WILL RETURN TO GR.0
```

In GTIA mode ten, you have all nine color registers available; hue and luminance may be set separately for each (it would otherwise allow 16 colors, but there are only nine registers). Try this to see:

```
10    N = 0: GRAPHICS 10
20    FOR Q = 1 TO 2
30    FOR B = 0 TO 8: POKE 704 + B, N
 *  16 + A
35    IF A > 15 THEN A = 0
40    COLOR B
45    A = A + 1: N = N + 1
50    IF N > 15 THEN N = 0
60    NEXT B
65    TRAP 70: NEXT Q
70    PUP: N = N + 1: FOR Z = 1 TO 200
   : NEXT Z
75    GOTO 30
```

GTIA mode eleven is similar to mode nine except that it allows 16 different hues, all of the same luminance. In BASIC, use SETCOLOR 4,0,luminance. Try this for a GTIA mode eleven demonstration:

```
10    GRAPHICS 11
20    FOR LOOP = 0 TO 79: COLOR LOOP:
   PLOT LOOP,0: DRAWTO LOOP,191: NEXT
   LOOP
30    GOTO 30
```

You can use these examples with the routine to rotate colors, described in the text preceding location 704. GTIA mode pixels are long and skinny; they have a four to one horizontal length to height ratio. This obviously isn't very good for drawing curves and circles!

GTIA modes are cleared on the OPEN command. How can you tell if you have the GTIA chip? Try POKE 623,64. If you have the GTIA, the screen will go all black. If not, you don't have it. Here is a short routine, written by Craig Chamberlain and Sheldon Leemon for **COMPUTE!**, which allows an Atari to test itself for the presence of a CTIA or GTIA chip. The routine flashes the answer on the screen, but can easily be modified so a program will "know" which chip is present so it can adapt itself accordingly:

```
10 POKE 66,1:GRAPHICS 8:POKE 709,0:PO
   KE 710,0:POKE 66,0:POKE 623,64:POK
   E 53248,42:POKE 53261,3:PUT#6,1
20 POKE 53278,0:FOR K=1 TO 300:NEXT K
   :GRAPHICS 18:POKE 53248,0:POSITION
    8,5:? #6;CHR$(71-PEEK(53252));"TI
   A"
30 POKE 708,PEEK(20):GOTO 30
```

How can you get the GTIA if you don't have one? Ask your local Atari service representative or dealer, or write directly to Atari in Sunnyvale, California.

See the GTIA/CTIA introduction at location 53248 ($D000) for more discussion of the chip. See *BYTE*, May 1982, **COMPUTE!**, July through September 1982, and *De Re Atari* for more on the GTIA chip, and the *GTIA Demonstration Diskette* from the Atari Program Exchange (APX).

Locations 624 to 647 ($270 to $287) are used for game controllers: paddle, joystick and lightpen values.

624   270   PADDL0

The value of paddle 0 (paddles are also called pots, short for *potentiometer*); PEEK 624 returns a number between zero and 228 ($E4), increasing as the knob is turned counter-clockwise. When used to move a player or cursor (i.e., PLOT PADDLE(0),0), test your screen first. Many sets will not display locations less than 48 ($30) or greater than 208 ($D0), and in many GRAPHICS modes you will get an ERROR 141 — cursor out of range. Paddles are paired in the controller jacks, so paddle 0 and paddle 1 both use jack one. PADDL registers are shadows for POKEY locations 53760 to 53767 ($D200 to $D207).

625   271   PADDL1

This and the next six bytes are the same as 624, but for the other paddles.

626   272   PADDL2

627	**273**	**PADDL3** ·
628	**274**	**PADDL4**
629	**275**	**PADDL5**
630	**276**	**PADDL6**
631	**277**	**PADDL7**

632	**278**	**STICK0**

The value of joystick 0. STICK registers are shadow locations for PIA locations 54016 and 54017 ($D300, $D301). There are nine possible decimal values (representing 45 degree increments) read by each joystick register (using the STICKn command), depending on the position of the stick:

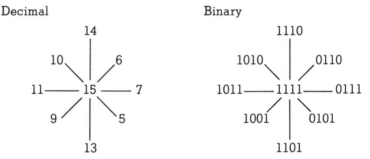

Decimal   Binary

15 (1111) equals stick in the upright (neutral) position.

See *Micro,* December 1981, for an article on making a proportional joystick. For an example of a machine language joystick driver you can add to your BASIC program, see **COMPUTE!**, July 1981.

One machine language joystick reader is listed below, based on an article in **COMPUTE!**, August 1981:

```
1    GOSUB 1000
10   LOOK = STICK(0)
20   X = USR(1764,LOOK): Y = USR(1781,
     LOOK)
30   ON X GOTO 120, 100, 110
     .
     .
     .
100 REM YOUR MOVE LEFT ROUTINE HERE
105 GOTO 10
110 REM YOUR MOVE RIGHT ROUTINE HERE
115 GOTO 10
```

```
120 ON Y GOTO 150, 130, 140
130 REM YOUR MOVE DOWN ROUTINE HERE
135 GOTO 10
140 REM YOUR MOVE UP ROUTINE HERE
145 GOTO 10
150 REM IF X <> 1 THEN NOTHING DOING,
    BRANCH TO YOUR OTHER ROUTINES OR
    TO 155
155 GOTO 10
.
.
.
1000 FOR LOOP = 1764 TO 1790: READ BY
    TE: POKE LOOP, BYTE: NEXT LOOP
1010 DATA 104,104,133,213,104,41,12,7
    4,74,73,2,24,105,1
1020 DATA 133,212,96,104,104,133,213,
    104,41,3,76,237,6
1030 RETURN
```

See locations 88, 89 ($58, $59) for an example of a USR call using a string instead of a fixed memory location.

633   279   STICK1

This and the next two locations are the same as 632, but for the other joysticks. These four locations are also used to determine if a lightpen (PEN 0 - 3) switch is pressed.

634   27A   STICK2
635   27B   STICK 3

636   27C   PTRIG0

Paddle trigger 0. Used to determine if the trigger or button on paddle 0 is pressed (zero is returned) or not (one is returned). Since these are the same lines as the joystick left/right switches, you can use PTRIG for horizontal movement. PTRIG(1) - PTRIG(0)returns –1 (left), 0 (center), +1 (right). The next seven locations are for the other paddle buttons. PTRIG 0 - 3 are shadows for PIA register 54016 ($D300).

637   27D   PTRIG1
638   27E   PTRIG2
639   27F   PTRIG3
640   280   PTRIG4

PTRIG 4 - 7 are shadows for PIA register 54017 ($D301).

641	281	PTRIG5
642	282	PTRIG6
643	283	PTRIG7
644	284	STRIG0

Stick trigger 0. This and the next three locations perform the same function as the PTRIG locations except for the joysticks. Like PTRIG, zero is returned when the button is pressed; one is returned when it is not. STRIG registers are shadow registers for GTIA/CTIA locations 53264 to 53267 ($D010 to $D013).

645	285	STRIG1
646	286	STRIG2
647	287	STRIG3

Locations 648 to 655 ($288 to $28F) are for miscellaneous OS use.

648   288   CSTAT

Cassette status register.

649   289   WMODE

Register to store either the read or the write mode for the cassette handler, depending on the operation: zero equals read, 128 ($80) equals write.

650   28A   BLIM

Cassette data record buffer size; contains the number of active data bytes in the cassette buffer for the record being read or written, at location 1021 ($3FD). Values range from zero to 128 (cassette record size is 128; $80). The pointer to the byte being read or written is at 61 ($3D). The value of BLIM is drawn from the control bytes that precede every cassette record, as explained in location 1021.

651-655   28B-28F   ....

Spare bytes. It is not recommended that you use the spare bytes for your own program use. In later upgrades of the OS, these bytes may be used, causing a conflict with your program. For example, the new OS ROMs use locations 652 and 653 ($28C, $28D) in the new IRQ interrupt handler routines. It is best to use a protected area of memory such as page six, locations 1536 to 1791 ($600 to $6FF).

Locations 656 to 703 ($290 to $2BF) are used for the screen RAM display handler (depending on GRAPHICS mode).

In split-screen mode, the text window is controlled by the screen editor
(E:), while the graphics region is controlled by the display handler
(S:), using two separate IOCB's. Two separate cursors are also
maintained. The display handler will set AUX1 of the IOCB to split-
screen option. Refer to the IOCB area, locations 832 to 959 ($340 to
$3BF). See **COMPUTE!**, February 1982, for a program to put GR.1
and GR.2 into the text window area. The text window uses 160 bytes of
RAM located just below RAMTOP (see location 106; $6A). See
location 88 ($58) for a chart of screen RAM use.

656   290   TXTROW
Text window cursor row; value ranges from zero to three (the text
window has only four lines). TXTROW specifies where the next
read or write in the text window will occur.

657,658   291,292   TXTCOL
Text window cursor column; value ranges from zero to 39. Unless
changed by the user, location 658 will always be zero (there are
only 40 columns in the display, so the MSB will be zero). Since
POSITION, PLOT, LOCATE and similar commands refer to the
graphics cursor in the display area above the text window, you
must use POKE statements to write to this area if PRINT
statements are insufficient.

659   293   TINDEX
Contains the current split-screen text window GRAPHICS mode.
It is the split-screen equivalent to DINDEX (location 87; $57) and
is always equal to zero when location 128 ($7B) equals zero.
Initialized to zero (which represents GR.0). You can alter the
display list to change the text window into any GRAPHICS mode
desired. If you do so, remember to change TINDEX to reflect that
alteration.

660,661   294,295   TXTMSC
Address of the upper left corner of the text window. Split-screen
equivalent of locations 88, 89 ($58, $59).

662-667   296-29B   TXTOLD
These locations contain the split-screen equivalents of OLDROW
(90; $5A), OLDCOL (91, 92; $5B, $5C), OLDCHR (location 93,
$5D) and OLDADR (locations 94, 95; $5E, $5F). They hold the
split-screen cursor data.

668   29C   TMPX1
Temporary register, used by the display handler for the scroll
loop count record.

669   29D   HOLD 3
Temporary register.

670	**29E**	**SUBTMP**

Temporary storage.

671	**29F**	**HOLD2**

Temporary register.

672	**2A0**	**DMASK**

Pixel location mask. DMASK contains zeroes for all bits which do
not correspond to the specific pixel to be operated upon, and
ones for bits which do correspond, according to the GRAPHICS
mode in use, as follows:

11111111	Modes 0, 1 and 2:	one pixel per screen display byte.
11110000 00001111	Modes 9, 10 and 11:	two pixels per byte.
11000000 00110000 00001100 00000011	Modes 3, 5 and 7:	four pixels per byte.
10000000 01000000	Modes 4, 6 and 8:	eight pixels per byte.

etc. to:

00000001

A pixel (short for picture cell or picture element) is a logical unit
of video size which depends on the GRAPHICS mode in use for
its dimensions. The smallest pixel is in GR.8 where it is only ½
color clock wide and one scan line high. In GR.0 it is also only ½
color clock wide, but it is eight scan lines high. Here is a chart of
the pixel sizes for each mode:

	Text Modes					Graphics modes			
GR. mode	0	1	2	3	4	5	6	7	8
Scan lines per pixel	8	8	16	8	4	4	2	2	1
Bits per pixel	1	1	1	2	1	2	1	2	1
Color clocks per pixel	.5	1	1	4	2	2	1	1	.5
Characters per line	40	20	20	—	—	—	—	—	—
Pixels per width	—	—	—	40	80	80	160	160	320

The number of pixels per screen width is based on the normal
playfield screen. See location 559 ($22F) for information on

playfield size.

673   2A1   TMPLBT
Temporary storage for the bit mask.

674   2A2   ESCFLG
Escape flag. Normally zero, it is set to 128 ($80) if the ESC key is pressed (on detection of the ESC character; 27, $1B). It is reset to zero following the output of the next character. To display ATASCII control codes without the use of an ESC character, set location 766 ($2FE) to a non-zero value.

675-689   2A3-2B1   TABMAP
Map of the TAB stop positions. There are 15 bytes (120 bits) here, each bit corresponding to a column in a logical line. A one in any bit means the TAB is set; to clear all TABs simply POKE every location with zero. There are 120 TAB locations because there are three physical lines to one logical line in GRAPHICS mode zero, each consisting of 40 columns. Setting the TAB locations for one logical line means they will also be set for each subsequent logical line until changed. Each physical line in one logical line can have different TAB settings, however.

To POKE TAB locations from BASIC, you must POKE in the number (i.e., set the bit) that corresponds to the location of the bit in the byte (there are five bytes in each line). For example:

To set tabs at locations 5, 23, 27 and 32, first visualize the line as a string of zeros with a one at each desired tab setting:

00001000000000000000001000100001000000000

Then break it into groups of eight bits (one byte units). There are three bytes with ones (bits set), two with all zeros:

00001000 = 8
00000000 = 0
00000010 = 2
00100001 = 33
00000000 = 0

Converting these to decimal, we get the values listed at the right of each byte. These are the numbers you'd POKE into locations 675 (the first byte) to 679 (the fifth byte on the line). On powerup or when you OPEN the display screen (S: or E:), each byte is given a value of one (i.e., 00000001) so that there are tab default tab stops at 7, 15, 23, etc., incrementing by eight to 119. Also, the leftmost screen edge is also a valid TAB stop (2, 42, and 82). In BASIC, these are set by the SET-TAB and CLR-TAB keys. TABMAP also works for the lines in the text display window in split-screen formats. TABMAP is reset to the default values on pressing RESET or changing GRAPHICS modes.

See location 201 ($C9) about changing the TAB settings used when a PRINT statement encounters a comma.

690-693   2B2-2B5   LOGMAP

Logical line start bit map. These locations map the beginning physical line number for each logical line on the screen (initially 24, for GR.0). Each bit in the first three bytes shows the start of a logical line if the bit equals one (three bytes equals eight bits * three equals 24 lines on the screen). The map format is as follows:

Bit	7	6	5	4	3	2	1	0	Byte
Line	0	1	2	3	4	5	6	7	690
	8	9	10	11	12	13	14	15	691
	16	17	18	19	20	21	22	23	692
	—	—	—	—	—	—	—	—	693

The last byte is ignored. The map bits are all set to one when the text screen is OPENed or CLEARed, when a GRAPHICS command is issued or RESET is pressed. The map is updated as logical lines are entered, edited, or deleted.

694   2B6   INVFLG

Inverse character flag; zero is normal and the initialization value (i.e., normal ATASCII video codes have BIT 7 equals zero). You POKE INVFLG with 128 ($80) to get inverse characters (BIT 7 equals one). This register is normally set by toggling the Atari logo key; however, it can be user-altered. The display handler XOR's the ATASCII codes with the value in INVFLG at all times. See location 702 ($2BE) below.

INVFLG works to change the input, not the output. For example, if you have A$ = "HELLO", POKE 694, 128 will not change A$ when you PRINT it to the screen. However, if you POKE 694, 128 before an INPUT A$, the string will be entered as inverse.

695   2B7   FILFLG

Right fill flag for the DRAW command. If the current operation is a DRAW, then this register reads zero. If it is non-zero, the operation is a FILL.

696   2B8   TMPROW

Temporary register for row used by ROWCRS (location 84; $54).

697,698   2B9,2BA   TMPCOL

Temporary register for column used by COLCRS (locations 85, 86; $55, $56).

699   2BB   SCRFLG

Scroll flag; set if a scroll occurs. It counts the number of physical lines minus one that were deleted from the top of the screen. This moves the entire screen up one physical line for each line scrolled off the top. Since a logical line has three physical lines, SCRFLG ranges from zero to two.

Scrolling the text window is the equivalent to scrolling an entire GR.0 screen. An additional 20-line equivalent of bytes (800) is scrolled upwards in the memory below the text window address. This can play havoc with any data such as P/M graphics you have stored above RAMTOP.

700   2BC   HOLD4

Temporary register used in the DRAW command only; used to save and restore the value in ATACHR (location 763; $2FB) during the FILL process.

701   2BD   HOLD5

Same as the above register.

702   2BE   SHFLOK

Flag for the shift and control keys. It returns zero for lowercase letters, 64 ($40) for all uppercase (called caps lock: uppercase is required for BASIC statements and is also the default mode on powerup). SHFLOK will set characters to all caps during your program if 64 is POKEd here. Returns the value 128 ($80; control-lock) when the CTRL key is pressed. Forced control-lock will cause all keys to output their control-code functions or graphics figures. Other values POKEd here may cause the system to crash. You can use this location with 694 ($2B6) above to convert all keyboard entries to uppercase, normal display by:

```
10    OPEN #2,4,0,"K:"
20    GET #2,A
30    GOSUB 1000
40    PRINT CHR$(A);: GOTO 20
.
.
.
1000  IF A = 155 THEN 1030: REM RETURN
      KEY
1010  IF A > = 128 THEN A = A - 128: R
      EM RESTORE TO NORMAL DISPLAY
1020  IF PEEK(702) = 0 AND A > 96 THEN
      A = A - 32: REM LOWERCASE TO UP
      PER
1030  POKE 702,64: POKE 694,0
1040  RETURN
```

703   2BF   BOTSCR

Flag for the number of text rows available for printing. 24 ($18) is normal for text mode GR.0; four for the text window, zero for all graphics modes. In all GRAPHICS modes except zero, if there is no text window then 703 will also read zero. The large-text displays in GR.1 and GR.2 are treated as graphics displays for this purpose. The display handler specifically checks for split-screen mode by looking for the variable 24 or four here. If it finds 24 here, it assumes there is no text window; if not, it looks for the variable four.

You can add a text window to GR.0 by POKEing here with four. The top portion (20 lines) of the screen will not scroll with the bottom. To write to the top part of the screen you will have to use the PRINT#6 statement as with modes one and two. One possible application of this would be to keep a fixed menu at the top of the screen while scrolling the bottom part, as done with the DOS menu.

Locations 704 to 712 ($2C0 to $2C8) are the color registers for players, missiles, and playfields. These are the RAM shadow registers for locations 53266 to 53274 ($D012 to $D01A). For the latter, you can use the SETCOLOR command from BASIC. For all registers you can POKE the desired color into the location by using this formula:

COLOR = HUE * 16 + LUMINANCE

It is possible to get more colors in GR.8 than the one (and a half) that Atari says is possible by using a technique called *artifacting*. There is a small example of artifacting shown at location 710 ($2C6). See *De Re Atari, Your Atari 400/800, Creative Computing*, June 1981, and **COMPUTE!**, May 1982.

Here are the 16 colors the Atari produces, along with their POKE values for the color registers. The POKE values assume a luminance of zero. Add the luminance value to the numbers to brighten the color. The color registers ignore BIT 0; that's why there are no "odd" values for luminance, just even values.

Color	Value		Color	Value	
Black	0,	0	Medium blue	8,	128
Rust	1,	16	Dark blue	9,	144
Red-orange	2,	32	Blue-grey	10,	160
Dark orange	3,	48	Olive green	11,	176
Red	4,	64	Medium green	12,	192
Dk lavender	5,	80	Dark green	13,	208
Cobalt blue	6,	96	Orange-green	14,	224
Ultramarine	7,	112	Orange	15,	240

The bit use of the PCOLR and COLOR registers is as follows:

Bit   7 6 5 4 3 2 1 0
       — color — luminance unused

....

Grey   0 0 0 0 0 0 0   Darkest
Rust   0 0 0 1 0 0 1

       etc. to: etc. to:

Orange 1 1 1 1 1 1 1   Lightest

When you enable the color overlap at location 623 ($26F), ANTIC performs a logical OR on the overlap areas. For example:

```
     01000010   Red, luminance two
OR   10011010   Dark blue, luminance ten
Result = 10011010   Dark green, luminance ten
```

Here's a short machine language routine which will rotate the colors in registers 705 to 712:

```
 10     DIM ROT$(30)
 20     FOR LOOP = 1 TO 27: READ BYTE: R
        OT$(LOOP,LOOP) = CHR$(BYTE): NEXT
        LOOP
 .
 .      PUT YOUR GRAPHICS ROUTINE HERE
 .
100     CHANGE = USR(ADR(ROT$))
105     FOR LOOP = 1 TO 200: NEXT LOOP:
        GOTO 100
110     DATA 104,162,0,172,193,2,189,194
        ,2,157
120     DATA 193,2,232,224,8,144,245,140
        ,200,2
130     DATA  96,65,65,65,65,65,65
```

If you wish to rotate the colors in registers 704 to 711 instead, change lines 110 and 120 to read as follows:

```
110     DATA 104,162,0,172,192,2,189,193
        ,2,157
120     DATA 192,2,232,224,8,144,245,140
        ,199,2
```

If you wish to include all of the registers 704 to 712 in the routine, make the changes as above and change the eight in line 120 to nine and restore the 199 to 200 in line 120. This routine works well with the GTIA demos at location 623 ($26F).

For further detail, refer to your *Atari BASIC Reference Manual,* pp. 45

704

- 56, and the *GTIA Demo Disk* from APX.

704   **2C0**   **PCOLR0**

Color of player 0 and missile 0. Locations 704 to 707 are also called COLPM# in some sources. This is the shadow for 53266 ($D012). In GTIA mode ten, 704 holds the background color (BAK; normally held by 712). You cannot use the SETCOLOR commands to change the PCOLR registers; color values must be POKEd into them.

705   **2C1**   **PCOLR1**

Color of player and missile 1. Shadow for 53267 ($D013).

706   **2C2**   **PCOLR2**

Color of player and missile 2. Shadow for 53268 ($D014).

707   **2C3**   **PCOLR3**

Color of player and missile 3. When the four missiles are combined to make a fifth player, it takes on the color in location 711 (COLOR3). Shadow for 53269 ($D015).

708   **2C4**   **COLOR0**

Color register zero, color of playfield zero, controlled by the BASIC SETCOLOR0 command. In GRAPHICS 1 and GRAPHICS 2, this color is used for the uppercase letters. Shadow for 53270 ($D016). You can change the values in all of the COLOR registers from BASIC by using either the SETCOLOR command or a POKE.

709   **2C5**   **COLOR1**

The next four locations are the same as location 708 for the different playfields and SETCOLOR commands. In GR.1 and GR.2, this register stores the color for lowercase letters. COLOR1 is also used to store the luminance value of the color used in GR.0 and GR.8. Shadow for 53271 ($D017).

710   **2C6**   **COLOR2**

The same as above for playfield two; in GR.1 and GR. 2, this register stores the color of the inverse uppercase letters. Shadow for 53272 ($D018). Used for the background color in GR.0 and GR.8. Both use COLOR1 for the luminance value.

Despite the official limitations of color selection in GR.8, it is possible to generate additional colors by "artifacting," turning on specific pixels (½ color clock each) on the screen. Taking advantage of the physical structure of the TV set itself, we selectively turn on vertical lines of pixels which all show the same color. For example:

```
10   A = 40: B = 30: C = 70: D = 5: F
   = 20   GRAPHICS 8: POKE 87,7: POK
```

64

```
E 710,0: POKE 709,15: COLOR 1
30   PLOT A,D: DRAWTO A,C: COLOR 2: P
LOT F,D: DRAWTO F,C:
40   PLOT A + 1,D: DRAWTO A + 1,C
50   COLOR 3: PLOT B,D: DRAWTO B,C
60   GOTO 60
```

A little experimentation with this will show you that the colors obtained depend on which pixels are turned on and how close together the pixel columns are. There are four "colors" you can obtain, as shown before. Pixels marked one are on; marked zero means they are off. Each pair of pixels is one color clock. Three color clocks are shown together for clarity:

00:01:00 = color A   00:11:00 = color B
00:10:00 = color C   00:01:10 = color D

See *BYTE,* May 1982, *De Re Atari,* and *Your Atari 400/800.*

711   2C7   COLOR3

The same as the above but for playfield three. Also, the color for GR.1 and GR.2 inverse lowercase letters. Shadow for 53273 ($D019).

712   2C8   COLOR4

The same as the above but for the background (BAK) and border color. Shadow for 53274 ($D01A). In GTIA mode ten, 704 stores the background color (BAK), while 712 becomes a normal color register.

Here are the default (powerup) values for the COLOR registers (PCOL registers are all set to zero on powerup):

Register	Color	=	Hue	Luminance
708 (CO.0)	40		2	8
709 (CO.1)	202		12	10
710 (CO.2)	148		9	4
711 (CO.3)	70		4	6
712 (CO.4)	0		0	0

Locations 713 to 735 ($2C9 to $2DF) are spare bytes. Locations 736 to 767 ($2E0 to $2FF) are for miscellaneous use.

736-739   2E0-2E3   GLBABS

Global variables, or, four spare bytes for non-DOS users. For DOS users they are used as below:

736-737   2E0-2E1   RUNAD

Used by DOS for the run address read from the disk sector one or from a binary file. Upon completion of any binary load, control will normally be passed back to the DOS menu. However, DOS can be forced to pass control to any specific address by storing that address here. If RUNAD is set to 40960 ($A000), then the left cartridge (BASIC if inserted) will be called when the program is booted.

With DOS 1.0, if you POKE the address of your binary load file here, the file will be automatically run upon using the DOS Binary Load (selection L). Using DOS 1.0's append (/A) option when saving a binary file to disk, you can cause the load address POKEd here to be saved with the data. In DOS 2.0, you may specify the initialization and the run address with the program name when you save it to disk (i.e., GAME.OBJ,2000,4FFF,4F00,4000). DOS 2.0 uses the /A option to merge files. In order to prevent your binary files from running automatically upon loading in DOS 2.0, use the /N appendage to the file name when loading the file.

For users of CompuServe, there is an excellent little BASIC program (with machine language subroutines) to create autoboot files, chain machine language files with BASIC and to add an 850 autoboot file in the *Popular Electronics Magazine* (PEM) access area. It is available free for downloading.

738-739   2E2-2E3   INITAD
Initialization address read from the disk. An autoboot file must load an address value into either RUNAD above or INITAD. The code pointed to by INITAD will be run as soon as that location is loaded. The code pointed to by RUNAD will be executed only after the entire load process has been completed. To return control to DOS after the execution of your program, end your code with an RTS instruction.

740   2E4   RAMSIZ
RAM size, high byte only; this is the number of pages that the top of RAM represents (one page equals 256 bytes). Since there can never be less than a whole page, it becomes practical to measure RAM in those page units. This is the same value as in RAMTOP, location 106 ($6A), passed here from TRAMSZ, location 6. Space saved by moving RAMSIZ or RAMTOP has the advantage of being above the display area. Initialized to 160 for a 48K Atari.

741,742   2E5,2E6   MEMTOP
Pointer to the top of free memory used by both BASIC (which calls it HIMEM) and the OS, passed here from TRAMSZ, location 6 after powerup. This address is the highest free location in RAM for programs and data. The value is updated on powerup, when RESET is pressed, when you change GRAPHICS mode, or when a channel (IOCB) is OPENed to the display. The display list starts

at the next byte above MEMTOP.

The screen handler will only OPEN the S: device if no RAM is needed below this value (i.e., there is enough free RAM below here to accommodate the requested GRAPHICS mode change). Memory above this address is used for the display list and the screen display RAM. Also, if a screen mode change would extend the screen mode memory below APPMHI (locations 14, 15: $E, $F), then the screen is set back for GR.0, MEMTOP is updated, and an error is returned to the user. Otherwise the mode change will take place and MEMTOP will be updated.

Space saved by moving MEMTOP is below the display list. Be careful not to overwrite it if you change GRAPHICS modes in mid-program. When using memory below MEMTOP for storage, make sure to set APPMHI above your data to avoid having the screen data descend into it and destroy it.

743,744   2E7,2E8   MEMLO

Pointer to the bottom of free memory, initialized to 1792 ($700) and updated by the presence of DOS or any other low-memory application program. It is used by the OS; the BASIC pointer to the bottom of free memory is at locations 128, 129 ($80, $81). The value in MEMLO is never altered by the OS after powerup.

This is the address of the first free location in RAM available for program use. Set after all FMS buffers have been allocated (see locations 1801 and 1802; $709 and $70A). The address of the last sector buffer is incremented by 128 (the buffer size in bytes) and the value placed in MEMLO. The value updates on powerup or when RESET is pressed. This value is passed back to locations 128, 129 ($80, $81) on the execution of the BASIC NEW command, but not RUN, LOAD or RESET.

If you are reserving space for your own device driver(s) or reserving buffer space, you load your routine into the address specified by MEMLO, add the size of your routine to the MEMLO value, and POKE the new value plus one back into MEMLO.

When you don't have DOS or any other application program using low-memory resident, MEMLO points to 1792 ($700). With DOS 2.0 present, MEMLO points to 7420 ($1CFC). If you change the buffer defaults mentioned earlier, you will raise or lower this latter value by 128 ($80) bytes for every buffer added or deleted, respectively. When you boot up the 850 Interface with or without disk, you add another 1728 ($6C0) bytes to the value in MEMLO.

You can alter MEMLO to protect an area of memory below your program. This is an alternative to protecting an area above RAMTOP (location 106; $6A) and avoids the problem of the CLEAR SCREEN routine destroying data. However, unless you have created a MEM. SAV file, the data will be wiped out when you call DOS. To alter MEMLO, you start by POKEing WARMST (location 8) with zero, then doing a JMP to the BASIC cartridge entry point at 40960($A000) after defining your area to protect. For example, try this:

```
10 DIM MEM$(24):PROTECT=700:REM NUMBE
   R OF BYTES TO CHANGE
15 HIBYTE=INT(PROTECT/256):LOBYTE=PRO
   TECT-256*HIBYTE
20 FOR N=1 TO 24:READ PRG:MEM$(N)=CHR
   $(PRG):NEXT N
30 MEM$(6,6)=CHR$(LOBYTE):MEM$(14,14)
   =CHR$(HIBYTE)
40 RESERVE=USR(ADR(MEM$))
50 DATA 24,173,231,2,105,0,141,231,2,
   173,232,2,105
60 DATA 0,141,232,2,169,0,133,8,76,0,
   160
```

You will find the address of your reserved memory by: PRINT PEEK(743) + PEEK(744) * 256 before you run the program. This program will wipe itself out when run. Altering MEMLO is the method used by both DOS and the RS-232 port driver in the 850 Interface. See **COMPUTE!**, July 1981.

745   2E9   ....

Spare byte.

746-749   2EA-2ED   DVSTAT

Four device status registers used by the I/O status operation as follows:

746 ($2EA) is the device error status and the command status byte. If the operation is a disk I/O, then the status returned is that of the 1771 controller chip in your Atari disk drive. Bits set to one return the following error codes:

Bit	Decimal	Error
0	1	An invalid command frame was received (error).
1	2	An invalid data frame was received.
2	4	An output operation was unsuccessful.
3	8	The disk is write-protected.
4	16	The system is inactive (on standby).
7	32	The peripheral controller is "intelligent" (has its own microprocessor: the disk drive). All Atari devices are intelligent except the cassette recorder, so BIT 7 will normally be one when a device is attached.

747 ($2EB) is the device status byte. For the disk, it holds the

value of the status register of the drive controller. For the 850 Interface, it holds the status for DSR,CTS,CRX and RCV when concurrent I/O is not active (see the *850 Interface Manual*). It also contains the AUX2 byte value from the previous operation (see the IOCB description at 832 to 959; $340 to $3AF).

748 ($2EC) is the maximum device time-out value in seconds. A value of 60 here represents 64 seconds. This value is passed back to location 582 ($246) after every disk status request. Initialized to 31.

749 ($2ED) is used for number of bytes in output buffer. See *850 Manual*, p. 43.

When concurrent I/O is active, the STATUS command returns the number of characters in the input buffer to locations 747 and 748, and the number of characters in the output buffer to location 749.

750,751   2EE,2EF   CBAUDL/H

Cassette baud rate low and high bytes. Initialized to 1484 ($5CC), which represents a nominal 600 baud (bits per second). After baud rate calculations, these locations will contain POKEY values for the corrected baud rate. The baud rate is adjusted by SIO to account for motor variations, tape stretch, etc. The beginning of every cassette record contains a pattern of alternating off/on bits (zero/one) which are used solely for speed (baud) correction.

752   2F0   CRSINH

Cursor inhibit flag. Zero turns the cursor on; any other number turns the cursor off. A visible cursor is an inverse blank (space) character. Note that cursor visibility does not change until the next time the cursor moves (if changed during a program). If you wish to change the cursor status without altering the screen data, follow your CRSINH change with a cursor movement (i.e., up, down) sequence. This register is set to zero (cursor restored) on powerup, RESET, BREAK, or an OPEN command to either the display handler (S:) or screen editor (E:). See location 755 for another means to turn off the cursor.

753   2F1   KEYDEL

Key delay flag or key debounce counter; used to see if *any* key has been pressed. If a zero is returned, then no key has been pressed. If three is returned, then any key. It is decremented every stage two VBLANK (1/60 or 1/30th second) until it reaches zero. If any key is pressed while KEYDEL is greater than zero, it is ignored as "bounce." See **COMPUTE!**, December 1981, for a routine to change the keyboard delay to suit your own typing needs.

754   2F2   CH1

Prior keyboard character code (most recently read and accepted). This is the previous value passed from 764 ($2FC). If the value of the new key code equals the value in CH1, then the code is accepted only if a suitable key debounce delay has taken place since the prior value was accepted.

755   2F3   CHACT

Character Mode Register. Zero means normal inverse characters, one is blank inverse characters (inverse characters will be printed as blanks, i.e., invisible), two is normal characters, three is solid inverse characters. Four to seven is the same as zero to three, but prints the display upside down.

This register also controls the transparency of the cursor. It is transparent with values two and six, opaque with values three and seven. The cursor is absent with values zero, one, four and five.

Toggling BIT 0 on and off can be a handy way to produce a blinking effect for printed inverse characters (characters with ATASCII values greater than 128 — those that have BIT 7 set). Shadow for 54273 ($D401). There is no visible cursor for the graphics mode output. CHACT is initialized to two.

Here's an example of blinking text using this register:

```
10 CHACT=755:REM USE INVERSE FOR WORD
   S BELOW
15 PRINT "THIS IS A TEST OF BLINKING
   TEXT"
20 POKE CHACT,INT(RND(0)*4)
30 FOR N=1 TO 100:NEXT N:GOTO 15
```

See **COMPUTE!**, December 1981.

Using a machine language routine and page six space, try:

```
10 PAGE=1536:EXIT=1568
20 FOR N=PAGE TO EXIT:READ BYTE:POKE
   N,BYTE:NEXT N
30 PGM=USR(PAGE)
40 PRINT "THIS IS A TEST OF BLINKING
   TEXT":REM MAKE SOME WORDS INVERSE
50 GOTO 50
60 DATA 104,169,17,141,40,2,169,6,141
   ,41
70 DATA 2,169,30,141,26,2,98,173,243,
   2
80 DATA 41,1,73,1,141,243,2,169,30,14
   1,26,2,96
```

The blink frequency is set to ½ second; to change it, change the 30 in line 80 to any number from one (1/30 second) to 255 (eight ½ seconds). For another way to make the cursor visible or invisible, see locations 752 above.

756   2F4   CHBAS

Character Base Register, shadow for 54281 ($D409). The default (initialization value) is 224 ($E0) for uppercase characters and numbers; POKE CHBAS with 226 ($E2) to get the lowercase and the graphics characters in GR.1 and GR.2. In GR.0 you get the entire set displayed to the screen, but in GR.1 and GR.2, you must POKE 756 for the appropriate half-set to be displayed.

How do you create an altered character set? First you must reserve an area in memory for your set (512 or 1024 bytes; look at location106; $6A to see how). Then either you move the ROM set (or half set, if that's all you intend to change) into that area and alter the selected characters, or you fill up the space with bytes which make up your own set. Then you POKE 756 with the MSB of the location of your set so the computer knows where to find it.

What does an altered character set look like? Each character is a block one byte wide by eight bytes high. You set the bits for the points on the screen you wish to be "on" when displayed. Here are two examples:

one byte wide:
```
00100000 = 32        #
00010000 = 16        #
00010000 = 16        #
00010000 = 16        #
00011110 = 30        ####
00000010 =  2           #
00001100 = 12         ##
00010000 = 16        #
```
Hebrew letter Lamed

one byte wide:
```
10000001 = 129    #        #
10011001 = 153    #  ##  #
10111101 = 189    # #### #
11111111 = 255    ########
11111111 = 255    ########
10111101 = 189    # #### #
10011001 = 153    #  ##  #
10000001 = 129    #        #
```
Tie-fighter

You can turn these characters into DATA statements to be POKEd into your reserved area by using the values for the bytes as in the above examples. To change the ROM set once it is moved, you look at the internal code (see the *BASIC Reference Manual*, p. 55) and find the value of the letter you want to replace — such as the letter A — code 33. Multiply this by eight bytes for each code number from the start of the set (33 * eight equals 264). You then replace the eight bytes used by the letter A, using a FOR-NEXT loop with the values for your own character. For example, add these lines to the machine language found a few pages further on:

```
1000 FOR LOOP=1 TO 4:READ CHAR:SET=CH
     ACT+CHAR*8
1010 FOR TIME=0 TO 7:READ BYTE:POKE S
     ET+TIME,BYTE:NEXT TIME
1020 NEXT LOOP
1030 DATA 33,0,120,124,22,22,124,120,
     0
1040 DATA 34,0,126,82,82,82,108,0,0
1050 DATA 35,56,84,254,238,254,68,56,
     0
1060 DATA 36,100,84,76,0,48,72,72,48
2000 END
```

RUN it and type the letters A to D.

Why 224 and 226? Translated to hex, these values are $E0 and $E2, respectively. These are the high bytes (MSB) for the location of the character set stored in ROM: $E000 (57344) is the address for the start of the set (which begins with punctuation, numbers and uppercase letters), and $E200 (57856), for the second half of the ROM set, lowercase and graphic control characters (both start on page boundaries). The ROM set uses the internal order given on page 55 of your *BASIC Reference Manual,* not the ATASCII order. See also location 57344 ($E000).

You will notice that using the PRINT#6 command will show you that your characters have more than one color available to them in GR.1 and GR.2. Try PRINTing lowercase or inverse characters when you are using the uppercase set. This effect can be very useful in creating colorful text pages. Uppercase letters, numbers, and special characters use color register zero (location 708; $2C4 - orange) for normal display, and color register two (710; $2C6 - blue) for inverse display. Lowercase letters use register one (709; $2C5 - aqua) for normal display and register three (711; $2C7 - pink) for inverse. See **COMPUTE!**, December 1981, page 98, for a discussion of using the CTRL keys with letter keys to get different color effects.

One problem with POKEing 756 with 226 is that there is no blank space character in the second set: you get a screen full of hearts. You have two choices: you can change the color of register zero to the same as the background and lose those characters which use register zero — the control characters — but get your blanks (and you still have registers one, two and three left). Or you can redefine your own set with a blank character in it. The latter is obviously more work. See "Ask The Readers," **COMPUTE!**, July 1982.

It is seldom mentioned in the manuals, but you cannot set 756 to 225 ($E1) or any other odd number. Doing so will only give you screen garbage. The page number 756 points to must be evenly divisible by two.

When you create your own character set and store it in memory, you need to reserve at least 1K for a full character set (1024 bytes — $400 or four pages), and you must begin on a page boundary. In hex these are the numbers ending with $XX00 such as $C000 or $600 because you store the pointer to your set here in 756; it can only hold the MSB of the address and assumes that the LSB is always zero — or rather a page boundary. You can reserve memory by:

POKE 106, PEEK(106) –4 (or any multiple of four)

And do a GRAPHICS command immediately after to have your new memory value accepted by the computer. If you are using only one half of the entire set, for GR.1 or GR.2, you need only reserve 512 bytes, and it may begin on a ½K boundary (like $E200; these are hexadecimal memory locations that end in $X200). If you plan to switch to different character sets, you will need to reserve the full 1K or more, according to the number of different character sets you need to display. RAM for half-K sets can be reserved by:

POKE 106, PEEK (106) –2 (or a multiple of two)

The location for your set will then begin at PEEK(106) * 256. Because BASIC cannot always handle setting up a display list for GR.7 and GR.8 when you modify location 106 by less than 4K (16 pages), you may find you must use PEEK(106) –16. See location 88,89 ($58,$59) and 54279 ($D407) for information regarding screen use and reserving memory.

Make sure you don't have your character set overlap with your player/missile graphics. Be very careful when using altered character sets in high memory. Changing GRAPHICS modes, a CLEAR command, or scrolling the text window all clear memory past the screen display. When you scroll the text window, you don't simply scroll the four lines; you actually scroll a full 24 (20 additional lines * 40 bytes equals 800 bytes scrolled past memory)! This messes up the memory past the window display address, so position your character sets below all possible interference (or don't scroll or clear the screen).

You can create and store as many character sets as your memory will allow. You switch back and forth between them and the ROM set by simply POKEing the MSB of the address into 756. Of course, you can display only one set at a time unless you use an altered display list and DLI to call up other sets. There are no restrictions outside of memory requirements on using altered character sets with P/M graphics as long as the areas reserved for them do not overlap.

A GRAPHICS command such as GR.0, RESET or a DOS call restores the character set pointer to the ROM location, so you must always POKE it again with the correct location of your new set after any such command. A useful place to store these sets is one page after the end of RAM, assuming you've gone back to location 106 ($6A) and subtracted the correct number of pages from the value it holds (by POKE 106, PEEK(106) minus the number of pages to be reserved; see above). Then you can reset the character set location by simply using POKE 756,PEEK(106) + 1 (the plus one simply makes sure you start at the first byte of your set).

A full character set requires 1024 bytes (1K: four pages) be reserved for it. Why? Because there are 128 characters, each represented by eight bytes, so 128 * eight equals 1024. If you are using a graphics mode that uses only half the character set, you need only reserve 512 bytes (64 * eight equals 512). Remember to begin either one on a page boundary (1K boundary for full sets or ½K for half sets). By switching back and forth between two character sets, you could create the illusion of animation.

Many magazines have published good utilities to aid in the design of altered character sets, such as the January 1982 *Creative Computing*, and *SuperFont* in **COMPUTE!**, January 1982. I suggest that you examine *The Next Step* from Online, *Instedit* from APX, or *FontEdit* from the Code Works for very useful set generators. One potentially useful way to alter just a few of the characters is to duplicate the block of memory which holds the ROM set by moving it byte by byte into RAM. A BASIC FOR-NEXT loop can accomplish this, although it's very slow. For example:

```
5 CH=57344
10 START=PEEK(106)-4:PLACE=START*256:
   POKE 106,PEEK(106)-5:GRAPHICS 0:RE
```

```
    M RESERVE EXTRA IN CASE OF SCREEN
    CLEAR
20  FOR LOOP=0 TO 1023:POKE PLACE+LOOP
    ,PEEK(CH+LOOP):NEXT LOOP:REM MOVE
    THE ROM SET
30  POKE 756,PLACE/256:REM TELL ANTIC
    WHERE CHSET IS
```

Here's a machine language routine to move the set:

```
10  DIM BYTE$(80)
15  REM MEM-1 TO PROTECT SET FROM CLEA
    R SCREEN DESTRUCTION (SEE LOC.88)
20  MEM=PEEK(106)-4:POKE 106,MEM-1:CHA
    CT=MEM*256:GRAPHICS 0
30  FOR LOOP=1 TO 32:READ PGM:BYTE$(LO
    OP,LOOP)=CHR$(PGM):NEXT LOOP
40  DATA 104,104,133,213,104,133,212
50  DATA 104,133,215,104,133,214,162
60  DATA 4,160,0,177,212,145,214
70  DATA 200,208,249,230,213,230,215
80  DATA 202,208,240,96
90  Z=USR(ADR(BYTE$),224*256,CHACT)
.
. ADD YOUR OWN ALTERATION PROGRAM OR
THE EARLIER EXAMPLE HERE
.
.
1500 POKE MEM-1,0:POKE 756,MEM
```

If you have Microsoft BASIC or BASIC A+, you can do this very easily with the MOVE command!

Remember, when altering the ROM set, that the characters aren't in ATASCII order; rather they are in their own internal order. Your own set will have to follow this order if you wish to have the characters correlate to the keyboard and the ATASCII values. See page 55 of your *BASIC Reference Manual* for a listing of the internal order. *Creative Computing*, January 1982, had a good article on character sets, as well as a useful method of transferring the ROM set to RAM using string manipulation. See also "Using Text Plot for Animated Games" in **COMPUTE!**, April 1982, for an example of using character sets for animated graphics.

757-761   2F5-2F9   ....
Spare bytes.

762   **2FA**   **CHAR**

Internal code value for the most recent character read or written (internal code for the value in ATACHR below). This register is difficult to use with PEEK statements since it returns the most recent character; most often the cursor value (128, $80 for a visible, zero for an invisible cursor).

763   **2FB**   **ATACHR**

Returns the last ATASCII character read or written or the value of a graphics point. ATACHR is used in converting the ATASCII code to the internal character code passed to or from CIO. It also returns the value of the graphics point. The FILL and DRAW commands use this location for the color of the line drawn, ATACHR being temporarily loaded with the value in FILDAT, location 765; $2FD. To force a color change in the line, POKE the desired color number here (color * sixteen + luminance). To see this register in use as character storage, try:

```
10 OPEN#2,4,0,"K:"
20 GET#2,A
30 PRINT PEEK(763);" ";CHR$(A)
40 GOTO 20
```

Make sure the PEEK statement comes before the PRINT CHR$ statement, or you will not get the proper value returned. When the RETURN key is the last key pressed, ATACHR will show a value of 155.

764   **2FC**   **CH**

Internal hardware value for the last key pressed. POKE CH with 255 ($FF; no key pressed) to clear it. The keyboard handler gets all of its key data from CH. It stores the value 255 here to indicate the key code has been accepted, then passes the code to CH1, location 754 ($2F2). If the value in CH is the same as in CH1, a key code will be accepted only if the proper key debounce delay time has transpired. If the code is the CTRL-1 combination (the CTRL and the "1" keys pressed simultaneously), then the start/stop flag at 767 ($2FF) is complemented, but the value is not stored in CH. The auto repeat logic will also store store key information here as a result of the continuous pressing of a key.

This is neither the ATASCII nor the internal code value; it is the "raw" keyboard matrix code for the key pressed. The table for translation of this code to ATASCII is on page 50 of the *OS User's Manual.* In a two-key operation, BIT 7 is set if the CTRL key is pressed, BIT 6 if the SHIFT key is pressed. The rest of the bytes are the code (ignored if both BITs 7 and 6 are set). Only the code for the last key pressed is stored here (it is a global variable for keyboard).

When a read request is issued to the keyboard, CH is set to 255 by the handler routine. After a keycode has been read from this register, it is reset to 255. BREAK doesn't show here, and CTRL and SHIFT will not show here on their own. However, the inverse toggle (Atari logo key), CAPS/LOWR, TAB and the ESC keys will show by themselves. You can examine this register with:

```
10 LOOK=PEEK(764)
20 PRINT "KEY PRESSED = ";LOOK
30 POKE 764,255
40 FOR LOOP=1 TO 250:NEXT LOOP
50 GOTO 10
```

See COMPUTE!'s First Book of Atari for an example of using this register as a replacement for joystick input.

765   2FD   FILDAT

Color data for the fill region in the XIO FILL command.

766   2FE   DSPFLG

Display flag, used in displaying the control codes not associated with an ESC character (see location 674; $2A2). If zero is returned or POKEd here, then the ATASCII codes 27 - 31, 123 - 127, 187 - 191 and 251 - 255 perform their normal display screen control functions (i.e., clear screen, cursor movement, delete/insert line, etc.). If any other number is returned, then a control character is displayed (as in pressing the ESC key with CTRL-CLEAR for a graphic representation of a screen clear). POKEing any positive number here will force the display instead of the control code action. There is, however, a small bug, not associated with location 766, in Atari BASIC: a PRINTed CTRL-R or CTRL-U are both treated as a semicolon.

767   2FF   SSFLAG

Start/stop display screen flag, used to stop the scrolling of the screen during a DRAW or graphics routine, a LISTing or a PRINTing. When the value is zero, the screen output is not stopped. When the value is 255 ($FF; the one's complement), the output to the screen is stopped, and the machine waits for the value to become zero again before continuing with the scrolling display. Normally SSFLAG is toggled by the user during these operations by pressing the CTRL-1 keys combination to both start and stop the scroll. Set to zero by RESET and powerup.

PAGE THREE

Locations 768 to 831 ($300 to $33F) are used for the device handler and vectors to the handler routines (devices S:, P:, E:, D:, C:, R: and K:).

A device handler is a routine used by the OS to control the transfer of data in that particular device for the task allotted (such as read, write, save, etc.). The resident D: handler does not conform entirely with the other handler — SIO calling routines. Instead, you use the DCB to communicate directly with the disk handler. The device handler for R: is loaded in from the 850 interface module. See *De Re Atari*, the *850 Interface Manual*, and the *OS Listings* pages 64 - 65.

Locations 768 to 779 ($300 to $30B) are the resident Device Control Block (DCB) addresses, used for I/O operations that require the serial bus; also used as the disk DCB. DUP.SYS uses this block to interface the FMS with the disk handler. The Atari disk drive uses a serial access at 19,200 baud (about 20 times slower than the Apple!). It has its own microprocessor, a 6507, plus 128 bytes of RAM, a 2316 2K masked ROM chip (like a 2716), a 2332 RAM-I/O timer chip with another 128 bytes of RAM (like the PIA chip) and a WD 1771 FD controller chip. See the "Outpost Atari" column, *Creative Computing*, May 1982, for an example of using the disk DCB.

All of the parameters passed to SIO are contained in the DCB. SIO uses the DCB information and returns the status in the DCB for subsequent use by the device handler.

768   300   DDEVIC

Device serial bus ID (serial device type) set up by the handler, not user-alterable. Values are:

Disk drives	D1 - D4	49-52	($31-$34)
Printer	P1	64	($40)
Printer	P2	79	($4F)
RS232 ports	R1-R4	80-83	($50-$53)

769   301   DUNIT

Disk or device unit number: one to four, set up by the user.

770   302   DCOMND

The number of the disk or device operation (command) to be performed, set by the user or by the device handler prior to calling SIO. Serial bus commands are:

Read	82	($52)
Write (verify)	87	($57)
Status	83	($83)
Put (no verify)	80	($50)
Format	33	($21)
Download	32	($22)
Read address	84	($54)
Read spin	81	($81)
Motor on	85	($55)
Verify sector	86	($56)

All of the above are disk device commands, except write and status, which are also printer commands (with no verify).

771   303   DSTATS

The status code upon return to user. Also used to set the data direction; whether the device is to send or receive a data frame. This byte is used by the device handler to indicate to SIO what to do after the command frame is sent and acknowledged. Prior to the SIO call, the handler examines BIT 6 (one equals receive data) and BIT 7 (one equals send data). If both bits are zero, then no data transfer is associated with the operation. Both bits set to one is invalid. SIO uses it to indicate to the handler the status of the requested operation after the SIO call.

772,773   304,305   DBUFLO/HI

Data buffer address of the source or destination of the data to be transferred or the device status information (or the disk sector data). Set by the user, it need not be set if there is no data transferred, as in a status request.

774   306   DTIMLO

The time-out value for the handler in one-second units, supplied by the handler for use by SIO. The cassette time-out value is 35, just over 37 seconds. The timer values are 64 seconds per 60 units of measurement. Initialized to 31.

775   307   DUNUSE

Unused byte.

776,777   308,309   DBYTLO/HI

The number of bytes transferred to or from the data buffer (or the disk) as a result of the most recent operation, set by the handler. Also used for the count of bad sector data. There is a small bug in SIO which causes incorrect system actions when the last byte in a buffer is in a memory location ending with $FF, such as $A0FF.

778,779   30A,30B   DAUX1/2

Used for device-specific information such as the disk sector number for the read or write operation. Loaded down to locations 572, 573 ($23C, $23D) by SIO.

There are only five commands supported by the disk handler: GET sector (82; $52), PUT sector (80; $50), PUT sector with VERIFY (87; $57), STATUS request (83; $53) and FORMAT entire disk (33; $21). There is no command to FORMAT a portion of the disk; this is done by the INS 1771-1 formatter/controller chip in the drive itself and isn't user-accessible. There is a new disk drive ROM to replace the current "C" version. It is the "E" ROM. Not only is it faster than the older ROMs, but it also allows for selective formatting of disk sectors. Atari has not announced yet whether this new 810 ROM will be made available. For more information, see the *OS User's Manual*.

Locations 780 to 793 ($30C to $319) are for miscellaneous use. Locations 794 to 831 ($31A to $33F) are handler address tables. To use these DCBs, the user must provide the required parameters to this block and then do a machine language JSR to $E453 (58451) for disk I/O or $E459 (58457; the SIO entry point) for other devices.

780,781   30C,30D TIMER1

Initial baud rate timer value.

782   30E   ADDCOR

Addition correction flag for the baud rate calculations involving the timer registers.

783   30F   CASFLG

Cassette mode when set. Used by SIO to control the program flow through shared code. When set to zero, the current operation is a standard SIO operation; when non-zero, it is a cassette operation.

784,785   310,311 TIMER2

Final timer value. Timer one and timer two contain reference times for the start and end of the fixed bit pattern receive period. The first byte of each timer contains the VCOUNT value (54283; $D40B), and the second byte contains the current realtime clock value from location 20 ($14). The difference between the timer values is used in a lookup table to compute the interval for the new values for the baud rate passed on to location 750, 751 ($2EE, $2EF).

786,787   312,313 TEMP1

Two-byte temporary storage register used by SIO for the VCOUNT calculation during baud timer routines. See location 54283 ($D40B).

788   314   TEMP2

Temporary storage register.

789   315   TEMP3

Ditto.

790   316   SAVIO

Save serial data-in port used to detect, and updated after, each bit arrival. Used to retain the state of BIT 4 of location 53775 ($D20F; serial data-in register).

791   317   TIMFLG

Time-out flag for baud rate correction, used to define an unsuccessful baud rate value. Initially set to one, it is decremented during the I/O operation. If it reaches zero (after two seconds) before the first byte of the cassette record is read, the operation will be aborted.

792   318   STACKP

SIO stack pointer register. Points to a byte in the stack being used in the current operation (locations 256 to 511; $100 to $1FF).

793   319   TSTAT

Temporary status holder for location 48 ($30).

794-831   31A-33F   HATABS

Handler Address Table. Thirty-eight bytes are reserved for up to 12 entries of three bytes per handler, the last two bytes being set to zero. On powerup, the HATABS table is copied from ROM. Devices to be booted, such as the disk drive, add their handler information to the end of the table. Each entry has the character device name (C,D,E,K,P,S,R) in ATASCII code and the handler address (LSB/MSB). Unused bytes are all set to zero. FMS searches HATABS from the top for a device "D:" entry, and when it doesn't find it, it then sets the device vector at the end of the table to point to the FMS vector at 1995 ($7CB). CIO searches for a handler character from the bottom up. This allows new handlers to take precedence over the old. Pressing RESET clears HATABS of all but the resident handler entries!

794   31A   Printer device ID (P:), initialized to 58416 ($E430).
797   31D   Cassette device ID (C:), initialized to 58432 ($E440).
800   320   Display editor ID (E:), initialized to 58368 ($E400).
803   323   Screen handler ID (S:), initialized to 58384 ($E410).
806   326   Keyboard handler ID (K:), initialized to 58400 ($E420).

HATABS unused entry points:
809 ($329), 812 ($32C), 815 ($32F), 818 ($332), 821 ($335), 824 ($338), 827 ($33B), and 830 ($33E). These are numbered sequentially from one to eight. There are only two bytes in the last entry (unused), both of which are set to zero. When DOS is present, it adds an entry to the table with the ATASCII code for the letter "D" and a vector to address 1995 ($7CB).

The format for the HATABS table is:

Device name
Handler vector table address
More entries
Zero fill to the end of the table

The device handler address table entry above for the specific handler points to the first byte (low byte/high byte) of the vector table which starts at 58368 ($E400). Each handler is designed with the following format:

OPEN vector
CLOSE vector
GET BYTE vector
PUT BYTE vector
GET STATUS vector
SPECIAL vector
Jump to initialization code (JMP LSB/MSB)

CIO uses the ZIOCB (see location 32; $20) to pass parameters to the originating IOCB, the A, Y and X registers and CIO. It is possible to add your own device driver(s) to OS by following these rules:

1) Load your routine, with necessary buffers at the address pointed to by MEMLO: location 743 ($2E7).
2) Add the size of your routine to the MEMLO value and POKE the result back into MEMLO.
3) Store the name and address of your driver in the handler address table; HATABS.
4) Change the vectors so that the OS will re-execute the above steps if RESET has been pressed. This is usually done by adjusting locations 12 ($C: DOSINIT) and 10 ($A; DOSVEC).

See the "Insight: Atari" columns in **COMPUTE!**, January and April 1982, for details. The APX program "T: A Text Display Device" is a good example of a device handler application.

See *De Re Atari* for more information on the DCB and HATABS, including the use of a null handler.

Locations 832 to 959 ($340 to $3BF) are reserved for the eight IOCB's (input/output control blocks). IOCB's are channels for the transfer of information (data bytes) into and out of the Atari, or between devices. You use them to tell the computer what operation to perform, how much data to move and, if necessary, where the data to be moved is located. Each block has 16 bytes reserved for it.

What is an IOCB? Every time you PRINT something on the screen or the printer, every time you LOAD or SAVE a file, every time you OPEN a channel, you are using an IOCB. In some cases, operations have automatic OPEN and CLOSE functions built in — like LPRINT. In others, you must tell the Atari to do each step as you need it. Some IOCB's are dedicated to specific use, such as zero for the screen display. Others can be used for any I/O function you wish. The information you place after the OPEN command tells CIO how you want the data transferred to or from the device. It is SIO and the device handlers that do the actual transfer of data.

You can easily POKE the necessary values into the memory locations and use a machine language subroutine through a USR function to call the CIO directly (you must still use an OPEN and CLOSE statement for the channel, however). This is useful because BASIC only supports either record or single byte data transfer, while the CIO will handle complete buffer I/O. See the CIO entry address, location 58454 ($E456), for more details. These blocks are used the same way as the page zero IOCB (locations 32 to 47; $20 to $2F). The OS takes the information here, moves it to the ZIOCB for use by the ROM CIO, then returns the updated information back to the user area when the operation is done.

Note that when BASIC encounters a DOS command, it CLOSEs all channels except zero. Refer to the *Atari Hardware Manual* and the *850 Interface Manual* for more detailed use of these locations.

832-847   340-34F IOCB0

I/O Control Block (IOCB) zero. Normally used for the screen editor (E:). You can POKE 838,166 and POKE 839,238 and send everything to the printer instead of to the screen (POKE 838,163, and POKE 839,246 to send everything back to the screen again). You could use this in a program to toggle back and forth between screen and printed copy when prompted by user input. This will save you multiple PRINT and LPRINT coding.

You can use these locations to transfer data to other devices as well since they point to the address of the device's "put one byte" routine. See the *OS Manual* for more information. Location 842 can be given the value 13 for read from screen and 12 for write to screen. POKE 842, 13 puts the Atari into "RETURN key mode" by setting the auxiliary byte one (ICAX1) to screen input and output. POKEing 842 with 12 returns it to keyboard input and screen output mode. The former mode allows for dynamic use of the screen to act upon commands the cursor is made to move across.

You can use this "forced read" mode to read data on the screen into BASIC without user intervention. For example, in the program below, lines 100 through 200 will be deleted by the program itself as it runs.

```
10 GRAPHICS 0:POSITION 2,4
20 PRINT 100:PRINT 150:PRINT 200
25 PRINT "CONT"
30 POSITION 2,0
50 POKE 842,13:STOP
60 POKE 842,12
70 REM THE NEXT LINES WILL BE DELETED
100 PRINT "DELETING..."
```

```
150 PRINT "DELETING..."
200 PRINT "DELETED!"
```

See **COMPUTE!**, August 1981, for a sample of this powerful technique. See Santa Cruz's Tricky Tutorial #1 (display lists) for another application. The last four bytes (844 to 847; $34C to $34F in this case) are spare (auxiliary) bytes in all IOCB's.

When you are in a GRAPHICS mode other than zero, channel zero is OPENed for the text window area. If the window is absent and you OPEN channel zero, the whole screen returns to mode zero. A BASIC NEW or RUN command closes all channels except zero. OPENing a channel to S: or E: always clears the display screen.

See **COMPUTE!**, October 1981, for an example of using an IOCB with the cassette program recorder, and September 1981 for another use with the Atari 825 printer.

848-863　　　350-35F IOCB1
IOCB one.

864-879　　　360-36F IOCB2
IOCB two.

880-895　　　370-37F IOCB3
IOCB three.

896-911　　　380-38F IOCB4
IOCB four.

912-927　　　390-39F IOCB5
IOCB five.

928-943　　　3A0-3AF IOCB6
IOCB six. The GRAPHICS statement OPENs channel six for screen display (S:), so once you are out of mode zero, you cannot use channel six unless you first issue a CLOSE#6 statement. If you CLOSE this channel, you will not be able to use the DRAWTO, PLOT or LOCATE commands until you reOPEN the channel. The LOAD command closes channel six; it also closes all channels except zero.

944-959　　　3B0-3BF IOCB7
IOCB seven. LPRINT automatically uses channel seven for its use. If the channel is OPEN for some other use and an LPRINT is done, an error will occur, the channel will be CLOSEd, and subsequent LPRINTs will work. The LIST command also uses channel seven, even if channel seven is already OPEN. However, when the LIST is done, it CLOSEs channel seven. The LOAD command uses channel seven to transfer programs to and from

the recorder or disk. LIST (except to the display screen), LOAD and LPRINT also close all sound voices. The RUN from tape or disk and SAVE commands use channel seven, as does LIST. The bytes within each IOCB are used as follows:

Label	Offset	Bytes	Description
ICHID	0	1	Index into the device name

table for the currently OPEN file. Set by the OS. If not in use, the value is 255 ($FF), which is also the initialization value.

ICDNO 1 1 Device number such as one for D1: or two for D2:. Set by the OS.

ICCOM 2 1 Command for the type of action to be taken by the device, set by the user. This is the first variable after the channel number in an OPEN command. See below for a command summary. Also called ICCMD.

ICSTA 3 1 The most recent status returned by the device, set by the OS. May or may not be the same value as that which is returned by the STATUS request in BASIC. See the *OS User's Manual*, pp. 165-166, for a list of status byte values.

ICBAL/H 4,5 2 Two-byte (LSB,MSB) buffer address for data transfer or the address of the file name for OPEN, STATUS, etc.

ICPTL/H 6,7 2 Address of the device's put-one-byte routine minus one. Set by the OS at OPEN command, but not actually used by the OS (it is used by BASIC, however). Points to CIO's "IOCB NOT OPEN" message at powerup.

ICBLL/H 8,9 2 Buffer length set to the maximum number of bytes to transfer in PUT and GET operations. Decremented by one for each byte transferred; updated after each READ or WRITE operation. Records the number of bytes actually transferred in and out of the buffer after each operation.

ICAX1 10 1 Auxiliary byte number one, referred to as AUX1. Used in the OPEN statement to specify the type of file access: four for READ, eight for WRITE, twelve for both (UPDATE). Not all devices can use both kinds of operations. This byte can be used in user-written drivers for other purposes and can be altered in certain cases once the IOCB has been OPENed (see the program example above). For the S: device, if AUX1 equals 32, it means inhibit the screen clear function when changing GRAPHICS modes. Bit use is as follows for most applications:

Bit	7	6	5	4	3	2	1	0
Use	....	unused	....		W	R	D	A

W equals write, R equals read, D equals directory, A equals append.

ICAX2 11 1   Auxiliary byte two, referred to as AUX2. Special use by each device driver; some serial port functions may use this byte. Auxiliary bytes two to five have no fixed use; they are used to contain device-dependent and/or user-established data.

ICAX3/4 12,13 2   Auxiliary bytes three and four; used to maintain a record of the disk sector number for the BASIC NOTE and POINT commands.

ICAX5 14 1   Auxiliary byte five. Used by NOTE and POINT to maintain a record of the byte within a sector. It stores the relative displacement in sector from zero to 124 ($7C). Bytes 125 and 126 of a sector are used for sector-link values, and byte 127 ($7F) is used as a count of the number of data bytes in actual use in that sector.

ICAX6 15 1   Spare auxiliary byte.

Offset is the number you would add to the start of the IOCB in order to POKE a value into the right field, such as POKE 832 + OFFSET, 12.

The following is a list of the values associated with OPEN parameter number 1. Most of these values are listed in *Your Atari 400/800*. These are the values found in ICAX1, not the ICCOM values.

Device	Task #	Description
Cassette	4	Read
recorder	8	Write (can do either, not both)
Disk	4	Read
file	6	Read disk directory
	8	Write new file. Any file OPENed in

this mode will be deleted, and the first byte written will be at the start of the file.

           9   Write — append. In this mode the file is left intact, and bytes written are put at the end of the file.

          12   Read and write — update. Bytes read or written will start at the first byte in the file.

D: if BIT 0 equals one and BIT 3 equals one in AUX1, then operation will be appended output.

Screen	8	Screen output
editor	12	Keyboard input and screen output

(E:)　　　13　　　Screen input and output

E: BIT 0 equals one is a forced read (GET command).

Keyboard　4　　Read

Printer　　8　　Write

RS-232　　5　　Concurrent read
serial　　　8　　Block write
port　　　　9　　Concurrent write
　　　　　13　　Concurrent read and write

		Clear Screen after GR.	Text Window also	Read Oper- ation
Screen	8	yes	no	no
display	12	yes	no	yes
(S:)	24	yes	yes	no
	28	yes	yes	yes
	40	no	no	no
	44	no	no	yes
	56	no	yes	no
	60	no	yes	yes

Note that with S:, the screen is always cleared in GR.0 and there is no separate text window in GR.0 unless specifically user-designed. Without the screen clear, the previous material will remain on screen between GRAPHICS mode changes, but will not be legible in other modes. The values with S: are placed in the first auxiliary byte of the IOCB. All of the screen values above are also a write operation.

The second parameter in an OPEN statement (placed in the second auxiliary byte) is far more restricted in its use. Usually set to zero. If set to 128 ($80) for the cassette, it changes from normal to short inter-record gaps (AUX2).

With the Atari 820 printer, 83 ($53; AUX byte two) means sideways characters (Atari 820 printer only). Other printer variables (all for AUX2 as well) are: 70 ($4E) for normal 40 character per line printing and 87 ($57) for wide printing mode. With the screen (S:), a number can be used to specify the GRAPHICS modes zero through eleven. If mode zero is chosen, then the AUX1 options as above are ignored.

For the ICCOM field, the following values apply (BASIC XIO commands use the same values):

Command	Decimal	Hex
Open channel	3	3

944-959

Get text record (line)	5	5	BASIC: INPUT #n,A
Get binary record (buffer)	7	7	BASIC: GET #n,A
Put text record (line)	9	9	
Put binary record (buffer)	11	B	BASIC: PUT #n,A
Close	12	C	
Dynamic (channel) status	13	D	

BASIC uses a special "put byte" vector in the IOCB to talk directly to the handler for the PRINT#n,A$ command.

Disk File Management System Commands (BASIC XIO command):

Rename	32	20
Erase (delete)	33	21
Protect (lock)	35	23
Unprotect (unlock)	36	24
Point	37	25
Note	38	26
Format	254	FE

In addition, XIO supports the following commands:

Get character	7	7	
Put character	11	B	
Draw line	17	11	Display handler only.
Fill area	18	12	Display handler only.

FILL is done in BASIC with XIO 18,#6,12,0,"S:" (see the *BASIC Reference Manual* for details).

For the RS-232 (R:), XIO supports:

Output partial block	32	20
Control RTS,XMT,DTR	34	22
Baud, stop bits, word size	36	24
Translation mode	38	26
Concurrent mode	40	28

(see the *850 Interface Manual* for details)

CIO treats any command byte value greater than 13 ($D) as a special case, and transfers control over to the device handler for processing. For more information on IOCB use, read Bill

88

Wilkinson's "Insight: Atari" columns in **COMPUTE!**, November and December 1981, and in *Microcomputing*, August 1982. Also refer to the *OS User's Manual* and *De Re Atari*.

960-999   3C0-3E7   PRNBUF

Printer buffer. The printer handler collects output from LPRINT statements here, sending them to the printer when an End of Line (EOL; carriage return) occurs or when the buffer is full. Normally this is 40 characters. However, if an LPRINT statement generates fewer than 40 characters and ends with a semicolon or 38 characters and ends with a comma, Atari sends the entire buffer on each FOR-NEXT loop, the extra bytes filled with zeros. The output of the next LPRINT statement will appear in column 41 of the same line. According to the *Operating System User's Manual,* the Atari supports an 80-column printer device called P2:. Using OPEN and PUT statements to P2: may solve this problem. Here is a small routine for a GR.0 BASIC screen dump:

```
10    DIM TEXT$(1000): OPEN#2,4,0,"S:":
      TRAP1050
      .
      .
      .
1000  FOR LINE = 1 TO 24: POSITION PE
      EK(82),LINE
1010  FOR COL = 1 TO 38: GET#2,CHAR:
      TEXT$(COL,COL)=CHR$(CHAR)
1020  NEXT COL: GET#2,COL
1030  LPRINT TEXT$
1040  NEXT LINE
1050  RETURN
```

You can use the PTABW register at location 201 ($C9) to set the number of spaces between print elements separated by a comma. The minimum number of spaces accepted is two. LPRINT automatically uses channel seven for output. No OPEN statement is necessary and CLOSE is automatic.

Locations 1000 to 1020 ($3E8 to $3FC) are a reserved spare buffer area.

1021-1151   3FD-47F   CASBUF

Cassette buffer. These locations are used by the cassette handler to read data from and write data to the program (tape) recorder. The 128 ($80) data bytes for each cassette record are stored beginning at 1024 ($400 - page four). The current buffer size is found in location 650 ($28A). Location 61 ($3D) points to the current byte being written or read.

CASBUF is also used in the disk boot process; the first disk record is read into this buffer.

A cassette record consists of 132 bytes: two control bytes set to 85 ($55; alternating zeros and ones) for speed measurement in the baud rate correction routine; one control byte (see below); 128 data bytes (compared to 125 data bytes for a disk sector), and a checksum byte. Only the data bytes are stored in the cassette buffer. See *De Re Atari* for more information on the cassette recorder.

CONTROL BYTE VALUES

Value   Meaning

250 ($FA)   Partial record follows. The actual number of bytes is stored in the last byte of the record (127).

252 ($FC)   Record full; 128 bytes follow.

254 ($FE)   End of File (EOF) record; followed by 128 zero bytes.

Locations 1152 to 1791 ($480 to $6FF) are for user RAM (outer environment) requirements, depending on the amount of RAM available in the machine. Provided you don't use the FP package or BASIC, you have 640 ($280) free bytes here.

Locations 1152 to 1279 ($480 to $4FF) are 128 ($80) spare bytes.

The floating point package, when used, requires locations 1406 to 1535 ($57E to $5FF).

1406   57E   LBPR1
LBUFF prefix one.

1407   57F   LBPR2
LBUFF prefix two.

1408-1535   580-5FF   LBUFF
BASIC line buffer; 128 bytes. Used as an output result buffer for the FP to ASCII routine at 55526 ($D8E6). The input buffer is pointed to by locations 243, 244 ($F3, $F4).

1504   5E0   PLYARG
Polynomial arguments (FP use).

1510-1515   5E6-5EB   FPSCR
FP scratch pad use.

1516-1535   5EC-5FF   FPSCR1
Ditto. The end of the buffer is named LBFEND.

1536-1791   600-6FF   ....

Page six: 256 ($FF) bytes protected from OS use. Page six is not used by the OS and may be safely used for machine language subroutines, special I/O handlers, altered character sets, or whatever the user can fit into the space. Some problem may arise when the INPUT statement retrieves more than 128 characters. The locations from 1536 to 1663 ($600 to $67F) are then immediately used as a buffer for the excess characters. To avoid overflow, keep INPUT statements from retrieving more than 128 characters. The valFORTH implementation of fig-FORTH (from ValPar International) uses all of page six for its boot code, so it is not available for your use. However, FORTH allows you to reserve other blocks of memory for similar functions. BASIC A + uses locations $0600 - $67F.

Locations 1792 to the address specified by LOMEM (locations 128, 129; ($80, $81) - the pointer to BASIC low memory) are also used by DOS and the File Management System (FMS). Refer to the DOS source code and *Inside Atari DOS* for details. The addresses which follow are those for DOS 2.0S, the official Atari DOS at the time of this writing. Another DOS is available as an alternative to DOS 2.0 — K-DOS (TM), from K-BYTE (R). K-DOS is not menu driven but command driven. It does not use all of the same memory locations as the Atari DOS although it does use a modified version of the Atari FMS. (Another command-driven DOS, called OS/A + , is completely compatible with DOS 2.0S and is available from OSS, the creators of DOS 2.0S.)

1792-5377   700-1501

File management system RAM (pages seven to fifteen). FMS provides the interface between BASIC or DUP and the disk drive. It is a sophisticated device driver for all I/O operations involving the D: device. It allows disk users to use the special BASIC XIO disk commands (see the IOCB area 832 to 959: $340 to $3BF). It is resident in RAM below your BASIC RAM and provides the entry point to DOS when called by BASIC.

5440-13062   1540-3306

DUP.SYS RAM. The top will vary with the amount of buffer storage space allocated to the drive and sector buffers.

6780-7547   1A7C-1D7B

Drive buffers and sector-data buffers. The amount of memory will vary with the number of buffers allocated.

7548-MEMLO 1D7C-3306 (maximum)

Non-resident portion of DUP.SYS, DOS utility routines. DUP provides the utilities chosen from the DOS menu page, not from BASIC. It is not resident in RAM when you are using BASIC or another cartridge; rather it is loaded when DOS is called from BASIC or on autoboot powerup (and no cartridge supersedes it). When DUP is loaded, it overwrites the lower portion of memory. If you wish to save your program from destruction, you must have created a MEM.SAV file on disk *before* you called DOS from your program. See the *DOS Reference Manual.*

Locations 1792 to 2047 ($700 to $7FF; page seven) are the user boot area. MEMLO and LOMEM point to 1792 when no DOS or DUP program is loaded. This area can then be used for your BASIC or machine language programs. The lowest free memory address is 1792, and programs may extend upwards from here. There is a one-page buffer before the program space used for the tokenization of BASIC statements, pointed to by locations 128, 129 ($80, $81). Actually a program may start from any address above 1792 and below the screen display list as long as it does not overwrite this buffer if it is a BASIC program. Also, 1792 is the start of the FMS portion of DOS when resident.

When software is booted, the MEMLO pointer at 743,744 ($2E7,$2E8) in the OS data base (locations 512 to 1151; $512 to $47F) points to the first free memory location above that software; otherwise, it points to 1792. The DUP portion of DOS is partly resident here, starting at 5440 ($1540) and running to 13062 ($1540 to $3306). The location of the OS disk boot entry routine (DOBOOT) is 62189 ($F2ED). The standard Atari DOS 2.0S takes up sectors one through 83 ($53) on a disk. Sector one is the boot sector. Sectors two through 40 ($28) are the FMS portion, and sectors 41 ($29) through 83 are the DUP.SYS portion of DOS. For more information, see the DOS and OS source listings and *Inside Atari DOS.*

FMS, DOS.SYS and DUP.SYS

Disk boot records (sector one on a disk) are read into 1792 ($700). Starting from $700 (1792), the format is:

Byte	Hex	Label and use
0	700	BFLAG: Boot flag equals zero (unused).
1	701	BRCNT: Number of consecutive sectors to read (if the file is DOS, then BRCNT equals one).
2,3	702,703	BLDADR: Boot sector load address ($700).
4,5	704,705	BIWTARR: Initialization address.
6	706	JMP XBCONT: Boot continuation vector; $4B

(75): JMP command to next address in bytes seven and eight.

7,8   707,708   Boot read continuation address (LSB/MSB).

9   709   SABYTE: Maximum number of concurrently OPEN files. The default is three (see 1801 below).

10   70A   DRVBYT: Drive bits: the maximum number of drives attached to the system. The default is two (see 1802 below).

11   70B   (unused) Buffer allocation direction, set to zero.

12,13   70C,70D   SASA: Buffer allocation start address. Points to 1995 ($7CB) when DOS is loaded.

14   70E   DSFLG: DOS flag. Boot flag set to non-zero Must be non-zero for the second phase of boot process. Indicates that the file DOS.SYS has been written to the disk; zero equals no DOS file, one equals 128 byte sector disk, two equals 256 byte sector disk.

15,16   70F,710   DFLINK: Sector point to the DOS.SYS file. Sector count for the DOS.SYS file but actually unused.

17   711   BLDISP: Displacement to the sector link byte 125 ($7D). The sector link byte is the pointer to the next disk sector to be read. If it is zero, the end of the file has been reached.

18,19   712,713   DFLADR: Address of the start of DOS.SYS file.

20+   714+   Continuation of the boot load file. See the *OS User's Manual* and Chapter 20 of *Inside Atari DOS*.

Data from the boot sector is placed in locations 1792 to 1916 ($700 to $77C). Data from the rest of DOS.SYS is located starting from 1917 ($77D). All binary file loads start with 255 ($FF). The next four bytes are the start and end addresses (LSB/MSB), respectively.

1801   709   SABYTE

This records the limit on the number of files that can be open simultaneously. Usually set to three, the maximum is seven (one for each available IOCB — remember IOCB0 is used for the screen display). Each available file takes 128 bytes for a buffer, so if you increase the number of buffers, you decrease your RAM space accordingly. You can POKE 1801 with your new number to increase or decrease the number of files and then rewrite DOS (by calling DOS from BASIC and choosing menu selection "H") and have this number as your default on the new DOS.

1802   70A   DRVBYT

The maximum number of disk drives in your system, the DOS 2.0 default value is two. The least four bits are used to record which drives are available, so if you have drives one, three and four, this location would read:

00001101 or 13 in decimal.

Each drive has a separate buffer of 128 bytes reserved for it in RAM. If you have more or less than the default (two), then POKE 1802 with the appropriate number:

1 drive =	1 BIT 0	Binary 00000001
2 drives =	3 BITS 0 & 1	00000011
3 drives =	7 BITS 0, 1 & 2	00000111
4 drives =	15 BITS 0, 1, 2 & 3	00001111

This assumes you have them numbered sequentially. If not, POKE the appropriate decimal translation for the correct binary code: each drive is specified by one of the least four bits from one in BIT 0 to four in BIT 3. If you PEEK (1802) and get back three, for example, it means drives one and two are allocated, not three drives.

You can save your modification to a new disk by calling up DOS and choosing menu selection "H." This new DOS will then boot up with the number of drives and buffers you have allocated. A one-drive system can save 128 bytes this way (256 if one less data buffer is chosen). See the *DOS Manual*, page G.87.

1900   76C   BSIO

Entry point to FMS disk sector I/O routines.

1906   772   BSIOR

Entry point to the FMS disk handler (?).

1913   779   ....

Write verify flag for disk I/O operations. POKE with 80 ($50) to turn off the verify function, 87 ($57) to turn it back on. Disk write without verify is faster, but you may get errors in your data. I have had very few errors generated by turning off the verify function, but even one error in critical material can destroy a whole program. Be careful about using this location. You can save DOS (as above with menu selection "H") without write verify as your new default by writing DOS to a new disk. See the *DOS Manual*, page F.85. K-DOS's write-verify flag is located at 1907 ($773).

1995   7CB   DFMSDH

Entry point to a 21-byte FMS device (disk) handler. The address of this handler is placed in HATABS (locations 794 to 831; $31A to $33F) by the FMS initialization routine. When CIO needs to call an FMS function, it will locate the address of that function via the handler address table. See Chapters 8-11 of *Inside Atari DOS*, published by **COMPUTE! Books.**

2016   7E0   DINT
FMS initialization routine. The entry point is 1995 ($7CB). DUP calls FMS at this point. K-DOS uses the same location for its initialization routine.

2219   8AB   DFMOPN
OPEN routines, including open for append, update, and output.

2508   900   DFMPUT
PUT byte routines.

2591   A1F   WTBUR
Burst I/O routines.

2592-2773   A20-AD5   ....
In **COMPUTE!**, May and July 1982, Bill Wilkinson discussed BURST I/O, which should not take place when a file is OPEN for update, but does, due to a minor bug in DOS 2.0 (see also *Inside Atari DOS*, Chapter 12). This will cause update writes to work properly, but update reads to be bad. The following POKEs will correct the problem. Remember to save DOS back to a new disk.

```
POKE 2592,130     ($A20,82)
POKE 2593,19      ($A21,13)
POKE 2594,73      ($A22,49)
POKE 2595,12      ($A23,0C)
POKE 2596,240     ($A24,F0)
POKE 2597,36      ($A25,24)
POKE 2598,106     ($A26,6A)
POKE 2599,234     ($A27,EA)
POKE 2625,16      ($A41,10)
POKE 2773,31      ($AD5,1F)
```

(Note that the July 1982 issue of **COMPUTE!** contained a typo where the value to be POKEd into 2773 was mistakenly listed as 13, not 31!) Wilkinson points out that one way to completely disable BURST I/O (useful in some circumstances such as using the DOS BINARY SAVE to save the contents of ROM to disk!) is by:

POKE 2606,0   ($A2E,0)

This, however, will make the system LOAD and SAVE files considerably more slowly, so it's not recommended as a permanent change to DOS.

2751   ABF   DFMGET
GET byte routines, including GET file routines.

2817   B01   DFMSTA
Disk STATUS routines.

2837   B15   DFMCLS
IOCB CLOSE routines.

2983   BA7   DFMDDC
Start of the device-dependent command routines, including the BASIC XIO special commands:

3033   BD9   XRENAME
RENAME a file.

3122   C32   XDELETE
DELETE a file.

3196   C7C   XLOCK, XUNLOCK
LOCK and UNLOCK files. UNLOCK routines begin at 3203 ($C83).

3258   CBA   XPOINT
BASIC POINT command.

3331   D03   XNOTE
BASIC NOTE command. See the *DOS Manual* for information regarding these two BASIC commands, and see *De Re Atari* for a sample use.

3352   D18   XFORMAT
Format the entire diskette.

3501   DAD   LISTDIR
List the disk directory.

3742   E9E   FNDCODE
File name decode, including wildcard validity test. The current file name is pointed to by ZBUFP at locations 67, 68 ($43, $44).

3783   EC7   ....
By POKEing the desired ATASCII value here, you can change the wildcard character (*; ATASCII 42, $2A) used by DOS to any other character of your choice. Your altered DOS can be saved back to disk with DOS menu selection "H".

3818,3822   EEA,EEE   ....
By POKEing 3818 with 33 and 3822 with 123 ($21,$7B;), you can modify DOS to accept file names with punctuation, numbers and lowercase as valid; 33 is the low range of the ATASCII code and 127 the high range (lower or higher values are control and

graphics codes and inverse characters). Of course, any
unmodified DOS still won't accept such file names. You could
actually change the range to any value from zero to 255 at your
discretion. This, however, may cause other problems with such
ATASCII codes as spaces and the wildcard (*; see above). Can
be saved back to disk with menu selection "H".

3850   F0A   FDSCHAR
Store the file name characters that result from the file name
decode routines.

3873   F21   SFDIR
Directory search routines; search for the user-specified file
name.

3988   F94   WRTNXS
Write data sector routine.

4111   100F   RDNXTS
Read data sector routine.

4206   106E   RDDIR
Read and write directory sector routines.

4235   108B   RDVTOC
Read or write the volume table of contents (VTOC) sectors.

4293   10C5   FRESECT
Free sector(s) routine; returns the number of free sectors on a
disk that are available to the user.

4358   1106   GETSECTOR
Get sector routine; retrieves a free sector for use from the disk.

4452   1164   SETUP
SETUP — initialization of the FMS parameters. Prepares FMS to
deal with the operation to be performed and to access a
particular file. See *Inside Atari DOS,* Chapter seven.

4618   120A   WRTDOS
Write new DOS.SYS file to disk routine, including new FMS file
to DOS.SYS file.

4789   12B5   ERRNO
Start of the FMS error number table.

4856-4978   12F8-1372   ....
Miscellaneous FMS storage area: sector length, drive tape, stack
level, file number, etc.

4993-5120   1381-1400   FCB
Start of the FMS File Control Blocks (FCB's). FCB's are used to

store information about files currently being processed. The eight FCB's are 16-byte blocks that correspond in a one-on-one manner with the IOCB's. Each FCB consists of:

Label	Bytes	Purpose

FCBFNO 1   File number of the current file being processed.

FCBOTC 1   Which mode the file has been OPENed for: append is one, directory read is two, input is four, output is eight, update is twelve.

SPARE 1   Not used.

FCBSLT 1   Flag for the sector length type; 128 or 256 bytes.

FCBFLG 1   Working flag. If equal to 128 ($80), then the file has been OPENed for output or append and may acquire new data sectors. If the value is 64, then sector is in the memory buffer awaiting writing to disk.

FCBMLN 1   Maximum sector data length; 125 or 253 bytes depending on drive type (single or double density). The last three sector bytes are reserved for sector link and byte count data.

FCBDLN 1   Current byte to be read or modified in the operation in a data sector.

FCBBUF 1   Tells FMS which buffer has been allocated to the file being processed.

FCBCSN 2   Sector number of the sector currently in the buffer.

FCBLSN 2   Number of the next sector in data chain.

FCBSSN 2   Starting sectors for appended data if the file has been OPENed for append.

FCBCNT 2   Sector count for the current file.

DUP doesn't use these FCB's; it writes to the IOCB's directly. CIO transfers the control to FMS as the operation demands, then on to SIO.

5121   1401   FILDIR

File directory, a 256 ($100) byte sequential buffer for entries to the disk directory.

5377   1501   ENDFMS

Disk directory (VTOC — Volume Table Of Contents) buffer. 64 ($40) bytes are reserved, one byte for each possible file. It also marks the end of FMS. The VTOC (sector 360; $168) is a sequential bit map of each of the 720 sectors on the disk. It starts at byte ten and continues through to byte 99. When a bit is set (one), it indicates that the sector associated is in use.

5440   1540   DOS

DUP.SYS initialization address. Beginning of mini-DOS; the RAM-resident portion of DUP. Used for the same purpose in K-DOS.

5446,5450   1546,154A   ....

Contains the location (LSB/MSB) of the DOSVEC (location 10; $A). This is the pointer to the address BASIC will jump to when DOS is called.

5533   159D   DUPFLG

Flag to test if DUP is already resident in memory. Zero equals DUP is not there.

5534   159E   OPT

Used to store the value of the disk menu option chosen by the user.

5535   159F   LOADFLG

If this location reads 128, then a memory file (MEM.SAV) file doesn't have to be loaded.

5540   15A4   SFLOAD

Routines to load a MEM.SAV file if it exists.

5888   1700   USRDOS

Listed in the DUP.SYS equates file but never explained in the listings.

5899   170B   MEMLDD

Flags that the MEM.SAV file has been loaded. Zero means it has not been loaded.

5947   173B   ....

The MEM.SAV (MEMSAVE) file creation routines begin here. They start with the file name MEM.SAV stored in ATASCII format. The write routines begin at MWRITE, 5958 ($1746). The DOS utility MEMSAVE copies the lower 6000 bytes of memory to disk to save your BASIC program from being destroyed when you call DOS, which then loads DUP.SYS into that area of memory.

6044,6045   179C-179D   INISAV

DOSINI (see location 12, 13; $C, $D) vector save location. Entry point to DOS on a call from BASIC.

6046   179E   MEMFLG

Flag to show if memory has been written to disk using a MEM.SAV file.

6418   1912   CLMJMP
Test to see if DOS must load MEM.SAV from the disk before it does a run at cartridge address, then jumps to the cartridge address.

6432   1920   LMTR
Test to see if DOS must load MEM.SAV before it performs a run at address command from the DOS menu.

6457   1939   LDMEM
MEMSAVE load routines (for the MEM.SAV file).

6518   1979   INITIO
DUP.SYS warmstart entry. An excellent program to eliminate the need for DUP.SYS and MEM.SAV (not to mention the time required to load them!) was presented in **COMPUTE!**, July 1982, called *MicroDOS*; it's well worth examining. See also "The Atari Wedge," **COMPUTE!**, December 1982.

6630   19E6   ISRODN
Start of the serial interrupt service routine to output data needed routines in DUP.SYS.

6691   1A23   ISRSIR
Start of the serial interrupt ready service routines in DUP.SYS.

6781   1A7D   ....
Start of the drive and data buffers. Drive buffers are numbered sequentially one to four, data buffers one to eight, assuming that many are allocated for each. Normally, the first two buffers are allocated for drives and the next three for data. Buffers are 128 ($80) bytes long each and start at 6908 ($1AFC), 7036 ($1B7C), 7162 ($1BFA) and 7292 ($1C7C). See locations 1801 and 1802 ($709, $70A).

7420   1CFC   ....
MEMLO (743, 744; $2E7, $2E8) points here when DOS is resident unless the buffer allocation has been altered. MEMLO will point to 7164 for a one drive, two data buffer setup, a saving of 256 bytes. Loading the RS-232 handler from the 850 Interface will move MEMLO up another 1728 bytes. The RS-232 handler in the 850 Interface will only boot (load into memory) if you first boot the AUTORUN.SYS file on your Atari master diskette or use another RS-232 boot program such as a terminal package. The RS-232 handler will boot up into memory if you do not have a disk attached and you have turned it on before turning on the computer. You may still use the printer (parallel) port on the 850 even if the RS-232 handler is not booted.

7548   1D7C   ....
Beginning of non-resident portion of DUP; 40 ($28) byte
parameter buffer.

7588   1DA4   LINE
80 ($50) byte line buffer.

7668   1DF4   DBUF
256 ($100) byte data buffer for COPY routines. Copy routines
work in 125-byte passes, equal to the number of data bytes in
each sector on the disk. There are 256 bytes because Atari had
planned a double density drive which has 253 data bytes in each
sector.

7924   1EF4   ....
Miscellaneous variable storage area and data buffers.

7951-8278   1F0F-2056   DMENU
Disk menu screen display data is stored here.

8191   1FFF   ....
This is the top of the minimum RAM required for operation (8K).
To use DOS, you must have a minimum of 16K.

DUP.SYS ROUTINES

Locations 8192 to 32767 ($2000 to $7FFF) are the largest part of the
RAM expansion area; this space is generally for your own use. If you
have DOS.SYS or DUP.SYS loaded in, they also use a portion of this
area to 13062 ($3306) as below:

8309   2075   DOSOS
Start of the DOS utility monitor, including the utilities called
when a menu selection function is completed and the display of
the "SELECT ITEM" message.

8505   2139   DIRLST
Directory listing.

8649   21C9   DELFIL
Delete a file.

8990   231E   ....
Copy a file. This area starts with the copy messages. The copy
routines themselves begin at PYFIL, 9080 ($2378).

9783   2637   RENFIL
Rename a disk file routines.

9856   2680   FMTDSK
Format the entire disk. There is no way to format specific sectors

of a disk with the "C" ROMs currently used in your 810 drives. There is a new ROM, the "E" version, which not only allows selective sector formatting, but is also considerably faster. It was not known at the time of this writing whether Atari would release the "E" version.

9966   26EE   STCAR
Start a cartridge.

10060   274C   BRUN
Run a binary file at the user-specified address.

10111   277F   . . . .
Start of the write MEM.SAV file to disk routine. The entry point is at MEMSAV, 10138 ($279A).

10201   27D9   WBOOT
Write DOS/DUP files to disk.

10483   28F3   TESTVER2
Test for version two DOS. DOS.20S is the latest official DOS, considerably improved over the earlier DOS 1.0. The S stands for single density. Atari had planned to release a dual density drive (the 815), but pulled it out of the production line at the last minute for some obscure high-level reason. A double density drive is available from the Percom company.

10522   291A   LDFIL
Load a binary file into memory. If it has a run address specified in the file, it will autoboot.

10608   2970   LKFIL, ULFIL
Lock and unlock files on a disk.

10690   29C2   DDMG
Duplicate a disk.

11528   2D08   DFFM
Duplicate a file.

11841   2E41   . . . .
Miscellaneous subroutines.

12078   2F2E   SAVFIL
Save a binary file.

12348   303C   . . . .
Miscellaneous subroutines.

13062   3306   . . . .
End of DUP.SYS.
The rest of RAM is available to location 32767 ($7FFF).

CARTRIDGE B: 8K

Locations 32768 to 40959 ($8000 to $9FFF) are used by the right
cartridge (Atari 800 only), when present. When not present, this RAM
area is available for use in programs. When the 8K BASIC cartridge is
being used, this area most frequently contains the display list and screen
memory. As of this writing, the only cartridge that uses this slot is
Monkey Wrench from Eastern House Software.

It is possible to have 16K cartridges on the Atari by either combining
both slots using two 8K cartridges or simply having one with large
enough ROM chips and using one slot. In this case, the entire area from
32768 to 49151 ($8000 to $BFFF) would be used as cartridge ROM.

Technically, the right cartridge slot is checked first for a resident
cartridge and initialized, then the left. You can confirm this by putting
the Assembler Editor cartridge in the right and BASIC in the left slots.
BASIC will boot, but not the ASED. Using FRE(0), you will see,
however, that you have 8K less RAM to use; and PEEKing through this
area will show that the ASED program is indeed in memory, but that
control was passed to BASIC. Control will pass to the ASED cartridge if
the cartridges are reversed. This is because the last six bytes of the
cartridge programs tell the OS where the program begins — in both
cases, it is a location in the area dedicated to the left cartridge. The six
bytes are as follows:

Byte		Purpose
Left (A)	Right(B)	
49146 ($BFFA)	40954 ($9FFA)	Cartridge start address (low byte)
49147 ($BFFB)	40955 ($9FFB)	Cartridge start address (high byte)
49148 ($BFFC)	40956,($9FFC)	Reads zero if a cartridge is

inserted, non-zero when no cartridge is present. This information
is passed down to the page zero RAM: if the A cartridge is plugged
in, then location 6 will read one; if the B cartridge is plugged in,
then location 7 will read one; otherwise they will read zero.

49149 ($BFFD)	40957 ($9FFD)	Option byte. If BIT 0 equals one,

then boot the disk (else there is no disk boot). If BIT 2 equals one,
then initialize and start the cartridge (else initialize but do not
start). If BIT 7 equals one, then the cartridge is a diagnostic
cartridge which will take control, but not initialize the OS (else
non-diagnostic cartridge). Diagnostic cartridges were used by
Atari in the development of the system and are not available to the
public.

49150 ($BFFE)	40958 ($9FFE)	Cartridge initialization address

low byte.

49151 ($BFFF)	40959 ($9FFF)	Cartridge initialization address

high byte. This is the address to which the OS will jump during all powerup and RESETs.

The OS makes temporary use of locations 36876 to 36896 ($900C to $9020) to set up vectors for the interrupt handler. See the OS listings pages 31 and 81. This code was only used in the development system used to design the Atari.

CARTRIDGE A: 8K

Locations 40960 to 49151 ($A000 to $BFFF) are used by the left cartridge, when present. When not present, this RAM area is available for other use. The display list and the screen display data will be in this area when there is no cartridge present.

Most cartridges use this slot (see above) including the 8K BASIC, Assembler-Editor, and many games. Below are some of the entry points for the routines in Atari 8K BASIC. There is no official Atari listing of the BASIC ROM yet. Many of the addresses below are listed in *Your Atari 400/800*. Others have been provided in numerous magazine articles and from disassembling the BASIC cartridge.

BASIC ROUTINES

40960-41036   A000-A04C
Cold start.

41037-41055   A04D-A05F
Warm start.

41056-42081   A060-A461
Syntax checking routines.

42082-42158   A462-A4AE
Search routines.

42159-42508   A4AF-A60C
STATEMENT name table. The statement TOKEN list begins at 42161 ($A4B1). You can print a list of these tokens by:

```
 5    ADDRESS = 42161
10    IF NOT PEEK(ADDRESS) THEN PRINT:
      END
15    PRINT TOKEN,
20    BYTE = PEEK(ADDRESS): ADDRESS = A
      DDRESS + 1
30    IF BYTE < 128 THEN PRINT CHR$(BYT
      E);: GOTO 20
40    PRINT CHR$(BYTE - 128)
50    ADDRESS = ADDRESS + 2: TOKEN = TO
      KEN + 1: GOTO 10
```

42509-43134   A60D-A87E
Syntax tables. The OPERATOR token list begins at 42979 ($A7E3). You

can print a list of these tokens by:

```
5    ADDRESS = 42979: TOKEN = 16
10   IF NOT PEEK(ADDRESS) THEN PRINT:
     END
15   PRINT TOKEN,
20   BYTE = PEEK(ADDRESS): ADDRESS = A
     DDRESS + 1
30   IF BYTE < 128 THEN PRINT CHR$(BYT
     E);: GOTO 20
40   PRINT CHR$(BYTE - 128)
50   TOKEN = TOKEN + 1
60   GOTO 10
```

See **COMPUTE!**, January and February 1982; *BYTE*, February 1982, and *De Re Atari* for an explanation of BASIC tokens.

43135-43358 A87F-A95E
Memory manager.

43359-43519 A95F-A9FF
Execute CONT statement.

43520-43631 AA00-AA6F
Statement table.

43632-43743 AA70-AADF
Operator table.

43744-44094 AAE0-AC3E
Execute expression routine.

44095-44163 AC3F-AC83
Operator precedence routine.

44164-45001 AC84-AFC9
Execute operator routine.

45002-45320 AFCA-B108
Execute function routine.

45321-47127 B109-B817
Execute statement routine.

47128-47381 B818-B915
CONT statement subroutines.

47382-47542 B916-B9B6
Error handling routines.

47543-47732 B9B7-BA74
Graphics handling routines.

47733-48548 BA75-BDA4
I/O routines.

48549-49145 BDA5-BFF9
Floating point routines (see below).

48551   BDA7   SIN

Calculate SIN(FR0). Checks DEGFLG (location 251; $FB) to see if trigonometric calculations are in radians (DEGFLG equals zero) or degrees (DEGFLG equals six).

48561   BDB1   COS

Calculate Cosine (FR0) with carry. FR0 is Floating Point register zero, locations 212-217; $D4-$D9. See the Floating Point package entry points from location 55296 on.

48759   BE77   ATAN

Calculate Atangent using FR0, with carry.

48869   BEE5   SQR

Calculate square root (FR0) with carry.

Note that there is some conflict of addresses for the above routines. The addresses given are from the first edition of *De Re Atari*. The *Atari OS Source Code Listing* gives the following addresses for these FP routines:

These are entry points, not actual start addresses.

SIN	48513	($BD81)
COS	48499	($BD73)
ATAN	48707	($BE43)
SQR	48817	($BEB1)

However, after disassembling the BASIC ROMs, I found that the addresses in *De Re Atari* appear to be correct.

49146,7   BFFA,B

Left cartridge start address.

49148   BFFC

A non-zero number here tells the OS that there is no cartridge in the left slot.

49149   BFFC

Option byte. A cartridge which does not specify a disk boot may use all of the memory from 1152 ($480) to MEMTOP any way it sees fit.

49150,1   BFFE,F

Cartridge initialization address. See the above section on the right slot, 32768 to 40959, for more information.

When a BASIC program is SAVEd, only 14 of the more than 50 page zero locations BASIC uses are written to the disk or cassette with the program. The rest are all recalculated with a NEW or SAVE command, sometimes with RUN or GOTO. These 14 locations are:

128,129	80,81	LOMEM
130,131	82,83	VNTP
132,133	84,85	VNTD
134,135	86,87	VVTP
136,137	88,89	STMTAB
138,139	8A,8B	STMCUR
140,141	8C,8D	STARP

The string/array space is not loaded; STARP is included only to point to the end of the BASIC program.

The two other critical BASIC page zero pointers, which are not SAVEd with the program, are:

142,143	8E,8F	RUNSTK
144,145	90,91	MEMTOP

For more information concerning Atari BASIC, see the appendix. For detailed description, refer to the *Atari BASIC Reference Manual*. For more technical information, see *De Re Atari*, BYTE, February 1982, and *COMPUTE!'s First Book of Atari* and *COMPUTE!'s Second Book of Atari*.

Locations 49152 to 53247 ($C000 to $CFFF) are unused. Unfortunately, this rather large 4K block of memory cannot be written to by the user, so it is presently useless. Apparently, this area of ROM is reserved for future expansion. Rumors abound about new Atari OS's that allow 3-D graphics, 192K of on-board RAM and other delights. Most likely this space will be consumed in the next OS upgrade. PEEKing this area will show it not to be completely empty; it was apparently used for system development in Atari's paleozoic age.

Although the Atari is technically a 64K machine (1K equals 1024 bytes, so 64K equals 65536 bytes), you don't really have all 64K to use. The OS takes up 10K; there is the 4K block here that's unused, plus a few other unused areas in the ROM and, of course, there are the hardware chips. BASIC (or any cartridge) uses another 8K. The bottom 1792 bytes are used by the OS, BASIC, and floating point package. Then DOS and DUP take up their memory space, not to mention the 850 handler if booted — leaving you with more or less 38K of RAM to use for your BASIC programming.

Locations 53248 to 55295 ($D000 to $D7FF) are for ROM for the special I/O chips that Atari uses. The CTIA (or GTIA, depending on which you have) uses memory locations 53248 to 53503 ($D000 to $D0FF). POKEY uses 53760 to 54015 ($D200 to $D2FF). PIA uses 54016 to 54271

($D300 to $D3FF). ANTIC uses 54272 to 54783 ($D400 to $D5FF). ANTIC, POKEY and G/CTIA are Large Scale Integration (LSI) circuit chips. Don't confuse this chip ROM with the OS ROM which is be found in higher memory. For the most extensive description of these chips, see the *Atari Hardware Manual*.

There are two blocks of unused, unavailable memory in the I/O areas: 53504 to 53759 ($D100 to $D1FF) and 54784 to 55295 ($D600 to $D7FF).

Many of the following registers can't be read directly, since they are hardware registers. Writing to them can often be difficult because in most cases the registers change every 30th second (stage two VBLANK) or even every 60th second (stage one VBLANK)! That's where the shadow registers mentioned earlier come in. The values written into these ROM locations are drawn from the shadow registers; to effect any "permanent" change in BASIC (i.e., while your program is running), you have to write to these shadow registers (in direct mode or while your program is running; these values will all be reset to their initialization state on RESET or powerup).

Shadow register locations are enclosed in parentheses; see these locations for further descriptions. If no shadow register is mentioned, you may be able to write to the location directly in BASIC. Machine language is fast enough to write to the ROM locations and may be able to bypass the shadow registers entirely.

Another feature of many of these registers is their dual nature. They are read for one value and written to for another. The differences between these functions are noted by the (R) for *read* and (W) for *write* functions. You will notice that many of these dual-purpose registers also have two labels.

CTIA or GTIA
53248-53505   D000-D0FF

GTIA (or CTIA) is a special television interface chip designed exclusively for the Atari to process the video signal. ANTIC controls most of the C/GTIA chip functions. The GTIA shifts the display by one-half color clock off what the CTIA displays, so it may display a different color than the CTIA in the same piece of software. However, this shift allows players and playfields to overlap perfectly.

There is no text window available in GTIA modes, but you can create a defined area on your screen with either a DLI (see **COMPUTE!**, September 1982) or by POKEing the GTIA mode number into location 87 ($57), POKEing 703 with four and then setting the proper bits in location 623 ($26F) for that mode. Only in the former method will you be able to get a readable screen, however. In the latter you will only create a four line, scrolling, unreadable window. You will be able to input and output as with any normal text window; you just won't be able to read it! GTIA, by the way, apparently stands for "George's Television Interface Adapter." Whoever George is, thanks, but what is CTIA?

See the *OS User's Manual,* the *Hardware Manual, De Re Atari* and **COMPUTE!**, July 1982 to September 1982, for more information.

53248   D000   HPOSP0

(W) Horizontal position of player 0. Values from zero to 227 ($E3) are possible but, depending on the size of the playfield, the range can be from 48 ($30) as the leftmost position to 208 ($D0) as the rightmost position. Other positions will be "off screen."

Here are the normal screen boundaries for players and missiles. The values may vary somewhat due to the nature of your TV screen. Players and missiles may be located outside these boundaries, but will not be visible (off screen):

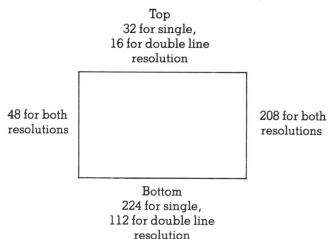

Top
32 for single,
16 for double line
resolution

48 for both
resolutions

208 for both
resolutions

Bottom
224 for single,
112 for double line
resolution

Although you can POKE to these horizontal position registers, they are reset to zero immediately. The player or missile will stay on the screen at the location specified by the POKE, but in order to move it using the horizontal position registers, you can't use:

POKE 53248, PEEK (53248) + n (or -n)

which will end up generating an error message. Instead, you need to use something like this:

```
10    POKE 704,220: GRAPHICS 1: HPOS =
      53248: POKE 623,8
```

53248

```
20    N = 100: POKE HPOS,N: POKE 53261
    ,255
30    IF STICK(0) = 11 THEN N = N - 1:
    POKE HPOS,N: PRINT N
40    IF STICK(0) = 7 THEN N = N + 1:
    POKE HPOS,N: PRINT N
50    GOTO 30
```

There are no vertical position registers for P/M graphics, so you must use software routines to move players vertically. One idea for vertical motion is to reposition the player within the P/M region rather than the screen RAM. For example, the program below uses a small machine language routine to accomplish this move:

```
1 REM LINES 5 TO 70 SET UP THE PLAYER
5 KEEP=PEEK(106)-16
10 POKE 106,KEEP:POKE 54279,KEEP
20 GRAPHICS 7+16:POKE 704,78:POKE 559
    ,46:POKE 53277,3
30 PMBASE=KEEP*256
40 FOR LOOP=PMBASE+512 TO PMBASE+640:
    POKE LOOP,0:NEXT LOOP:REM CLEAR OU
    T MEMORY FIRST
50 X=100:Y=10:POKE 53248,X
60 FOR LOOP=0 TO 7:READ BYTE:POKE PMB
    ASE+512+Y+LOOP,BYTE:NEXT LOOP:REM
    PLAYER GRAPHICS INTO MEMORY
70 DATA 129,153,189,255,255,189,153,1
    29
80 REM LINES 100 TO 170 SET UP MACHIN
    E LANGUAGE ROUTINE
100 DIM UP$(21),DOWN$(21):UP=ADR(UP$)
    :DOWN=ADR(DOWN$)
110 FOR LOOP=UP TO UP+20:READ BYTE:PO
    KE LOOP,BYTE:NEXT LOOP
120 FOR LOOP=DOWN TO DOWN+20:READ BYT
    E:POKE LOOP,BYTE:NEXT LOOP
130 DATA 104,104,133,204,104,133,203,
    160,1,177
140 DATA 203,136,145,203,200,200,192,
    11,208,245,96
150 DATA 104,104,133,204,104,133,203,
    160,10,177
160 DATA 203,200,145,203,136,136,192,
    255,208,245,96
200 REM VERTICAL CONTROL
210 IF STICK(0)=14 THEN GOSUB 300
```

```
220 IF STICK(0)=13 THEN D=USR(DOWN,PM
    BASE+511+Y):Y=Y+1
250 GOTO 210
300 U=USR(UP,PMBASE+511+Y):Y=Y-1
310 RETURN
```

This will move any nine-line (or less) size player vertically with the joystick. If you have a larger player size, increase the 11 in line 140 to a number two larger than the number of vertical lines the player uses, and change the ten in line 150 to one greater than the number of lines. To add horizontal movement, add the following lines:

```
6    HPOS = 53248
230  IF STICK(0) = 11 THEN X = X - 1:
     POKE HPOS, X
240  IF STICK(0) = 7 THEN X = X + 1:
     POKE HPOS, X
```

You can use the routine to move any player by changing the number 511 in the USR calls to one less than the start address of the object to be moved. See the appendix for a map of P/M graphics memory use. Missiles are more difficult to move vertically with this routine, since it moves an entire byte, not bits. It would be useful for moving all four missiles vertically if you need to do so; they could still be moved horizontally in an individual manner.

See **COMPUTE!**, December 1981, February 1982, and May 1982, for some solutions and some machine language move routines, and **COMPUTE!**, October 1981, for a solution with animation involving P/M graphics.

M0PF

(R) Missile 0 to playfield collision. This register will tell you which playfield the object has "collided" with, i.e., overlapped. If missile 0 collides with playfield two, the register would read four and so on. Bit use is:

Bit	7	6	5	4	3	2	1	0
Playfield	....	unused	....		3	2	1	0
Decimal	....	....	....		8	4	2	1

53249   **D001**   **HOPSP1**

(W) Horizontal position of player 1.

M1PF

(R) Missile 1 to playfield collision.

53250   **D002**   **HPOSP2**

(W) Horizontal position of player 2.

M2PF

53251

(R) Missile 2 to playfield collision.

53251   D003   HPOSP3

(W) Horizontal position of player 3.

M3PF

(R) Missile 3 to playfield collision.

53252   D004   HPOSM0

(W) Horizontal position of missile 0. Missiles move horizontally like players. See the note in 53248 ($D000) concerning the use of horizontal registers.

P0PF

(R) Player 0 to playfield collisions. There are some problems using collision detection in graphics modes nine to eleven. There are no obviously recognized collisions in GR.9 and GR. 11. In GR.10, collisions work only for the playfield colors that correspond to the usual playfield registers. Also, the background (BAK) color is set by PCOLR0 (location 704; $2C0) rather than the usual COLOR4 (location 712; $2C8), which will affect the priority detection. In GR.10, playfield colors set by PCOLR0 to PCOLR3 (704 to 707; $2C0 to $2C3) behave like players where priority is concerned. Bit use is:

Bit	7	6	5	4	3	2	1	0
Playfield	. . . .	unused	. . . .		3	2	1	0
Decimal	. . . .	. . . .	. . . .		8	4	2	1

53253   D005   HPOSM1

(W) Horizontal position of missile 1.

P1PF

(R) Player 1 to playfield collisions.

53254   D006   HPOSM2

(W) Horizonal position of missile 2.

P2PF

(R) Player 2 to playfield collisions.

53255   D007   HPOSM3

(W) Horizontal position of missile 3.

P3PF

(R) Player 3 to playfield collisions.

53256   D008   SIZEP0

(W) Size of player 0. POKE with zero or two for normal size (eight color clocks wide), POKE with one to double a player's width (sixteen color clocks wide), and POKE with three for quadruple width (32 color clocks wide). Each player can have its own width set.

A normal size player might look something like this:

```
00011000
00111100
01111110
11111111
11111111
01111110
00111100
00011000
```

In double width, the same player would like this:

```
0000001111000000
0000111111110000
0011111111111100
1111111111111111
1111111111111111
0011111111111100
0000111111110000
0000001111000000
```

In quadruple width, the same player would become:

```
00000000000011111111000000000000
00000000111111111111111100000000
00001111111111111111111111110000
11111111111111111111111111111111
11111111111111111111111111111111
00001111111111111111111111110000
00000000111111111111111100000000
00000000000011111111000000000000
```

Bit use is:

Bit	7	6	5	4	3	2	1	0	
Size:		....	unused	....			0	0	Normal (8 color clocks)
							0	1	Double (16 color clocks)
							1	0	Normal
							1	1	Quadruple (32 color clocks)

M0PL

(R) Missile 0 to player collisions. There is no missile-to-missile collision register. Bit use is:

Bit	7	6	5	4	3	2	1	0
Player		..	unused	..	3	2	1	0
Decimal		...	.....	...	8	4	2	1

53257   **D009**   **SIZEP1**

(W) Size of player 1.

M1PL

(R) Missile 1 to player collisions.

53258   D00A   SIZEP2

(W) Size of player 2.

M2PL

(R) Missile 2 to player collisions.

53259   D00B   SIZEP3

(W) Size of player 3.

M3PL

(R) Missile 3 to player collisions.

53260   D00C   SIZEM

(W) Size for all missiles; set bits as below (decimal values included):

Bits	Size:		
	Normal	Double	Quadruple
7 & 6: missile 3	0,128	64	192
5 & 4: missile 2	0, 32	16	48
3 & 2: missile 1	0, 8	4	12
1 & 0: missile 0	0, 2	1	3

where turning on the bits in each each pair above does as follows:

0 and 0: normal size — two color clocks wide
0 and 1: twice normal size — four color clocks wide
1 and 0: normal size
1 and 1: four times normal size — eight color clocks wide

So, to get a double-sized missile 2, you would set BITs 5 and 6, or POKE 53260,48. Each missile can have a size set separately from the other missiles or players when using the GRAF registers.

A number of sources, including *De Re Atari*, say that you can set neither missile sizes nor shapes separately. Here's a routine to show that you can in fact do both:

```
10   POKE 53265,255: REM SHAPE START
15   GR.7
20   POKE 623,1: REM SET PRIORITIES
30   FOR X = 1 TO 25
35   F = 50
40   FOR C = 704 TO 707: POKE C,F + X:
     F = F + 50: NEXT C: REM COLOURS
45   S = 100
50   FOR P = 53252 TO 53255: POKE P,S
     + X: S = S + 20: NEXT P : REM SCRE
     EN POSITIONS
```

```
60   NEXT X
70   INPUT A,B: REM MISSILE SIZE AND S
     HAPES
80   POKE 53260,A: POKE 53265,B
100  GOTO 30
```

Here's another example using DMA; GRACTL and DACTL (53277 and 54272; $D01D and $D400):

```
10   POKE 623,1: POKE 559,54: POKE 542
     79, 224: POKE 53277,1
20   FOR N = 53252 TO 53255: POKE N, 1
     00 + X: X = X + 10: NEXT N: X = 0
30   INPUT SIZE: POKE 53260, SIZE
40   GOTO 30
```

See 54279 ($D407) for more information on P/M graphics.

POPL

(R) Player 0 to player collisions. Bit use is:

Bit	7	6	5	4	3	2	1	0
Player	. . .	unused	. . .		3	2	1	0
Decimal	. . .	. . .	. . .	. . .	8	4	2	1

53261   D00D   GRAFP0

(W) Graphics shape for player 0 written directly to the player graphics register. In using these registers, you bypass ANTIC. You only use the GRAFP# registers when you are not using Direct Memory Access (DMA: see GRACTL at 53277). If DMA is enabled, then the graphics registers will be loaded automatically from the area specified by PMBASE (54279; $D407).

The GRAF registers can only write a single byte to the playfield, but it runs the entire height of the screen. Try this to see:

```
10   POKE 53248, 160: REM SET HORIZONT
     AL POSITION OF PLAYER 0
20   POKE 704, 245: REM SET PLAYER 0 C
     OLOUR TO ORANGE
30   POKE 53261, 203: REM BIT PATTERN
     11001011
```

To remove it, POKE 53261 with zero. The bit order runs from seven to zero, left to right across the TV screen. Each bit set will appear as a vertical line on the screen. A value of 255 means all bits are set, creating a wide vertical line. You can also use the size registers to change the player width. Using the GRAF registers will allow you to use players and missiles for such things as boundaries on game or text fields quite easily.

P1PL

(R) Player 1 to player collisions.

53262   **D00E**   **GRAFP1**

(W) Graphics for player 1.

P2PL

(R) Player 2 to player collisions.

53263   **D00F**   **GRAFP2**

(W) Graphics for player 3.

P3PL

(R) Player 3 to player collisions.

53264   **D010**   **GRAFP3**

(W) Graphics for player 3.

TRIG0

(R) Joystick trigger 0 (644). Controller jack one, pin six. For all triggers, zero equals button pressed, one equals not pressed. If BIT 2 of GRACTL (53277; $D01D) is set to one, then all TRIG BITs 0 are latched when the button is pressed (set to zero) and are only reset to one (not pressed) when BIT 2 of GRACTL is reset to zero. The effect of latching the triggers is to return a constant "button pressed" read until reset.

53265   **D011**   **GRAFM**

(W) Graphics for all missiles, not used with DMA. GRAFM works the same as GRAFP0 above. Each pair of bits represents one missile, with the same allocation as in 53260 ($D00C) above.

> Bit   7 6   5 4   3 2   1 0
> Missile - 3 -   - 2 -   - 1 -   - 0 -

Each bit set will create a vertical line running the entire height of the TV screen. Missile graphics shapes may be set separately from each other by using the appropriate bit pairs. To mask out unwanted players, write zeros to the bits as above.

TRIG1

(R) Joystick trigger 1 (645). Controller jack two, pin six.

53266   **D012**   **COLPM0**

(W) Color and luminance of player and missile 0 (704). Missiles share the same colors as their associated players except when joined together to make a fifth player. Then they take on the same value as in location 53733 ($D019; color register 3).

TRIG 2

(R) Joystick trigger 2 (646). Controller jack three, pin six.

53267   **D013**   **COLPM1**

(W) Color and luminance of player and missile 1 (705).

TRIG3

(R) Joystick trigger 3 (647). Controller jack four, pin six.

53268   D014   COLPM2

(W) Color and luminance of player and missile 2 (706).

PAL

(R) Used to determine if the Atari is PAL (European and Israeli TV compatible when BITs 1 - 3 equal zero) or NTSC (North American compatible when BITs 1 - 3 equal one; 14 decimal, $E). European Ataris run 12% slower if tied to the VBLANK cycle (the PAL VBLANK cycle is every 50th second rather than every 60th second). They use only one CPU clock at three MHZ, so the 6502 runs at 2.217 MHZ — 25% faster than North American Ataris. Also, their $E000 and $F000 ROMs are different, so there are possible incompatibilities with North American Ataris in the cassette handling routines. There is a third TV standard called SECAM, used in France, the USSR, and parts of Africa. I am unaware if there is any Atari support for SECAM standards.

PAL TV has more scan lines per frame, 312 compared to 262. NTSC Ataris compensate by adding extra lines at the beginning of the VBLANK routine. Display lists do not have to be altered, and colors are the same because of a hardware modification.

53269   D015   COLPM3

Color and luminance of player and missile 3 (707).

53270   D016   COLPF0

Color and luminance of playfield zero (708).

53271   D017   COLPF1

Color and luminance of playfield one (709).

53272   D018   COLPF2

Color and luminance of playfield two (710).

53273   D019   COLPF3

Color and luminance of playfield three (711).

53274   D01A   COLBK

Color and luminance of the background (BAK). (712).

53275   D01B   PRIOR

(W) Priority selection register. PRIOR establishes which objects on the screen (players, missiles, and playfields) will be in front of other objects. Values used in this register are also described at location 623 ($26F), the shadow register. If you use conflicting priorities, objects whose priorities are in conflict will turn black in their overlap region.

Priority order
(Decimal values in brackets):

Bit 0 = 1 (1):	Bit 1 = 1 (2):
Player 0	Player 0
Player 1	Player 1
Player 2	Playfield 0
Player 3	Playfield 1
Playfield 0	Playfield 2
Playfield 1	Playfield 3 and Player 5
Playfield 2	Player 2
Playfield 3 and Player 5	Player 3
Background	Background

Bit 2 = 1 (4):	Bit 3 = 1 (8):
Playfield 0	Playfield 0
Playfield 1	Playfield 1
Playfield 2	Player 0
Playfield 3 and Player 5	Player 1
Player 0	Player 2
Player 1	Player 3
Player 2	Playfield 2
Player 3	Playfield 3 and Player 5
Background	Background

Bit 4 = 1: Enable a fifth player out of the four missiles.

Bit 5 = 1: Overlap of players 0 and 1, 2 and 3 is third color (else overlap is black). The resulting color is a logical OR of the two player colors.

Bits 6 and 7 are used to select GTIA modes:

0	0	= no GTIA modes
0	1	= GTIA GR.9
1	0	= GTIA GR.10
1	1	= GTIA GR.11

53276   D01C   VDELAY

(W) Vertical delay register. Used to give one-line resolution movement capability in the vertical positioning of an object when the two line resolution display is enabled. Setting a bit in VDELAY to one moves the corresponding object down by one TV line. If DMA is enabled, then moving an object by more than one line is accomplished by moving bits in the memory map instead.

Bit	Decimal	Object
7	128	Player 3
6	64	Player 2
5	32	Player 1
4	16	Player 0

3	8	Missile 3
2	4	Missile 2
1	2	Missile 1
0	1	Missile 0

53277   D01D   GRACTL

(W) Used with DMACTL (location 54272; $D400) to latch all stick and paddle triggers (to remember if triggers on joysticks or paddles have been pressed), to turn on players and to turn on missiles. To get the values to be POKEd here, add the following options together for the desired function:

	Decimal	Bit
To turn on missiles	1	0
To turn on players	2	1
To latch trigger inputs	4	2

To revoke P/M authorization and turn off both players and missiles, POKE 53277,0. Once latched, triggers will give a continuous "button pressed" read the first time they are pressed until BIT 2 is restored to zero. Triggers are placed in "latched" mode when each individual trigger is pressed, but you cannot set the latch mode for individual triggers.

Have you ever hit BREAK during a program and still had players or their residue left on the screen? Sometimes hitting RESET doesn't clear this material from the screen. There are ways to get rid of it:

POKE 623,4: This moves all players behind playfields.

POKE 53277,0: This should turn them off.

POKE 559,2: This should return you to a blank screen.

Make sure you SAVE your program before POKEing, just in case!

53278   D01E   HITCLR

(W) POKE with any number to clear all player/missile collision registers. It is important to clear this register often in a program — such as a game — which frequently tests for collisions. Otherwise, old collision values may remain and confuse the program. A good way to do this is to POKE HITCLR just before an event which may lead to a collision; for example, right before a joystick or paddle is "read" to move a player or fire a missile. Then test for a collision immediately after the action has taken place. Remember that multiple collisions cause *sums* of the collision values to be written to the collision registers; if you do not clear HITCLR often enough, a program checking for individual collisions will be thrown off by these sums.

53279   D01F   CONSOL

(W/R) Used to see if one of the three yellow console buttons has been pressed (not the RESET button!). To clear the register, POKE CONSOL with eight. POKEing any number from zero to eight will cause a click from the speaker. A FOR-NEXT loop that alternately POKEs CONSOL with eight and zero or just zero, since the OS put in an 8 every 1/60 second, will produce a buzz. Values PEEKed will range from zero to seven according to the following table:

Key	Value	0	1	2	3	4	5	6	7
OPTION		X	X	X	X				
SELECT		X	X			X	X		
START		X		X		X		X	
Bits 2		0	0	0	0	1	1	1	1
1		0	0	1	1	0	0	1	1
0		0	1	0	1	0	1	0	1

Where zero means all keys have been pressed, one means OPTION and SELECT have been pressed, etc., to seven, which means no keys have been pressed. CONSOL is updated every stage two VBLANK procedure with the value eight.

It is possible to use the console speaker to generate different sounds. Here is one idea based on an article in **COMPUTE!**, August 1981:

```
10    GOSUB 1000
20    TEST = USR(1536)
 .
 .
 .
999   END
1000  FOR LOOP = 0 TO 26: READ BYTE: P
      OKE 1536 + LOOP, BYTE: NEXT LOOP
      : RETURN
1010  DATA 104,162,255,169,255,141,31,
      208,169
1020  DATA 0,160,240,136,208,253,141,3
      1,208,160
1030  DATA 240,136,208,253,202,208,233
      ,96
```

To change the tone, you POKE 1547 and 1555 with a higher or

lower value (both are set to 240 above). To change the tone duration, you POKE 1538 with a lower value (it is set to 255 in the routine above). Do these before you do your USR call or alter the DATA statements to permanently change the values in your own program. Turn off DMA (see location 559) to get clearer tones.

Locations 53280 to 53503 ($D020 to $D0FF) are repeats of locations 53248 to 53279 ($D000 to $D01F). You can't use any of the repeated locations; consider them "filler." They may be used for other purposes in any Atari OS upgrade.

Locations 53504 to 53759 ($D100 to $DFFF) are unused. These locations are not empty; you can PEEK into them and find out what's there. They cannot, however, be user-altered.

POKEY
53760-54015   D200-D2FF

POKEY is a digital I/O chip that controls the audio frequency and control registers, frequency dividers, poly noise counters, pot (paddle) controllers, the random number generator, keyboard scan, serial port I/O, and the IRQ interrupts.

The AUDF# (audio frequency) locations are used for the pitch for the corresponding sound channels, while the AUDC# (audio control registers) are the volume and distortion values for those same channels. To POKE sound values, you must first POKE zero into locations 53768 ($D208) and a three into 53775 ($D20F).

Frequency values can range from zero to 255 ($FF), although the value is increased by the computer by one to range from one to 256. Note that the sum of the volumes should not exceed 32, since volume is controlled by the least four bits. It is set from zero as no volume to 15 ($F) as the highest. A POKE with 16 ($10) forces sound output even if volume is not set (i.e., it pushes the speaker cone out. A tiny "pop" will be heard). The upper four bits control distortion: 192 ($C0) is for pure tone; other values range from 32 to 192. Note that in BASIC, the BREAK key will not turn off the sound; RESET will, however. See *De Re Atari* and *BYTE*, April 1982, for more information on sound generation.

The AUDF registers are also used as the POKEY hardware timers. These are generally used when counting an interval less than one VBLANK. For longer intervals, use the software timers in locations 536 to 545 ($218 to $221). You load the AUDCTL register with the number for the desired clock frequency. You then set the volume to zero in the AUDC register associated with the AUDF register you plan to use as a timer. You load the AUDF register itself with the number of clock intervals you wish to count. Then you load your interrupt routine into memory, and POKE the address into the appropriate timer vector between locations 528 and 533 ($210 and $215). You must set the proper bit(s) in IRQEN and its shadow register POKMSK at location 16 ($10) to enable the interrupt. Finally, you load STIMER with any value to load and start the timer(s). The OS will force a jump to the timer vector and then to your routine when the AUDF register counts down to zero. Timer processing can be preempted by ANTIC's DMA, a DLI, or the VBLANK process.

POT values are for the paddles, ranging from zero to 240, increasing as the paddle knob is turned counterclockwise, but values less than 40 and greater than 200 represent an area on either edge of the screen that may not be visible on all TV sets or monitors.

53760   D200   AUDF1
(W) Audio channel one frequency. This is actually a number (N) used in a "divide by N circuit"; for every N pulses coming in (as set by the POKEY clock), one pulse goes out. As N gets larger, output pulses will decrease, and thus the sound produced will be a lower note. N can be in the range from one to 256; POKEY adds one to the value in the AUDF register. See *BYTE*, April 1982, for a program to create chords instead of single tones.

POT0
(R) Pot (paddle) 0 (624); *pot* is short for *potentiometer*. Turning the paddle knob clockwise results in decreasing pot values. For machine language use: these pot values are valid only 228 scan lines after the POTGO command or after ALLPOT changes (see 53768; $D208 and 53771; $D20B). POT registers continually count down to zero, decrementing every scan line. They are reset to 228 when they reach zero or by the values read from the shadow registers. This makes them useful as system timers. See **COMPUTE!**, February 1982, for an example of this use.

The POTGO sequence (see 53771; $D20B) resets the POT registers to zero, then reads them 228 scan lines later. For the fast pot scan, BIT 2 of SKCTL at 53775 ($D20F) must be set.

53761   D201   AUDC1
(W) Audio channel one control. Each AUDF register has an associated control register which sets volume and distortion levels. The bit assignment is:

Bit	7 6 5	4	3 2 1 0	
	Distortion (noise)	Volume only	Volume level	
	0 0 0	0	0 0 0 0	Lowest
	0 0 1		0 0 0 1	
	etc. to:		etc. to:	
	1 1 1	1 (forced output)	1 1 1 1	Highest

The values for the distortion bits are as follows. The first process is to divide the clock value by the frequency, then mask the output using the polys in the order below. Finally, the result is divided by two.

Bit			
7	6	5	
0	0	0	five bit, then 17 bit, polys
0	0	1	five bit poly only
0	1	0	five bit, then four bit, polys
0	1	1	five bit poly only
1	0	0	17 bit poly only
1	0	1	no poly counters (pure tone)
1	1	0	four bit poly only
1	1	1	no poly counters (pure tone)

In general, the tones become more regular (a recognizable droning becomes apparent) with fewer and lower value polys masking the output. This is all the more obvious at low frequency ranges. POKE with 160 ($A0) or 224 ($E0) plus the volume for pure tones.

See *De Re Atari* and the *Hardware Manual* for details.

POT1

(R) Pot 1 register (625).

53762   D202   AUDF2

(W) Audio channel two frequency. Also used with AUDF3 to store the 19200 baud rate for SIO.

POT2

(R) Pot 2 (626).

53763   D203   AUDC2

(W) Audio channel two control.

POT3

(R) Pot 3 (627).

53764

53764   D204   AUDF3
(W) Audio channel three frequency. Used with AUDF3 above and
with AUDF4 to store the 600 baud rate for SIO.

POT4
(R) Pot 4 (628).
53765   D205   AUDC3
(W) Audio channel three control.
POT5
(R) Pot 5 (629).
53766   D206   AUDF4
(W) Audio channel four frequency.
POT6
(R) Pot 6 (630).
53767   D207   AUDC4
(W) Audio channel four control.
POT7
(R) Pot 7 (631).
53768   D208   AUDCTL
(W) Audio control. To properly initialize the POKEY sound
capabilities, POKE AUDCTL with zero and POKE 53775,3
($D20F). These two are the equivalent of the BASIC statement
SOUND 0,0,0,0. AUDCTL is the option byte which affects all
sound channels. This bit assignment is:

Bit   Description:
7   Makes the 17 bit poly counter into nine bit poly
      (see below)
6   Clock channel one with 1.79 MHz
5   Clock channel three with 1.79 MHz
4   Join channels two and one (16 bit)
3   Join channels four and three (16 bit)
2   Insert high pass filter into channel one, clocked by channel
      two
1   Insert high pass filter into channel two, clocked by channel
      four
0   Switch main clock base from 64 KHz to 15 KHz

Poly (polynomial) counters are used as a source of random pulses
for noise generation. There are three polys: four, five and 17 bits
long. The shorter polys create repeatable sound patterns, while the
longer poly has no apparent repetition. Therefore, setting BIT 7
above, making the 17-bit into a nine-bit poly will make the pattern

in the distortion more evident. You chose which poly(s) to use by setting the high three bits in the AUDC registers. The 17-bit poly is also used in the generation of random numbers; see 53770 ($D20A).

The clock bits allow the user to speed up or slow down the clock timers, respectively, making higher or lower frequency ranges possible. Setting the channels to the 1.79 MHz will produce a much higher sound, the 64 KHz clock will be lower, and the 15 KHz clock the lowest. The clock is also used when setting the frequency for the AUDF timers.

Two bits (three and four) allow the user to combine channels one and two or three and four for what amounts to a nine octave range instead of the usual five. Here's an example from *De Re Atari* of this increased range, which uses two paddles to change the frequency: the right paddle makes coarse adjustments, the left paddle makes fine adjustments:

```
10 SOUND 0,0,0,0:POKE 53768,80:REM SE
   T CLOCK AND JOIN CHANNELS 1 AND 2
20 POKE 53761,160:POKE 53763,168:REM
   TURN OFF CHANNEL 1 AND SET 2 TO PU
   RE TONE GENERATION
30 POKE 53760,PADDLE(0):POKE 53762,PA
   DDLE(1):GOTO 30
```

High pass filters allow only frequencies higher than the clock value to pass through. These are mostly used for special effects. Try:

```
10 SOUND 0,0,0,0:POKE 53768,4:REM HIG
   H PASS FILTER ON CHANNEL 1
20 POKE 53761,168:POKE 53765,168:REM
   PURE TONES
30 POKE 53760,254:POKE 53764,127
40 GOTO 40
```

See the excellent chapter on sound in *De Re Atari:* it is the best explanation of sound functions in the Atari available. See also the *Hardware Manual* for complete details.

ALLPOT

(R) Eight line pot port state; reads all of the eight POTs together. Each bit represents a pot (paddle) of the same number. If a bit is set to zero, then the register value for that pot is valid (it's in use); if it is one, then the value is not valid. ALLPOT is used with the POTGO command at 53771 ($D20B).

53769   **D209**   **STIMER**

(W) Start the POKEY timers (the AUDF registers above). You

53770

POKE any non-zero value here to load and start the timers; the value isn't itself used in the calculations. This resets all of the audio frequency dividers to their AUDF values. If enabled by IRQEN below, these AUDF registers generate timer interrupts when they count down from the number you POKEd there to zero. The vectors for the AUDF1, AUDF2 and AUDF4 timer interrupts are located between 528 and 533 ($210 and $215). POKEY timer four interrupt is only enabled in the new "B" OS ROMs.

KBCODE

(R) Holds the keyboard code which is then loaded into the shadow register (764; $2FC) when a key is hit. Usually read in response to the keyboard interrupt. Compares the value with that in CH1 at 754 ($2F2). If both values are the same, then the new code is accepted only if a suitable key debounce delay time has passed. The routines which test to see if the key code will be accepted start at 65470 ($FFBE). BIT 7 is the control key flag, BIT 6 is the shift key flag.

53770   D20A   SKREST

(W) Reset BITs 5 - 7 of the serial port status register at 53775 to one.

RANDOM

(R) When this location is read, it acts as a random number generator. It reads the high order eight bits of the 17 bit polynomial counter (nine bit if BIT 7 of AUDCTL is set) for the value of the number. You can use this location in a program to generate a random integer between zero and 255 by:

10   PRINT PEEK(53770)

This is a more elegant solution than INT(RND(0) *256). For a test of the values in this register, use this simple program:

10 FOR N = 1 TO 20: PRINT PEEK(53770): NEXT N

53771   D20B   POTGO

(W) Start the POT scan sequence. You must read your POT values first and then start the scan sequence, since POTGO resets the POT registers to zero. Written by the stage two VBLANK sequence.

53772   D20C   ....

Unused.

53773   D20D   SEROUT

(W) Serial port data output. Usually written to in the event of a serial data out interrupt. Writes to the eight bit (one byte) parallel holding register that is transferred to the serial shift register when a full byte of data has been transmitted. This "holding" register is used to contain the bits to be transmitted one at a time (serially) as a one-byte unit before transmission.

SERIN

(R) Serial port input. Reads the one-byte parallel holding register that is loaded when a full byte of serial input data has been received. As above, this holding register is used to hold the bits as they are received one bit at a time until a full byte is received. This byte is then taken by the computer for processing. Also used to verify the checksum value at location 49 ($31).

The serial bus is the port on the Atari into which you plug your cassette or disk cable. For the pin values of this port, see the *OS User's Manual*, p. 133, and the *Hardware Manual*.

53774   D20E   IRQEN

(W) Interrupt request enable. Zero turns off all interrupt requests such as the BREAK key; to disable or re-enable interrupts, POKE with the values according to the following chart (setting a bit to one — i.e., true — enables that interrupt; decimal values are also shown for each bit):

Bit	Decimal	Interrupt	Vector
0	1	Timer 1 (counted down to zero)	VTIMR1 (528; $210)
1	2	Timer 2 (counted down to zero)	VTIMR2 (530; $212)
2	4	Timer 4 (counted down to zero)	VTIMR4 (532; $214), OS "B" ROMs only)
3	8	Serial output transmission done	VSEROC (526; $20E)
4	16	Serial output data needed	VSEROR (524; $20C)
5	32	Serial input data ready	VSERIN (522; $20A)
6	64	Other key pressed	VKEYBD (520; $208)
7	128	BREAK key pressed	see below

Here is the procedure for the BREAK key interrupt: clear the interrupt register. Set BRKKEY (17; $11) to zero; clear the start/stop flag SSFLAG at 767 ($2FF); clear the cursor inhibit flag CRSINH at 752 ($2F0); clear the attract mode flag at 77 ($4D), and return from the interrupt after restoring the 6502 A register. (There is now (in the OS "B" ROMs) a proper vector for BREAK key interrupts at 566, 567 ($236, $237) which is initialized to point to 59220 ($E754).) If the interrupt was due to a serial I/O bus proceed line interrupt, then vector through VPRCED at 514 ($202). If due to a serial I/O bus interrupt line interrupt, then vector through

VINTER at 516 ($204). If due to a 6502 BRK instruction, then vector through VBREAK at 518 ($206).

Timers relate to audio dividers of the same number (an interrupt is processed when the dividers count down to zero). These bits in IRQEN are not set on powerup and must be initiated by the user program before enabling the processor IRQ.

There are two other interrupts, processed by PIA, generated over the serial bus Proceed and Interrupt lines, set by the bits in the PACTL and PBCTL registers (54018 and 54019; $D302, $D303):

Bit	Decimal	Location	Interrupt
0	1	PACTL	Peripheral A (PORTA) interrupt enable bit.
7	128	PACTL	Peripheral A interrupt status bit.
0	1	PBCTL	Peripheral B (PORTB) interrupt enable bit.
7	128	PBCTL	Peripheral B interrupt status bit.

The latter PORT interrupts are automatically disabled on powerup. Only the BREAK key and data key interrupts are enabled on powerup. The shadow register is 16 ($10).

IRQST

(R) Interrupt request status. Bit functions are the same as IRQEN except that they register the interrupt request when it is zero rather than the enable when a bit equals one. IRQST is used to determine the cause of interrupt request with IRQEN, PACTL and PBCTL as above.

All IRQ interrupts are normally vectored through 65534 ($FFFE) to the IRQ service routine at 59123 ($E6F3), which determines the cause of the interrupt. The IRQ global RAM vector VIMIRQ at 534 ($216) ordinarily points to the IRQ processor at 59126 ($E6F6). The processor then examines 53774 ($D20E) and the PIA registers at 54018 and 54019 to determine the interrupt cause. Once determined, the routine vectors through one of the IRQ RAM vectors in locations 514 to 526 ($202 to $20E). For Non-Maskable Interrupts (NMI's), see locations 54286 to 54287 ($D40E; $D40F). See the *OS User's Manual* for complete details.

53775   D20F   SKCTL

(W) Serial port control. Holds the value 255 ($255) if no key is pressed, 251 ($FB) for most other keys pressed, 247 ($F7) for SHIFT key pressed (*M). See the (R) mode below for an explanation of the bit functions. POKE with three to stop the occasional noise from cassette after I/O to bring POKEY out of the two-tone mode. (562).

SKSTAT

(R) Reads the serial port status. It also returns values governed by a signal on the digital track of the cassette tape. You can generate certain values using the SOUND command in BASIC and a PEEK to SKSTAT:

SOUND 0,5,10,15 returns a value to here of 255 (or, on occasion, 127).
SOUND 0,8,10,3 returns a value of 239.

This is handy for adding a voice track to Atari tapes. You use the left channel for your voice track and the right for the tone(s) you want to use as cuing marks. You can use the speaker on your TV to generate the tones by placing the right microphone directly in front of the speaker. The computer will register these tones in this register when it encounters them during a later cassette load. See **COMPUTE!**, July 1981, for some other suggestions on doing this. Remember, you can turn the cassette off by POKEing 54018 ($D302) with 60 ($3C) and back on with 52 ($34).

Bits in the SKCTL (W) register are normally zero and perform the functions below when set to one. The status when used as (R) is listed below the write (W) function:

Bit   Function

0   (W) Enable keyboard debounce circuits.
       (R) Not used by SKSTAT.
1   (W) Enable keyboard scanning circuit.
       (R) Serial input shift register busy.
2   (W) Fast pot scan: the pot scan counter completes its sequence in two TV line times instead of one frame time (228 scan lines). Not as accurate as the normal pot scan, however.
       (R) the last key is still pressed.
3   (W) Serial output is transmitted as a two-tone signal rather than a logic true/false. POKEY two-tone mode.
       (R) The shift key is pressed.
4,5,6 (W) Serial port mode control used to set the bi-directional clock lines so that you can either receive external clock data or provide clock data to external devices (see the *Hardware Manual*, p. II.27). There are two pins on the serial port for Clock IN and Clock OUT data. See the *OS User's Manual*, p. 133.
4   (R) Data can be read directly from the serial input port, ignoring the shift register.
5   (R) Keyboard over-run. Reset BITs 7 to 5 (latches) to one using SKRES at 53770 ($D20A).
6   (R) Serial data input over-run. Reset latches as above.
7   (W) Force break (serial output to zero).

(R) Serial data input frame error caused by missing or extra bits. Reset latches as above.

BIT 2 is first set to zero to reset POT registers to zero (dumping the capacitors used to change the POT registers). Then BIT 2 is set to one to enable the fast scan. Fast scan is not as accurate as the normal scan routine. BIT 2 must be reset to zero to enable the normal scan mode; otherwise, the capacitors will never dump.

Locations 53776 to 54015 ($D210 to $D2FF) are duplications of locations 53760 to 53775 and have no particular use at present.

PIA: 6520 CHIP
54016-54271   D300-D3FF

The Peripheral Interface Adapter (PIA) integrated circuit is a special microprocessor used to control the Atari ports, controller jacks one to four. Ports can be used for both input and output simultaneously or alternately. Barely tapped at the time of this writing, the ports represent a major resource for external (and internal) control and expansion. PIA also processes two of the IRQ interrupts: VINTER and VPRCED, vectored at locations 514 to 517 ($202 to $205). These interrupts are unused by the OS, but also may be used to provide greater control over external devices.

54016   D300   PORTA

(W/R) Reads or writes data from controller jacks one and two if BIT 2 of PACTL (location 54018) is one. Writes to direction control if BIT 2 of PACTL is zero.

These two port registers also control the direction of data flow to the port, if the controller register (54018, below) is POKEd with 48 ($30). Then, if the bits in the register read zero, it is in input (R) mode; if they read one, it is in output (W) mode. A zero POKEd here makes all bits input, a 255 ($FF) makes all bits output. BITs 0 to 3 address pins one to four on jack one, BITs 4 to 7 address pins one to four on jack two. POKE 54018 with 52 to make this location into a data register again. Shadow registers are: STICK0 (632; $278, jack one), STICK1 (633; $279, jack two) and PTRIG0-3 (636-639; $27C-$27F).

Bits used as data register
```
7   6   5   4   3   2   1   0
 — Jack 0 —       — Jack 1 —
 — Stick 1 —      — Stick 0 —
Forward   = BIT 0, 4 = 1
Backward = BIT 1, 5 = 1
```

Left	= BIT 2, 6 = 1
Right	= BIT 3, 7 = 1
Neutral	= All four jack bits = 1

PORTA is also used to test if the paddle 0-3 triggers (PTRIG) have been pressed, using these bits:

Bit	7	6	5	4	3	2	1	0
PTRIG	3	2	—	—	1	0	—	—

Where zero in the appropriate bit equals trigger pressed, one equals trigger not pressed.

The PORT registers are also used in the keyboard controller (used with a keypad) operation where:

Bit	7	6	5	4	3	2	1	0
Row	4	3	2	Top	4	3	2	Top
Jack		.... 2				.... 1		

Columns for the keyboard operation are read through the POT (PADDL) and TRIG registers. See *Micro,* May 1982, and the *Hardware Manual* for more information on jacks and ports.

54017   D301   PORTB

(W/R) Port B. Reads or writes data to and/or from jacks three and four. Same as PORTA, above, for the respective jacks. Shadow registers are: STICK2 (634; $27A, jack three), STICK3 (635, $27B, jack four), and PTRIG4-7 (640-643; $280-$283).

54018   D302   PACTL

(W/R) Port A controller (see 54016 above). POKE with 60 ($3C) to turn the cassette motor off, POKE with 52 to turn it on. You can put a music cassette in your program recorder, press PLAY and then POKE 54018,52. Your music will play through the TV speaker or external amplifier while you work at the Atari. You can use this technique to add voice tracks to your programs. To turn off the music or voice, type POKE 54018,60.

PACTL can be used for other external applications by the user. Bit use is as follows:

Bit	Function
7 (read only)	Peripheral A interrupt (IRQ) status bit. Set by Peripheral (PORT) A. Reset by reading PORTA (53774; $D20E).
6	Set to zero.
5	Set to one.
4	Set to one.
3 (write)	Peripheral motor control line (turn the cassette on or off; zero equals on).
2 (write)	Controls PORTA addressing. One equals PORTA

	register; zero equals direction control register.
1	Set to zero.
0 (write)	Peripheral A interrupt (IRQ) enable. One equals
	enable. Set by the OS but available to the user;
	reset on powerup.

54019   D303   PBCTL

(W/R) Port B controller. Initialized to 60 ($3C) by the OS IRQ code. PBCTL is the same as PACTL, above, with the following exception (this may actually perform the same function as in PACTL, but I am not sure of the distinction between descriptions):

Bit	Function
3	Peripheral command identification (serial bus command), initialized to 60 ($3C).

Ports can be used for external control applications by the technically minded reader who is willing to do some soldering to develop cables and connectors. A good example can be found in **COMPUTE!**, February 1981, where the author gives directions for using jacks three and four as a printer port. The Macrotronic printer cables use just this method, bypassing the 850 interface entirely (one way of reducing your hardware costs). Theoretically, the entire Atari can be controlled through the ports!

Locations 54020 to 54271 ($D304 to $D3FF) are repeats of locations 54016 to 54019 ($D300 to $D303).

ANTIC
54272-54783   D400-D5FF

ANTIC is a special, separate microprocessor used in your Atari to control C/GTIA, the screen display, and other screen-related functions including processing the NMI interrupts. It uses its own instruction set, called the display list, which tells ANTIC where to find the screen data in RAM and how to display it. ANTIC also uses an internal four bit counter called the Delta Counter (DCTR) to control the vertical dimension of each block.

54272   D400   DMACTL

(W) Direct Memory Access (DMA) control. It is also used to define one- or two-line resolution for players and to turn on players and missiles. Values are POKEd into the shadow register, 559 ($22F), and are also described there. You POKE the shadow register with the following numbers in order to:

Turn off the playfield	0
Use narrow playfield	1

Use normal playfield	2
Use wide playfield	3
Enable missile DMA	4
Enable player DMA	8
Enable both player and missile DMA	12
Single line player resolution	16
Enable DMA Fetch instructions	32

Double line resolution is the default status. Use this register in conjunction with GRACTL at 53277 ($D01D). Both must be set properly or no display will result. BIT 5 enables DMA to fetch the display list instructions. If BIT 5 is not set (BIT 5 equals zero), ANTIC will not work. DMACTL is initialized to 34 ($22).

A player in single line resolution might look like this:

```
00011000     ##
00111100     ####
01111110     ######
11111111     ########
11111111     ########
01111110     ######
00111100     ####
00011000     ##
```

so that each byte is displayed on one TV line. The same player in double line resolution would look like this:

```
00011000     ##
00011000     ##
00111100     ####
00111100     ####
01111110     ######
01111110     ######
11111111     ########
11111111     ########
11111111     ########
11111111     ########
01111110     ######
01111110     ######
00111100     ####
00111100     ####
00011000     ##
00011000     ##
```

where every byte is displayed over two TV lines.

54273   D401   CHACTL

(W) Character mode control. See shadow register 755 for values that can be POKEd in. Only the least three bits (decimal zero to seven) are read, as below:

Decimal	0	1	2	3	4	5	6	7
Cursor								
Transparent	X		X		X		X	
Opaque		X		X		X		X
Present			X	X			X	X
Absent	X	X			X	X		
Characters								
Normal	X	X	X	X				
Inverted					X	X	X	X

54274,5   D402,3   DLISTL/H

Display list pointer. Tells the OS the address of the display list instructions about what screen mode(s) to display and where to find the screen data. See SDLIST (560, 561; $230, $231).

54276   D404   HSCROL

(W) Horizontal scroll enable, POKE HSCROL with from zero to 16 clock cycles for the number of cycles to scroll. Horizontal fine scrolls can be used only if BIT 4 of the display list instruction is set. The difficulty in horizontal scrolling lies in arranging the screen data to be scrolled in such a manner as to prevent wraparound (i.e., the bit or byte scrolled off screen in one line becomes the bit or byte scrolled on screen in an adjacent line). Normal data arranged for TV display looks like this on the screen:

where it is a one-dimensional memory area "folded" at the proper places to create the image of a two dimensional screen. This is done by the DL character or map mode instruction. Without other instructions, it reads the memory continuously from the first specified location, each line taking the correct number of bytes for the GRAPHICS mode specified. To properly scroll it horizontally, you must arrange it in relation to the TV screen like this:

Now you will have to make each display instruction for each line into a Load Memory Scan (LMS) instruction. To direct each LMS to the proper screen RAM for that line, you will have to increment each memory location by the total length of the line. For example, if you want to scroll a 256-byte horizontal screen, each LMS instruction will have to point to a location in memory 256 bytes above the last one. Of course, you will have to implement error-trapping routines so that your screen does not extend beyond your desired boundaries.

Coarse scrolling, one byte at a time, can be done without setting the HSCROL register by the method described above. For smooth scrolling, you will have to use this register. See *De Re Atari.*

54277   D405   VSCROL

(W) Vertical scroll enable, POKE VSCROL with from zero to 16 scan lines, depending on the GRAPHICS mode of the screen for the number of scan lines to scroll. Vertical fine scrolls can be used only if BIT 5 of the display list instruction has been set.

Coarse scrolling can be done without using this register, simply by moving the top of the screen address (as defined by the DL LMS instruction) up or down one mode line (plus or minus 40 or 20 bytes, depending on the GRAPHICS mode). The top of the screen address can be found by:

```
10    DLIST = PEEK(560) + PEEK(561) * 2
      56
20    SCRNLO = DLIST + 4: SCRNHI = DLIS
      T + 5: REM LSB/MSB OF SCREEN ADDRE
      SS
25    PRINT "SCREEN ADDRESS = " PEEK(SC
      RNLO) + PEEK(SCRNHI) * 256
```

You could then add a routine to this for a coarse - scroll vertically through the memory with a joystick, such as:

```
30    LOBYTE = 0: HIBYTE = 0
40    IF STICK(0) = 14 THEN LOBYTE = LO
      BYTE + 40:GOTO 100
50    IF STICK(0) = 13 THEN LOBYTE = LO
      BYTE - 40
60    IF LOBYTE < 0 THEN LOBYTE = LOBYT
      E + 256: HIBYTE = HIBYTE - 1
70    IF HIBYTE < 0 THEN HIBYTE = 0
80    GOTO 200
100   IF LOBYTE > 255 THEN LOBYTE = LOB
      YTE - 256
110   HIBYTE = HIBYTE + 1
```

```
200 POKE SCRNLOW, LOBYTE: POKE SCRNHI
    , HIBYTE
210 GOTO 40
```

Coarse scrolling is relatively easy to implement in the Atari: one basically alters the screen RAM to display the new material. Fine scrolling is more difficult: each scroll register must be POKEd with the number of units to be scrolled — color clocks or scan lines — and the corresponding display list instructions must have the proper bits set. This means you can selectively fine scroll any mode lines you wish by setting only those bits of the lines you intend to scroll. Other lines will be displayed normally. You can set a DL instruction for both horizontal and vertical scroll enable. See the *Hardware Manual* for a discussion of the problems in fine scrolling.

Fine scrolling will allow only a certain amount of data to be scrolled before the register must be reset (16 clock bits or scan lines maximum). In order to make the scrolling activity continuous, the register involved must be reset to zero when the desired value is reached, a coarse scroll must be implemented (usually during a DLI or VBLANK interval) and a new fine scroll begun. This is not easily done in BASIC since it is too slow, and changing registers during ANTIC's display process usually causes rough or jerky motion. Assembly routines are suggested for smooth display. See *De Re Atari, Micro,* November 1981, *BYTE,* January 1982, and Santa Cruz's *Tricky Tutorial #2* for more information.

54278   D406   ....
Unused.

54279   D407   PMBASE
(W) MSB of the player/missile base address used to locate the graphics for your players and missiles (the address equals PMBASE * 256. P/M graphics are tricky to use since there are no direct Atari 8K BASIC commands to either create or move them (there are, however, commands for P/M graphics in BASIC A + and in valFORTH utilities).

Your P/M graphics must always begin on a 1K boundary (PEEK(RAMTOP) –4 for double line resolution players) or 2K boundary (PEEK(RAMTOP) –5 for single line resolution), so the LSB is always zero (page numbers always end in $XX00). For example:

```
10   POKE 106, PEEK(106)  -  8: GRAPHIC
     S 8: SETCOLOR 2,3,4
20   POKE 559,62: POKE 53248,100: POK
```

```
    E 704,160: POKE 53256,2
30   MEM = PEEK(106) - 8
40   POKE 54279, MEM: POKE 53277,3: S
     TART = MEM * 256 + 1024
50   FOR LOOP = 100 TO 119: READ BYTE
     : POKE START + LOOP, BYTE: NEXT LO
     OP
60   DATA 16,16,56,40,40,56,40,40,40
70   DATA 124,84,124,84,254,146,254,1
     70,170,68
100  END
```

You can change the color, width, resolution, and horizontal position of the player in the example by altering the registers used above.

Each player is one byte (eight bits) wide. Single line resolution P/M characters (POKE 559,62) can be up to 256 bytes high. Double line resolution P/M characters (POKE 559,46) can be up to 128 bytes high. In either case, they can map to the height of the screen. Missiles have the same height, but are only two bits wide each. Four missiles can be combined into a fifth player by setting BIT 4 of location 623 ($26F). You need not fill the entire height of a P/M character, but you should POKE unused bytes with zero to eliminate any screen garbage. You can do this by:

FOR N = PMBASE + 1024 TO PMBASE + 2048:
POKE N,0: NEXT N

where PMBASE is the starting address of the reserve memory area. In double line resolution, change the loop value to N = PMBASE + 512 TO PMBASE + 1024. Here's a short machine language routine to do the same thing. You would put the start address of the area to be loaded with zero and the number of bytes to be cleared in with the USR call as the first two parameters. In this example, I have arbitrarily chosen 38012 and 2048 for these values.

```
10   START = 38012: BYTE = 2048: DIM
     PGM$(42)
20   FOR LOOP = 1 TO 42: READ ML: PGM
     $(LOOP, LOOP) = CHR$(ML): NEXT LOO
     P
30   DATA 104,104,133,204,104,133,203
     ,104,133,206,104
40   DATA 133,205,166,206,160,0,169,0
     ,145,203,136
50   DATA 208,251,230,204,202,48,6,20
     8,244,164
```

```
60    DATA 205,208,240,198,204,160,0,1
      45,203,96
70    A = USR(ADR(PGM$),START,BYTE)
```

You can use this routine to clear out memory anywhere in the Atari. You can also use it to load any one value into memory by changing the second zero (after the 169) in line 40 to the value desired.

Locating your graphics tables at the high end of memory may cause addressing problems for playfield graphics, or may leave some of the display unusable and cause PLOT to malfunction. If you locate your tables just before the screen display, it may be erased if you change graphics modes. You can look at your highest RAM use graphics statement and plan accordingly. To calculate a safe starting address below the display list, try:

100 DLIST = PEEK(560) + PEEK(561) * 256: PMBASE = INT (DLIST/SIZE –1) * SIZE

where SIZE is 2048 for single line resolution, 1024 for double line.

Once you have the starting address, determine the ending address of your table by adding the correct number of bytes for the size (same as the SIZE variable above), and POKE this number (LSB/MSB) into APPMHI at locations 14 and 15 ($E, $F). This sets the lower limit for playfield graphics memory use. If you change graphics modes in the program now, it should leave your player tables intact. For example, if the DL is at 39968, the PMBASE will equal 36864 in the equation above. Add 2048 (single line resolution) to get 38912. This is $9800. In decimal, the LSB is zero and the MSB is 152. POKE these values into APPMHI. This sets the lowest limit to which the screen and DL data may descend.

The unused portion of the RAM set aside for P/M use, or any RAM reserved for players, but not used, may be used for other purposes in your program such as machine language routines. See the appendix for a map of P/M memory use. The register stores the address as below:

Bit	7	6	5	4	3	2	1	0
One line resolution:	. . . . . MSB					. . . unused . . .		
Two line resolution:	. . . . MSB						unused . .	

There are some restrictions on locating your P/M data above the display list. If not positioned far enough above your screen data, you may end up with both the normal and screen data being displayed at once, resulting in garbage on the screen. A display list may not cross a 1K boundary without a jump instruction, and the screen display RAM cannot cross a 4K boundary without an LMS instruction to point to the proper byte(s). Due to problems that arise when moving the GR.7 and GR.8 screens and data less than 4K, you should never reserve less than 16 pages above RAMTOP in these modes. If you are reserving more, add the pages in blocks of 4K (16 pages).

See **COMPUTE!**, September 1981, for a discussion of the problems of positioning P/M graphics in memory, and using P/M graphics for animation.

See *De Re Atari*, **COMPUTE!**, June 1982, and *Creative Computing*, April 1982, for a discussion of using string manipulation with P/M graphics. See *Your Atari 400/800* for a general discussion of P/M graphics. Most of the popular magazines have also carried articles on simplifying P/M graphics.

54280   D408   ....
Unused.

54281   D409   CHBASE
(W) Character base address; the location of the start of the character set, either the standard Atari set or a user-designed set. The default is 224 ($E0), which points to the start of the Atari ROM character set. *Iridis*, a short-lived disk -and- documentation magazine, produced a good utility called *FontEdit* to aid in the design of altered character sets. Online Systems' program *The Next Step* is also very useful for this purpose, as is **COMPUTE!**'s *"SuperFont,"* January 1982. Uses shadow register 756 ($2F4).

Normally, this points to location 57344 or 57856 ($E000 or $E200) depending on your choice of characters used in which text mode. GRAPHICS mode zero uses the entire 128-character set; GR.1 and GR.2 use only half the set (64 characters). You POKE a different number into the shadow register at 756 ($2F4) to point to your own character set in RAM. This must be an even number that points to a page in memory that is evenly divisible by two. In GR.1 and GR.2 this number is 224 (pointing to $E000), giving you uppercase, punctuation and numbers. POKEing the shadow or this location (in machine language) with 226 will give you lowercase and control characters.

See the information about the ROM character set at 57344 ($E000).

54282   D40A   WSYNC
(W) Wait for horizontal synchronization. Allows the OS to synchronize the vertical TV display by causing the 6502 to halt and restart seven machine cycles before the beginning of the

next TV line. It is used to synchronize the VBI's or DLI's with the screen display.

To see the effect of the WSYNC register, type in the second example of a Display List Interrupt at location 512. RUN it and observe that it causes a clean separation of the colors at the change boundary. Now change line 50 to:

50　DATA 72,169,222,234,234,234,141,24,208,104,64

This eliminates the WSYNC command. RUN it and see the difference in the boundary line.

The keyboard handler sets WSYNC repeatedly while generating the keyboard click on the console speaker at 53279 ($D01F). When interrupts are generated during the WSYNC period, they get delayed by one scan line. To bypass this, examine the VCOUNT register below and delay the interrupt processing by one line when no WSYNC delay has occurred.

54283　　　D40B　　　VCOUNT

(R) Vertical line counter. Used to keep track of which line is currently being generated on the screen. Used during Display List Interrupts to change color or graphics modes. PEEKing here returns the line count divided by two, ranging from zero to 130 ($82; zero to 155 on the PAL system; see 53268; $D014) for the 262 lines per TV frame.

54284　　　D40C　　　PENH

(R) Light pen horizontal position (564). Holds the horizontal color clock count when the pen trigger is pressed.

54285　　　D40D　　　PENV

(R) Light pen vertical position (565). Holds the VCOUNT value (above) when the pen trigger is pressed. See the *Hardware Manual*, p. II-32, for a description of light pen operation.

54286　　　D40E　　　NMIEN

(W) Non-maskable interrupt (NMI) enable. POKE with 192 to enable the Display List Interrupts. When BIT 7 is set to one, it means DL instruction interrupt; any display list instruction where BIT 7 equals one will cause this interrupt to be enabled at the start of the last video line displayed by that instruction. When BIT 6 equals one, it allows the Vertical Blank Interrupt and when BIT 5 equals one, it allows the RESET button interrupt. The RESET interrupt is never disabled by the OS. You should never press RESET during powerup since it will be acted upon.

NMIEN is set to 64 ($40) by the OS IRQ code on powerup, enabling VBI's, but disabling DLI's. All NMI interrupts are vectored through 65530 ($FFFA) to the NMI service routine at

59316 ($E7B4) to determine their cause.

Bit	7	6	5	4	3	2	1	0
Interrupt:	DLI	VBI	RESET	.... unused				

54287   D40F   NMIRES

(W) Reset for NMIST (below); clears the interrupt request register; resets all of the NMI status together.

NMIST

(R) NMI status; holds cause for the NMI interrupt in BITs 5, 6 and 7; corresponding to the same bits in NMIEN above. If a DLI is pending, a jump is made through the global RAM vector VDSLST (512; $200). The OS doesn't use DLI's, so 512 is initialized to point to an RTI instruction and must be changed by the user before a DLI is allowed.

If the interrupt is not a DLI, then a test is made to see if the interrupt was caused by pressing RESET key and, if so, a jump is made to 58484 ($E474). If not a RESET interrupt, then the system assumes the interrupt was a VBLANK interrupt, and a jump is made through VVBLKI at 546 ($222), which normally points to the stage one VBLANK processor. From there it checks the flag at CRITIC (66; $42) and, if not from a critical section, jumps through VVBLKD at 548 ($224), which normally points to the VBLANK exit routine. On powerup, the VBLANK interrupts are enabled while the display list interrupts are disabled. See the end of the memory map for a description of the VBLANK procedures. For IRQ interrupts, see location 53744 ($D20E).

Locations 54288 to 54303 ($D410 to $D41F) are repeats of locations 54272 to 54287 ($D400 to $D40F).

Locations 54784 to 55295 ($D600 to $D7FF) are unused but not empty nor user alterable. See the note at 53504 ($D100).

OPERATING SYSTEM ROM

Locations 55296 to 65535 ($D800 to $FFFF) are the OS ROM.

These locations are contained in the 10K ROM cartridge, which sits in the front slot of the Atari 800 or inside the Atari 400. The OS is identical for both computers.

The locations given here are for the "A" version of the OS ROMs. There are changes in the new "B" version ROMs, which are explained in the appendix. Most of the changes affect the interrupt handler routines and SIO. In making these changes, Atari cured some bugs such as the device time-out problem. Unfortunately, there is a cloud with this silver lining: not all of your old software will run with the new ROMs. *Megalegs,* one of my favorite games, cannot run under the new ROMs. A pity that. There are others; I'm sure you'll find them. The solution is to have both sets of ROMs so you can use all of your software.

FLOATING POINT PACKAGE ROM

Locations 55296 to 57343 ($D800 to $DFFF) are reserved for the ROM's Floating Point Mathematics Package. There are other areas used by the FP package: page zero (locations 212 to 254; $D4 to $FE) and page five (locations 1406 to 1535; $57E to $5FF), which are used only if FP routines are called. There are also trigonometric functions in the BASIC cartridge located between 48549 and 49145 ($BDA5 to $BFF9) which use the FP routines. See *De Re Atari* for more information.

These are the entry points to some of the subroutines; unless otherwise noted, they use FP register zero (FR0 at 212 to 217, $D4 to $DB):

55296   D800   AFP
ASCII to Floating Point (FP) conversion.

55526   D8E6   FASC
FP value to ASCII conversion.

55722   D9AA   IFP
Integer to FP conversion.

55762   D9D2   FPI
FP to integer conversion.

55876   DA44   ZFR0
Clear FR0 at 212 to 217 ($D4-$DB) by setting all bytes to zero.

55878   DA46   ZF1
Clear the FP number from FR1, locations 224 to 229 ($E0 to $E5), by setting all bytes to zero. Also called AF1 by *De Re Atari.*

55904   DA60   FSUB
FP subtract routine; the value in FR0 minus the value in FR1.

55910   DA66   FADD
FP addition routine; FR0 plus FR1.

56027   DADB   FMUL
FP multiplication routine; FR0 times FR1.

56104   DB28   FDIV
FP division routine; FR0 divided by FR1.

56640   DD40   PLYEVL
FP polynomial evaluation.

56713 **DD89** **FLD0R**
Load the FP number into FR0 from the 6502 X,Y registers.

56717 **DD8D** **FLD0P**
Load the FP number into FR0 from user routine, using FLPTR at 252 ($FC).

56728 **DD98** **FLD1R**
Load the FP number into FR1 from the 6502 X,Y registers.

56732 **DD9C** **FLD1P**
Load the FP number into FR1 from user program, using FLPTR.

56743 **DDA7** **FSTOR**
Store the FP number into the 6502 X,Y registers from FR0.

56747 **DDAB** **FSTOP**
Store the FP number from FR0, using FLPTR.

56758 **DDB6** **FMOVE**
Move the FP number from FR0 to FR1.

56768 **DDC0** **EXP**
FP base e exponentiation.

56780 **DDCC** **EXP10**
FP base 10 exponentiation.

57037 **DECD** **LOG**
FP natural logarithm.

57041 **DED1** **LOG10**
FP base 10 logarithm.

Locations 57344 to 58367 ($E000 to $E3FF) hold the standard Atari character set: at $E000 the special characters, punctuation and numbers begin; at $E100 (57600) the capital letters begin; at $E200 (57856) the special graphics begin, and at $E300 (58112) the lowercase letters begin.

There are 1024 bytes here ($400), with each character requiring eight bytes, for a total of 128 characters (inverse characters simply manipulate the information here to reverse the bits by performing an OR with 128 — the value in location 694 ($2B6) when the Atari logo key is toggled — on the bits. To return to the normal ATASCII display, the inverse characters are EORed with 128). The first half of the memory is for numerals, punctuation, and uppercase characters; the second half ($E200 to $E3FF) is for lowercase and control characters. When you POKE 756 ($2F4) with 224 ($E0), you are POKEing it with the MSB of this address ($E000). When you POKE it with 226 ($E2), you are moving the address pointer to the second half of the character set. In GR.0, you have the entire character set to use. In GR.1 and GR.2, you can use only one half of the set at a time. You can't POKE it with 225 because the number POKEd must be evenly divisible by two.

The characters stored here aren't in ATASCII order; they have their own internal order for storage. The order of the characters is listed on page 55 of your *BASIC Reference Manual.*

Here's an example of how a letter (A) is stored in ROM. Each line represents a byte. The decimal values are those you'd find if you PEEKed the eight locations where "A" is stored (starting at 57608; $E108):

Bit	76543210	Decimal	
	00000000	0	
	00011000	24	##
	00111100	60	####
	01100110	102	## ##
	01100110	102	## ##
	01111110	126	######
	01100110	102	## ##
	00000000	0	

When you create your own character sets (or alter the Atari set when you move it to RAM — see location 756; $2F4 for a routine to do this), you do a "bit-map" for each character as in the example above. It could as easily be a spaceship, a Hebrew letter, an APL character, or a face. Chris Crawford's game *Eastern Front 1941* (APX) shows excellent use of an altered character set to create his large map of Russia, plus the symbols for the armies.

Here's an example of using the bit-mapping of the character set to provide text in GRAPHICS 8:

```
1   GRAPHICS 8
5   DLIST = PEEK(560) + PEEK(561)*256
6   LOBYTE = DLIST+4: HIBYTE = DLIST +
    5
7   REAL = PEEK(LOBYTE) + PEEK(HIBYTE)
    *256: SCREEN = REAL: TV = SCREEN
10  CHBASE = 57344
20  DIM A$(128),BYTE(128),WANT(128)
27  PRINT "INPUT A 40 CHARACTER STRIN
    G: "
30  INPUT A$
35  TIME = TIME + 1
40  FOR LOOK = 1 TO LEN(A$)
50  BYTE(LOOK) = ASC(A$(LOOK,LOOK))
```

```
51  IF BYTE(LOOK) > 127 THEN BYTE(LOO
    K) = BYTE(LOOK) - 128
52  IF BYTE(LOOK) < 32 THEN BYTE(LOOK
    ) = BYTE(LOOK) + 64: GOTO 55
53  IF BYTE(LOOK) < 97 THEN BYTE(LOOK
    ) = BYTE(LOOK) - 32
55  NEXT LOOK
59  FOR EXTRA = 0 TO 7
60  FOR LOOK = 1 TO LEN(A$)
70  WANT(LOOK) = PEEK(CHBASE + EXTRA
    + BYTE(LOOK)*8)
80  POKE TV + EXTRA, WANT(LOOK): TV =
    TV + 1
82  NEXT LOOK
85  SCREEN = SCREEN + 39: TV = SCREEN
90  NEXT EXTRA
100  SCREEN = REAL + TIME*320
110  IF SCREEN > REAL + 6080 THEN TIM
     E = 0: GOTO 100
120  GOTO 30
```

This program simply takes the bytes which represent the letters
you input as A$ and finds their places in the ROM character set.
It then proceeds to POKE the bytes into the screen RAM, using a
FOR-NEXT loop.

To convert ATASCII codes to the internal codes, use this table:

ATASCII value	Operation for internal code
0 — 31	add 64
32 — 95	subtract 32
96 — 127	remains the same
128 — 159	add 64
160 — 223	subtract 32
224 — 255	remains the same

See **COMPUTE!**, November 1981, for the program "TextPlot"
which displays text in different sizes in GRAPHICS modes three
to eight, and January 1982 for a program to edit character sets,
"SuperFont."

Locations 58368 to 58447 ($E400 to $E44F) are the vector tables, stored
as LSB, MSB. These base addresses are used by resident handlers.
Handler vectors use the following format:

OPEN vector
CLOSE vector

145

GET BYTE vector
PUT BYTE vector
GET STATUS vector
SPECIAL vector
Jump to handler initialization routine (JMP LSB/MSB)

The device tables in location 794 ($31A) point to the particular
vector(s) used in each appropriate table. In each case, the 6502 X
register is used to point to the originating IOCB.

58368   E400   EDITRV

Screen Editor (E:) entry point table.

58383   E40F   ....

If you PEEK here and get back 56, then you have the older ''A''
version of the OS ROMs. If you get back zero, then you have the
newer ''B'' version that was released in January 1982. The ''B''
version fixes some minor bugs, including the device time-out
problems, enables POKEY timer four, and provides a vector for
BREAK key interrupts. See Appendix 4.

58384   E410   SCRENV

Display handler (television screen) (S:).

58400   E420   KEYBDV

Keyboard handler (K:).

58416   E430   PRINTV

Printer handler (P:).

58432   E440   CASETV

Cassette handler (C:).

Locations 58448 to 58533 ($E450 to $E4A5) are more vectors: those to
location 58495 ($E47F) are Jump vectors, those from 58496 to 58533
($E480 to $E4A5) are the initial RAM vectors.

58448   E450   DISKIV

Disk handler initialization vector, initialized to 60906 ($EDEA).

58451   E453   DSKINV

Disk handler (interface) entry; checks the disk status. Initialized
to 60912 ($EDF0).

58454   E456   CIOV

Central Input/Output (CIO) utility entry. CIO handles all of the
I/O operations or data transfers. Information placed in the
IOCB's tells CIO what operations are necessary. CIO passes this
information to the correct device driver routine and then passes
control to the Device Control Block (DCB). This in turn calls up

SIO (below) to control the actual peripheral(s). CIO treats all I/O in the same manner: device independent. The differentiation between operations is done by the actual device drivers.

You jump to here to use the IOCB handler routines in ROM. BASIC supports only record I/O or one-byte-at-a-time I/O (GET and PUT). Addressing CIOV directly will allow the user to input or output a buffer of characters at a time, such as loading a machine language program directly into memory from a disk file. This is considerably faster than using BASIC functions such as GET. Here is a typical machine language subroutine to do this:

PLA, PLA, PLA, TAX, JMP $E456
(104,104,104,170,76,86,228)
($68,$68,$68,$AA,$4C,$56,$E4)

This gets the IOCB number into the 6502 X register and the return address on the stack. CIOV expects to find the IOCB number 16 in the 6502 X register (i.e., IOCB zero is zero, IOCB one is 16; $10, IOCB two is 32, $20, etc.). $E456 is the CIO initialization entry point (this address).

To use CIOV in a program, first you must have OPENed a channel for the appropriate actions, POKEd the correct IOCB (locations 848 to 959; $350 to $3BF) with the correct values, and established a location in which to load your file (IOCB address plus four and plus five). One use is calling up a high-res picture from a disk and storing it in the screen memory (locations 88, 89; $58, $59). You can POKE the appropriate decimal values into memory and call it with a USR call, or make it into a string (START$ = "hhh*LVd" where the * and the d are both inverse characters) and call it by:

JUMP = USR(ADR(START$))

This method is used to start the concurrent mode in the RS-232 of the 850 interface in the *850 Interface Manual.* See location 88, 89 ($58, $59) for another example of the machine language routine technique. Still another use of this method can be found in *De Re Atari.* Initialized to 58564 ($E4C4).

58457   E459   SIOV

Serial Input/Output (SIO) utility entry point. SIO drives the serial bus and the peripherals. When a request is placed in the Device Control Block (DCB) by a device handler, SIO takes control and uses the data in the DCB to perform the operation required. SIO takes care of the transfer of data as defined by the DCB. CIO (above) is responsible for the "packaging" of the data and transfers control to SIO when necessary. See the DCB locations 768 to 779 ($300-$30B).

SIO first sends a command frame to the device, consisting of five bytes: the device ID, the command BYTE, two auxiliary bytes for device-specific information, then a checksum (which is the sum of the first four bytes). If the device acknowledges this frame, it is followed, if necessary, by the data frame of a fixed number of bytes depending on the device record size, plus a checksum byte. Initialized to 59737 ($E959).

58460   E45C   SETVBV

Set system timers during the VBLANK routine. Uses the 6502 X register for the MSB of vector/times, Y for the LSB and A for the number of the vector to hack (change). SETVBV insures that both bytes of the vector addressed will be updated while VBLANK is enabled. You can JSR here when creating your own timer routines. See **COMPUTE!**, November 1981, for an application. Initialized to 59666 ($E912) old ROMs, 59629 ($E8ED) new ROMs.

58463   E45F   SYSVBV

Stage one VBLANK calculations entry. It performs the processing of a VBLANK interrupt. Contains JMP instruction for the vector in the next two addresses (58464, 58465; $E460, $E461). This is the address normally found in VVBLKI (546, 547; $222, $223). It is initialized to 59345 ($E7D1), which is the VBLANK routine entry. Initialized to 59345 ($E7D1) old ROMs, 59310 ($E7AE) new ROMs.

58466   E462   XITVBV

Exit from the VBLANK routine, entry point. Contains JMP to the address stored in next two locations (58467, 58468; $E463, $E464). This is the address normally found in VVBLKD (548, 549; $224, $225). Initialized to 59710 ($E93E), which is the VBLANK exit routine. It is used to restore the computer to its pre-interrupt state and to resume normal processing. Initialized to 59710 ($E93E) old ROMs, 59653 ($E905) new ROMs.

58469   E465   SIOINV

SIO utility initialization, OS use only.

58472   E468   SENDEV

Send enable routine, OS use only.

58475   E46B   INTINV

Interrupt handler initialization, OS use only.

58478   E46E   CIOINV

CIO utility initialization, OS use only.

58481   E471   BLKBDV

Blackboard mode entry. Blackboard mode is the "ATARI MEMO

PAD" mode. It can be reached from BASIC by typing "BYE", "B." or by powering up with no peripherals or cartridges. Nothing you write to the screen in blackboard mode is acted upon by the computer. You can enter this mode to protect your programs temporarily from prying and curious fingers.

All of the screen editing commands continue to work in blackboard mode. You can enter blackboard mode from any graphics mode with a text window; the display screen will remain intact on the screen while the text window will be in blackboard mode. Pressing RESET will, of course, return the entire screen to GR.0. You can also enter blackboard mode from a program, but cannot get out of it in BASIC once you are in it.

If you entered blackboard mode from BASIC, you can return to it by pressing RESET. Any BASIC program will still be there. So will any RS-232 or DOS handlers previously booted. Initialized to 61987 ($F223).

58484   E474   WARMSV

Warmstart entry point (RESET button vector). Initializes the OS RAM region. The RESET key produces an NMI interrupt and a chip reset (see below). Jump to here on an NMI caused by pressing the RESET key. Initialized to 61723 ($F11B).

58487   E477   COLDSV

Coldstart (powerup) entry point. Initializes the OS and user RAM regions; wipes out any program in memory. Initialized to 61733 ($F125).

58490   E47A   RBLOKV

Cassette read block routine entry, OS use only.

58493   E47D   CSOPIV

Cassette OPEN for input vector, OS use only.

58496   E480   VCTABL

RAM vector initial value table.

The following are the addresses for the handler routines:

58534-59092 E4A6-E6D4 CIOORG

Addresses for the Central Input/Output routines (CIO):

58534 ($E4A6) CIOINT is the CIO initialization routine called by the monitor on powerup.

58577 ($E4D1); move the user IOCB to the ZIOCB.

58596 ($E4E4); check for a valid command.

58633 ($E509); OPEN command routines.

58675 ($E533); CLOSE command routines.

58702 ($E54E); STATUS and special command routines.

58729 ($E569) CIREAD; process the CIO commands for read and write, including buffer check for full or empty.

58907 ($E61B); routine to return to the user from CIO.

58941 ($E63D); routines to compute the device handler entry point, jump to the handler, transfer control, and then return to CIO after the operation.

59093-59715 E6D5-E943 INTORG

Addresses for the interrupt handler routines:

59123 ($E6F3) PIRQ; IRQ interrupt service routines start here.

59126 ($E6F6); the immediate IRQ vector to the IRQ handler. The global NMI and IRQ RAM vectors in locations 512 to 527 ($200 to $20F) are all initialized to this area (59142, $E706 for the new OS ROMs).

59314 ($E7B2); the vector for the IRQ interrupts on powerup; it points to a PLA and RTI instruction sequence (new OS ROMs; 59219; $E78F).

59316 ($E7B4) PNMI; the NMI handler, tests for the reason for the NMI, then jumps through the appropriate RAM vector. Also called the Interrupt Service Routine (ISR).

59345 ($E7D1) SYSVBL; the VBLANK routines start here, including frame counter, update timer, update hardware registers from shadow registers, update the attract mode counter and the realtime clock. The vertical blank immediate vector, VVBLKL1, normally pointed to by locations 546, 547 ($222, $223), points to here. The Updated OS ROMs point to 59310 ($E7AE).

59666 ($E912) SETVBL; subroutines to set the VBLANK timers and vectors.

The vertical blank deferred interrupt, normally vectored from locations 548, 549 ($224, $225), points to 59710 ($E93E). In the Updated OS ROMs, it points to 59653 ($E905). In both cases they point to the VBLANK exit routine.

See page 104 of the *OS User's Manual* for a list of the vectors and *MICRO*, January 1982, for an explanation of the VBLANK process.

59716-60905 E944-EDE9 SIOORG

Routines for the Serial Input/Output (SIO) routines:

60011 ($EA6B) SEND; is the SIO send buffer routine entry.

60048 ($EA90) ISRODN; is the serial output ready IRQ vector.

60113 ($EAD1) ISRTD; is the serial output complete IRQ vector. This is at 60111 ($EACF) in the new OS ROMs.

60177 ($EB11) ISRSIR; is the serial input ready IRQ vector. This is 60175 ($EB0F) in the new OS ROMs.

60292 ($EB84) CASENT; is the start of the cassette handling code SIO subroutine to set baud rate, tone values, inter-record gap, to load the buffer from the cassette and to turn on the recorder motor. Write routines are located in 61249 to 61666 ($EFF5 to $F0E2).

60515 ($EC63) is the start of the disable POKEY interrupts routine entry, which also disables the send and receive functions.

60583 ($ECA7) COMPUT; is the subroutine to calculate baud rate using the POKEY frequency registers and the VCOUNT timer. The tables for the AUDF and VCOUNT values are between 60882 and 60905 ($EDD2 and $EDE9).

60906-61047 EDEA-EE77 DSKORG
Routines for the disk handler.
Initialization is at DINIT, 60906 ($EDEA), entry is at DSKIF, 60912 ($EDF0).

61048-61248 EE78-EF40 PRNORG
Routines for the printer handler.

61249-61666 EF41-F0E2 CASORG
Routines for the cassette handler.

The buzz used in the cassette CLOAD command can be called up from BASIC by:

BUZZ = USR(61530).

You can turn it off with the RESET key. While this isn't terribly exciting, it points to the potential of using the console speaker for sound instead of merely for beeps (the RAM location for the speaker is at 53279; $D01F). See the speaker location and **COMPUTE!**, August 1981, for a short routine to use the speaker for sound effects.

61667-62435 F0E3-F3E3 MONORG
Routines for the monitor handler. This is also the address area of PWRUP, the powerup module (61733; $F125). Coldstart routines are initialized to this location. The routine to check for cartridge installation begins at 61845 ($F195). Hardware initialization begins at 62081 ($F281).

61723 ($F11B) RESET; the RESET button routine starts here.

62081 ($F281) HARDI; the start of the hardware initialization routines.

62100 ($F294) OSRAM; the start of the OS RAM initialization and setup routines.

62159 ($F2CF) BOOT; the entry point for the disk boot routine.

62189 ($F2ED) DOBOOT; the disk boot routine activation.

62334 ($F37E) DOPEN; the entry point for the reinitialization of disk software.

62436-65535   F3E4-FFFF   KBDORG

Routines for the display and keyboard handler. The display handler begins at 62454 ($F3F6) and the keyboard handler begins at 63197 ($F6DD), below.

63038   F63E   EGETCH

Like the BASIC INPUT command, EGETCH gets a line from the screen and keyboard, but only one character at a time. You must do a JSR $F63E for each character input. This is also the address of the beginning of the screen editor routines.

63140   F6A4   EOUTCH

This routine puts the character currently in the accumulator onto the screen in the next print location. Similar to the BASIC PUT command.

63197   F6DD   KGETC2

Beginning of the keyboard handler.

63202   F6E2   KGETCH

This routine waits for a key to be pressed and returns its value to the accumulator (6502 register A). Similar to the BASIC GET command.

64428   FBAC   SCROLL

The screen scroll routine starts here.

64764   FCFC   DRAW

Screen draw routines begin here, end at 65092 ($FE44). See *Creative Computing*, March 1982, for an example of a modification to the draw routines to avoid the "out-of-bounds" error for use in GR.7 + .

65093-469   FE45-FFBD   ....

The ROM tables for display lists, ANTIC codes, control codes, and ATASCII conversion codes.

65470   FFBE   PIRQQ

Subroutines to test the acceptance of the last key pressed and to process the debounce delay routines start here.

When a key is pressed, it initiates an IRQ through VKEYBD at locations 520, 521 ($208, $209) to 65470 ($FFBE). This is the keyboard service routine. It processes debounce, and SHIFT-CTRL logic (see location 559; $22F); saves the internal keyboard code in 754 ($2F2) and 764 ($2FC); sets the ATTRACT mode flag at 77 ($4D) and sets location 555 ($22B — SRTIMR) to 48 ($30).

65528   FFF8   CHKSUN

According to *Softside Magazine*, December 1981, if a PEEK here returns 255, then you have the older OS ROM(s). There were some troubles with cassette loads in the older ROMs that sometimes require the following to cure:

Do an LPRINT without a printer attached before CLOAD. This clears the cassette buffer.

Press RESET before CSAVEing or CLOADing will restore the system to its initialization parameters and help with loading and saving routines.

There is a new OS available from Atari which fixes a bug that would cause the I/O operations to "time out" for a few seconds. It apparently does not alter any of the routines mentioned here.

The chip reset interrupt (powerup) vectors through location 65532 ($FFFC) to 58487 ($E477) where a JMP vector to the powerup routine is located. A chip reset is not the same as pressing the RESET key, which in itself does not generate a chip reset.

The NMI interrupts are vectored through 65530 ($FFFA) to the NMI service routine (ISR) at 59316 ($E7B4), and all IRQ interrupts are vectored through 65534 ($FFFE) to the IRQ service routine at 59123 ($E6F3). In these service routine areas, the cause of the interrupt is determined, and the appropriate action is taken, either by the OS or through a JMP to a RAM vector where a user routine exists.

APPENDIX ONE

VBLANK Processes

The VBLANK routines are all documented in the OS listings, pages 35 to 38. In the "A" ROMs, they are processed in locations 59345 to 59665 ($E7D1 to $E911). In the "B" ROMs, they are processed at 59310 to 59628 ($E7AE to $E8EC). See also *De Re Atari* for more explanation.

Stage 1 VBLANK:

Performed every VBI:
1) Increment the realtime clock at 18 - 20 ($12-$14)
2) Process the attract mode variables (location 77; $4D)
3) Decrement system timer one at 536 ($218) and if zero JSR through 550 ($226).

Stage 2 VBLANK:

Performed every VBI which does not interrupt critical sections:
1) Update the hardware registers from the shadows as follows:

Shadow:	Hardware:	Update reason:
SDLISTL/H	DLISTL/H	DISPLAY LIST END
SDMCTL	DMACTL	
CHBAS	CHBASE	
CHACT	CHACTL	
GPRIOR	PRIOR	
COLOR0-4	COLPF0-4,BAK	ATTRACT MODE
PCOL0-3	COLPM0-3	
LPCNV/H	PENV/H	LIGHT PEN
STICK0-1	PORTA	JOYSTICKS
PTRIG0-3	PORTA	PADDLE TRIGGERS
STICK2-3	PORTB	
PTRIG4-7	PORTB	
PADDL0-7	POT0-7	PADDLES
STRIG0-3	TRIG0-3	JOYSTICK TRIGGERS
....	CONSOL	CONSOLE SPEAKER OFF

2) System timers two to five (locations 540,542,544; $21C,$21E,$220) are decremented and if the value is zero, the corresponding flags are set. A JSR is made through 552 ($228) if timer two equals zero.
3) A character is read from POKEY keyboard register at 53769 ($D209) and read into CH at 764 ($2FC) if the auto-repeat is active.
4) The keyboard debounce counter is decremented by one if it is not zero and if no key is being pressed.
5) Keyboard auto-repeat logic is processed.
6) Exit the VBLANK routine through 58466 ($E45C).

APPENDIX TWO

A Graphic Memory Map

This diagram is not to scale; it is merely meant to give you a visual idea of the structure of the Atari memory. The numbers on the right are the memory pointers: these locations point to the addresses shown. The numbers on the left are the actual locations in memory.

Location	Contents	Pointers
65535 ____	Top of memory _____	
	Operating System ROM	
60906-65535	Device handler routines	794-831 HATABS
59716-60905	Serial Input/Output (SIO) utilities	
59093-59715	Interrupt handler	512,513 VDSLST
		514-527 Vectors
58534-59092	Central Input/Output (CIO) utilities	
58533 ____	Operating System vectors _____	
58496-58533	Initial RAM vectors on powerup	
58448-58495	JMP vectors	
58432-58447	Cassette	
58416-58431	Printer	
58400-58415	Keyboard	
58384-58399	Screen	
58368-58383	Editor	
58367 ____	ROM Character set _____	756 CHBAS ____
57344		
57343 ____	Floating Point ROM package	
55295 ____	I/O chips _____	
54784-55295	Unused	
54272-54783	ANTIC	756 CHBAS
		755 CH1
		564-565 LPEN
		560-561 SDLSTL
		559 SDMCTL

54016-54271	PIA	636-639	PTRIG#
		632-635	STICK#
53760-54015	POKEY	624-631	PADDL#
		562	SSKCTL
		16	POKMSK
53504-53759	unused		
53248-53503	GTIA or CTIA	704-707	PCOLR#
		708-712	COLOR#
		644-647	STRIG#
		623	GPRIOR

53247 _____ | Unused 4K ROM block _____

49151 _____ | 8K BASIC ROM
or Left cartridge (A) _____

40959 _____ | Top of BASIC RAM or | 106 | RAMTOP

| | | 740 | RAMSIZ |

Right cartridge (B) ROM if present
(Atari 800 only)

**Size and
location
vary with
GRAPHICS
mode**

Text window screen RAM	60,661	TXTMSC
40800 for GR.0		

Bottom of screen RAM	88,89	SAVMSC
40000 for GR.0		

Display List:	560,561	SDLSTL
39968 for GR.0		

Top of BASIC RAM	741,742	MEMTOP

(OS)

32768		
32767 _____	User-program RAM _____	
	The amount of RAM can be ascertained by: PRINT FRE(0)	
(13062)	Bottom varies: see note below Depends on buffer area allocated.	
	RAM used by DOS and File System Manager	
		144,145 MEMTOP
	Stack for FOR-NEXT & GOSUB	142,143 RUNSTK
		14,15 APPMHI
Size and location vary with program size		
	String & array table & end of BASIC program	140,141 STARP
	BASIC program area	
	Statement table:	136,137 STMTAB
	Beginning of BASIC program	
	Variable variable table	134,135 VVTP
	VNTP + 1	132,133 VNTD
	Variable name table	130,131 VNTP
(7420)	BASIC bottom of memory	743,744 MEMLO
		128,129 LOMEM
	Sector buffers	4921,4937 SABUFL/H
6781	Drive & sector buffers	4905,4913 DBUFA1/H
6047	DOS vector	10, 11 DOSVEC
5440	DUP.SYS start	

APPENDIX TWO

5377	VTOC buffer DOS initialization or BASIC RAM without DOS resident FMS RAM	12,13 DOSINI (743,744 MEMLO) (128,129 LOMEM)
1792	DUP.SYS beginning	

1791 _____ RAM used by OS and cartridge.
(to bottom of RAM)

Page six RAM

1535 ____ RAM used by BASIC _____
(to bottom of RAM)

1406 Floating Point RAM
1405 BASIC RAM

1151   Operating System RAM

Cassette buffer

Printer buffer

IOCB's

512

511   Stack

256

255   BASIC zero page RAM

Floating Point pg. 0

Assembler Cart. pg. 0

	128	
	127	OS page zero RAM
		Zero page IOCB
	0	Bottom of memory

Notes

The bottom of the BASIC RAM depends on whether or not you have DOS files loaded in. Without DOS, LOMEM should be 1792, with DOS 7420. If you increase or decrease the number of disk and sector buffers by modifying DOS, this value will change again. See locations 743, 744 and 1801, 1802.

The size and location of the variable, string and array tables depend on the program use and size. The more variables and arrays, the larger the memory the tables use.

The size and address of the Display List and screen memory depend on the GRAPHICS mode in use.

The first 256 bytes pointed to by LOMEM are the token output buffer. The actual BASIC program starts at the address pointed to by VNTP.

APPENDIX THREE

Atari Timing Values

clock frequency = 1.79 MHZ
1 machine cycle = 0.558 μsec.
1 frame   = 1/60 second
scan lines   = 262/frame
color clocks   = 228/scan line
color clocks   = 2/machine cycle
machine cycles = 29868/frame
machine cycles = 114/scan line

VBLANK time = 7980 machine cycles or less, depending on GRAPHICS mode. The shortest 6502 instruction requires two cycles; during that time the electron beam moves four color clocks.

Horizontal blank time:
Wide playfield   18 machine cycles
Normal playfield   34 machine cycles
Narrow playfield   50 machine cycles

See the *Hardware Manual* for more information on cycle counting.

APPENDIX FOUR ━━━━━━━

Old (A) And New (B) ROMS

The new OS ROMs have been mentioned throughout the book. They fixed some of the earlier OS bugs, but also changed a few ROM locations in the process. The result is a better OS, but some of your earlier software which calls up old ROM locations may not work with the new.

There are two ways to test to see if you have the new or old ROMs; one is to PEEK location 58383, as described there. The other (the hardware solution) is to take out your ROM card, unscrew the metal top, and look inside. If the two chips facing you on your left have an "A" after their first code number, you have the earlier ROMs. If they have a "B", lucky you. You have the latest ROMs. There is also the empirical test: if your drive times out during I/O operations, you've got the old ROMs.

Here are the differences between the new and old ROM locations. There are also a number of changes made with the new ROMs to the vectors at locations 512 to 534, 546 to 549 and 550. Refer to those locations and the OS locations for more information. The list below first specifies the old ROM locations, then the changes in the new ROMs.

55296-57343 (FP package)   same

57344-58367 (character set)   same

58368-58477 (vector tables) are the same to 58459 ($E45B) where there are changes in the table between 58460-58466 ($E45C to $E462).

58467-59092 ($E463-$E6D4)   same

59093 ($E6D5) is the start of the IRQ handler. Changes to the new ROMs begin at 59126 ($E6F6) and continue to the end of the new IRQ handler at 59280 ($E790).

59316 ($E7B4) is the NMI interrupt handler in the old ROMs, now starts at 59281 ($E791). It is the same as the old version except moved 35 bytes lower.

59345 ($E7D1) is the start of the VBLANK routines in the old ROMs; they now start at 59310 ($E7AE) in the new ROMs. The routines remain the same until the SETVBL routine is reached at 59666 ($E912) old ROMs, 59629 ($E8ED) new ROMs. The changes to the VBLANK routine are mostly to adjust for the shift in the new memory locations.

58457 ($E459) is the SIO entry point for both versions. There are changes in the SIO routines to accommodate the new memory locations, but the entry point is still the same.

60048 ($EA90) output data needed interrupt service routine is changed, but the entry point is the same in both versions.

60113 ($EAD1) the transmit done interrupt service routine is the same,

APPENDIX FOUR

but has a new entry point at 60111 ($EACF).

60130 ($EAE2) the receive routine has some address changes and is moved to 60128 ($EAE0).

60177 ($EB11) the serial input ready interrupt service routine is the same, but the new entry point is 60175 ($EB0F).

60222 ($EB3E) the SIO subroutines have some changes and a new entry point at 60220 ($EB3C).

60270 ($EB6E) the load buffer subroutine is the same, but moved to 60266 ($EB6A).

60292 to 60905 ($EB84 to $EDE9) all of the routines in this area are the same, but have entry points four bytes lower in ROM (i.e., 60288; $EB80).

60906 to 62014 ($EDEA to $F23E) these routines are the same and at the same locations in both versions.

62015 ($F23F) test for RAM and special cartridge has the same entry point, but has some changes to the routine.

62038 ($F256) RAM check subroutine has changes and a new entry point, now at 62036 ($F254).

62081 ($F281) the hardware initialization routines, have changes and a new entry point at 62071 ($F277) in the new ROMs. The changes continue to 62159 ($F2CF) where everything again becomes the same for both versions until the end of ROM at 65535 ($FFFF).

APPENDIX FIVE ────────────

Color

Color is a very important aspect in the Atari computers; you may not fully appreciate it unless you've spent a long time working with computers or monitors with monochrome displays. The Atari has sixteen colors available for display in eight different luminance (brightness) factors. These colors are stored in memory locations 704 to 712. The first four of these registers are used to determine the color of your players and missiles. The second five determine the color of the playfields, background, lines drawn and areas filled.

The Atari has a default value for each of the five playfield registers that is assigned on powerup:

Playfield	Location	Color	Value
0	708	Orange	40
1	709	Light green	202
2	710	Dark blue	148
3	711	Red	70
4 (BAK)	712	Black	0

The figure in the value category represents the number you would get if you PEEKed into that location. For discussion of the locations, refer to the Memory Map.

To change these colors, you can use either a POKE statement or the BASIC command SETCOLOR (abbreviated to SE). You should refer to the description in the earlier Memory Map text. SETCOLOR has three parameters: the register to change (which always corresponds to one of the memory locations above); the hue (a number from zero to fifteen which corresponds to the available colors); and the luminance (an even number between zero and fourteen). The Atari will treat any odd number as if it were the next lowest even number where luminance is concerned. Your statement might look like this:

SETCOLOR 0,2,8

This will produce the orange color in playfield zero. To change it to red, you would use:

SETCOLOR 0,4,6

Unless you are changing the background or border or you are changing a register which has already been used for drawing on the screen, you won't see any change from using SETCOLOR. The effect comes when you follow up with a COLOR command, telling the Atari which register to use for the DRAWTO or fill command. You can easily POKE the location with the proper color value by using this formula:

COLOR = HUE * 16 + LUMINANCE

So the orange in the above example would be obtained by:

APPENDIX FIVE

POKE 708,40

and the red by:

POKE 708,70

These are the values listed in the chart above. It's quite simple to change them to your own colors using either method. Of course, you'll have to adjust your colors every time you change GRAPHICS modes or press RESET, since both restore the registers to their default values. What's more, the player/missile registers can only be changed using POKE; they have no corresponding SETCOLOR commands and are all preset to zero. The winter 81/82 edition of *The Atari Connection*, the house organ of Atari Inc., had a nice little chart in full color to display all of the colors available. The SETCOLOR number in the following list is the value you would place as the second number in the statement right after the register number.

Color	SETCOLOR number	POKE number
Black	0	0
Rust	1	16
Red-orange	2	32
Dark orange	3	48
Red	4	64
Dark lavender	5	80
Cobalt blue	6	96
Ultramarine blue	7	112
Medium blue	8	128
Dark blue	9	144
Blue-grey	10	166
Olive green	11	176
Medium green	12	192
Dark green	13	208
Orange-green	14	224
Orange	15	240

The next number in the SETCOLOR statement would be the luminance. You would add the luminance value to the POKE number.

When you want to use the DRAWTO or XIO 18 (FILL) commands, you must first specify what color register to use by the COLOR command. The confusing part for most people is that the number in the COLOR command doesn't correspond to the same number as the SETCOLOR register and, to make things worse, it's not always the same number in different GRAPHICS modes! Modes zero, one, and two are text modes; they print characters to the screen rather than graphics, so you don't use the COLOR command in these modes. In GR.0, you actually have only one color as chosen by SETCOLOR 2. The luminance is

ignored in this command and is instead set with SETCOLOR 1 —
where the color is ignored. You can use SETCOLOR to change the
colors of the text and the background as below:

GRAPHICS 0	SETCOLOR	Register
Character luminance	1	709
Background	2	710
Border (BAK)	4	712

GRAPHICS 1 and 2	SETCOLOR	Register
Uppercase and numbers	0	708
Lowercase characters	1	709
Inverse uppercase	2	710
Inverse lowercase	3	711
Background, border	4	712

When you want to draw or fill an area in modes three to eight, you must
use the proper COLOR statement for the SETCOLOR register:

GRAPHICS 3, 5, 7	SETCOLOR	COLOR	Register
Four color modes			
Graphics point or	0	1	708
fill area	1	2	709
	2	3	710
Background, border	4	0	712

GRAPHICS 4, 6	SETCOLOR	COLOR	Register
Two color modes			
Graphics point	0	1	708
Background, border	4	0	712

GRAPHICS 8	SETCOLOR	COLOR	Register
One color, two luminances			
Graphics luminance	1	1	709
Background color	2	0	710
Border	4	—	712

It's awkward, but not difficult to use. You will have to refer to this chart
or the chart on page 53 of your *BASIC Reference Manual* until you get
the hang of it. Remember to precede any COLOR statement with a
SETCOLOR somewhere in your program and to precede a DRAW or
XIO 18 with a COLOR or the computer will use the previously
designated register.

The GTIA chip confuses things somewhat: in GRAPHICS 10, register
704 stores the background color while 712 is used as a normal color
register. This means you must change it with a POKE rather than a
SETCOLOR statement. However, in the two other GTIA modes (GR.9
and GR.11), you still use location 712, SETCOLOR 4, for the
background; see the examples of GTIA modes at location 623.

APPENDIX FIVE

With GRAPHICS 9, the COLOR command is used to set the luminance level to one of sixteen possible values; the value you use with the COLOR statement is equal to the luminance used (so you can have COLOR 15, COLOR 10, etc. Actually you can use any value up to 255 with COLOR and not get an error message; see the demo program for GR.11 in location 623). SETCOLOR 4 defines the background and graphics color. There is only one color in GR.9. In GRAPHICS 11, COLOR is used to define the color the same way it is used for luminance in GR.9, while the luminance of each color is the same value; you can have sixteen colors all of the same luminance. GRAPHICS 10 allows you to set the nine color registers to individual colors and luminances, but you must use POKE commands for the registers 704 to 707.

For more information on the GTIA modes, see **COMPUTE!**, July to September 1982, and *De Re Atari*. There are many good programs for drawing your own pictures in various GRAPHICS modes; *Micropainter* from Datasoft is one of my favorites; then there's *Drawpic* from Artworx, *The Graphics Machine* from Santa Cruz, *Graphic Master* from Datasoft, *Graphics Composer* from Versaware and *The Next Step* from Online which is really a utility for character creation and color set selection. **COMPUTE!** published an interesting program called "Supercube" over many issues in 1980 and 1981.

APPENDIX SIX ⎯⎯⎯⎯

Sound And Music

Sound on the Atari can be quite sophisticated or quite simple, depending on your needs and programming abilities. Simple sounds may be input using the SOUND command; you enter the voice (zero to three), the pitch (zero to 255), the distortion (even numbers from zero to fourteen) and the volume (one to fifteen) in this manner:

SOUND 0,121,10,8

This will give you a pure tone middle C, moderate volume.

The SOUND command is only one way to adjust your music or sound in the Atari. You can also POKE directly into the POKEY registers to effect changes. For example, you can increase the normal five octave range to nine by setting the proper bits in location 53768. This method reduces the number of voices to two or three, but does give you quite a range. You can use all sorts of tricks with filters, clock channels, and poly counters, as described in the POKEY locations. For the best description of sound control technique, see *De Re Atari*.

Here are the pitch values for the major notes when used with a pure tone in the sound command:

Note	Octave 1	2	3	4	5
C	14	29	60	121*	243
B	15	31	64	128	255
A# or Bb	16	33	68	136	
A	17	35	72	144	
G# or Ab	18	37	76	153	
G	19	40	81	162	
F# or Gb	21	42	85	173	
F	22	45	91	182	
E	23	47	96	193	
D# or Eb	24	50	102	204	
D	26	53	108	217	
C# or Db	27	57	114	230	

You can see that the intervals between notes increase as the pitch decreases (the larger the number, the lower the pitch). Middle C is marked with "*". Here's a simple routine to test pitch and distortion with one voice:

```
5    PRINT CHR$(125): POKE 752,2
10   A = 0: B = 0: C = 0
20   SOUND 0,A,B,C: POSITION 0,0
30   PRINT "PITCH", "DISTORTION", "VO
     LUME"
35   POSITION 0,2: PRINT A, B;"    ",,
     C;"   "
```

```
40    IF STICK(0) = 14 THEN A = A + 1:
      IF A > 255 THEN A = 0: GOTO 20
50    IF STICK(0) = 13 THEN A = A - 1:
      IF A < 0 THEN A = 255: GOTO 20
60    IF STICK(0) = 7 THEN B = B + 2:
   IF B > 14 THEN B = 0: GOTO 20
70    IF STICK(0) = 11 THEN B = B - 2:
      IF B < 0 THEN B = 14: GOTO 20
80    IF STRIG(0) = 0 THEN C = C + 1:
      IF C > 15 THEN C = 0: GOTO 20
90    GOTO 20
```

You move the stick up or down to change pitch, right or left to change the distortion level. Press the trigger to change the volume level. See *Softside,* #30 for a similar program using all four voices and Santa Cruz's *Tricky Tutorial #6* (sound). You should also examine Atari's Music Composer cartridge; it is not only a fine program, but it also has excellent documentation on music, sound, and composition. There are two excellent programs from APX, *Sound Editor* and *Insomnia,* both of which allow you to create sounds to include in your programs (not tunes however). *Insomnia* is particularly interesting in that it creates sound which is played during the VBLANK intervals.

APPENDIX SEVEN ▬▬▬▬▬

Player/Missile Graphics Memory Map

You have no doubt seen this little map in dozens of publications. It shows you where your PM graphics are located in memory. The problem is: what does it mean? I'll attempt to explain it below. First, the map:

Double Line Resolution Offset	One byte wide	Single Line Resolution Offset
0	unused area	0
+ 384	0 | 1 | 2 | 3 missiles	+ 768
+ 512	Player 0	+ 1024
+ 640	Player 1	+ 1280
+ 768	Player 2	+ 1536
+ 896	Player 3	+ 1792
+ 1024		+ 2048

No matter where in memory you reserve your PM graphics area, the location of the space used by the players and missiles will be offset the same number of bytes from the beginning of the reserved area. That's what the offset numbers represent: the number of bytes from the beginning of the PM area where that object's graphics begin.

So, if you decide to reserve sixteen pages (4096 bytes) from the top of your memory (40960), your PM graphics will begin at 36864. Depending on which resolution you have chosen, the missile graphics area will begin either 384 or 768 bytes from that location: or at 37248 and 37632 respectively. In double line resolution, you can define your objects up to 128 bytes in length; in single line they can be 256 bytes long.

Even if your object is only eight or ten bytes in height, the boundaries for their placement are always the same relative offset from the top of PM graphics memory.

APPENDIX SEVEN

This map is only eight bits — one byte — wide. You can see that all four missiles share the same width byte, each using two bits for resolution. If you combine the missiles to form a fifth player, you use this area exactly as you would the area for any other player.

One means of moving your players vertically is to move the players within their reserved area rather than on the screen itself. In BASIC, this is considerably faster than having to move the player on the screen, but it's a slow process anyway. As far as the boundaries of the TV set are concerned, all players in both resolutions are mapped to the entire height of the screen.

There are many good programs to create and edit PM graphics, mentioned earlier in the Memory Map text. PM graphics are one of the Atari's most powerful and least understood capabilities. I suggest you read up on them and try to master their use; they're not as difficult as they seem.

APPENDIX EIGHT _____

Display Lists

A display list is a short program for the ANTIC chip, telling it how to display data on the screen. This program includes such instructions as how many blank lines to place on the screen for top boundaries, where the screen display data is stored, what mode the line(s) to be displayed are in, whether or not there is an interrupt to execute and where to find the display list itself.

There are nine pre-programmed display lists (ten with the GTIA) you use in BASIC, one for each GRAPHICS mode. You can examine the display lists for each mode by running the program at location 560. You can change these lists to suit your own needs without much effort. It is quite easy to design and implement your own display list once you know where it's located and what the proper instructions are.

Certain techniques, such as horizontal and vertical fine scrolling, require that you modify the display list in order to properly display your screen data. Sometimes you want to be able to display data in more than one mode or mix graphics and text in the same screen. These are all done by modifying the display list.

The smallest display list is for GRAPHICS 2, so I'll use it as an example. It consists of a mere twenty odd bytes, but the format is the same for every list; it's just the instructions that change. Use the program listed in the Memory Map to examine the list or use a simple two-liner such as:

```
10    GRAPHICS 2: P = PEEK(560) + PEEK
      (561) * 256
20    FOR N = 0 TO 23: PRINT PEEK(P +
      N);" ";: NEXT N
```

When you RUN this example, you should get this:

```
112  112  112  71  112  158  7  7  7  7  7  7  7  7  7  66
96  159  2  2  2  65  88  158
```

Or something similar depending on your available memory. If you change the GR.2 to GR.2 + 16, you will get:

```
112  112  112  71  112  158  7  7  7  7  7  7  7  7  7  7
65  92  158
```

The display list instruction set is discussed at location 560, but here's a chart to summarize it:

Instruction Decimal	Hex	BASIC mode	Scan lines	Pixels line	Bytes line	Comments
						Blank instructions
0	0	—	1	—	—	1 blank line
16	10	—	2	—	—	2 blank lines
32	20	—	3	—	—	3 blank lines

48	30	—	4	—	—	4 blank lines
64	40	—	5	—	—	5 blank lines
80	50	—	6	—	—	6 blank lines
96	60	—	7	—	—	7 blank lines
112	70	—	8	—	—	8 blank lines
						Display instructions
2	2	0	8	40	40	text mode 0
3	3	—	10	40	40	text mode *
4	4	—	8	40	40	text mode *
5	5	—	16	40	40	text mode *
6	6	1	8	20	20	text mode 1
7	7	2	16	20	20	text mode 2
8	8	3	8	40	10	graphics mode 3
9	9	4	4	80	10	graphics mode 4
10	A	5	4	80	20	graphics mode 5
11	B	6	2	160	20	graphics mode 6
12	C	—	1	160	20	graphics mode *
13	D	7	2	160	40	graphics mode 7
14	E	—	1	160	40	graphics mode *
15	F	8	1	320	40	graphics mode 8
						Jump instructions (three bytes long)
1	1	—	—	—	—	jump to location
65	41	—	—	—	—	jump and wait for VBLANK

Modes marked with an asterisk (*) have no equivalent in BASIC. These are the instructions in the display list. You can alter the display instructions by setting the bits for horizontal or vertical scroll, load memory scan (tells ANTIC where the next line(s) to be displayed are in memory and what mode to use for them) and enable a display list interrupt. These are:

Function	add decimal	hex	bit
Vertical scroll	16	10	4
Horizontal scroll	32	20	5
Load memory scan	64	40	6
Display list interrupt	128	80	7

The LMS instruction is a three-byte instruction; the second and third bytes are the LSB and MSB of the address where the line or screen data is to be displayed. You can add any or all of these modifications to the text or graphics mode instructions. You can only add the interrupt modification to blank line or jump instructions. The two bytes that follow the jump instructions are the LSB and MSB of the address to which the ANTIC jumps to continue or repeat the list.

So let's analyze the DL for GRAPHICS 2 that we printed above:

112	These three instructions print
112	24 blank scan lines at the top
112	of the screen
71	GR.2 with LMS instruction added
112	Address of the first line of screen data
158	158 * 256 + 112 = 40560
7	Display the rest of the data in
7	GR. 2, so we have a total of
7	ten GR.2 lines, or 10 * 16 =
7	160 scan lines used.
7	
7	
7	
7	
7	
66	GR.0 with LMS instruction added
96	Address of the text window at bottom
159	159 * 256 + 96 = 40800
2	GR.0 for text window, so we have
2	a total of four lines
2	
65	Jump and wait for vertical blank
88	Address of display list itself
158	158 * 256 + 88 = 40536
	(return to the top of this list)

Now examine the list for GR.2 + 16. You can see that it adds two 7's to replace the GR.0 lines at the bottom of the screen. A little math shows us that the screen in both cases has a total of 192 scan lines. That's an important number; if you want your screen to come out properly, you must insure that you get as close to this figure as possible; otherwise you'll end up with blank lines at the bottom of your screen, or worse — in the display itself.

You will find the value 112 in every Atari display list. The three of them are used to bring the display to a readable location on your set. Try replacing one or more of them with a zero to see what happens without them. The jump instructions are also used to skip across a 1K boundary, since the DL itself cannot cross a 1K boundary without such a jump. Also, DL data cannot cross a 4K boundary, so you must use an LMS instruction before crossing one.

The critical factor in designing your own display list is to make sure that the data and the scan lines match. This may require you to manipulate your data so that you have the proper number of bytes per line so that the display appears correctly on the screen. Here are the

APPENDIX EIGHT

number of bits per pixel for each of the ANTIC modes:

Mode decimal	hex	BASIC	Bits per pixel	
2	2	0	8	text modes
3	3	—	8	
4	4	—	8	
5	5	—	8	
6	6	1	8	
7	7	2	8	
8	8	3	2	graphics modes
9	9	4	1	
10	A	5	2	
11	B	6	1	
12	C	—	1	
13	D	7	2	
14	E	—	2	
15	F	8	1	

You can have as many DL's as you wish, using the jump/vertical blank instruction at the end of the DL to tell ANTIC where your new DL is located. When placing your new DL (page six, unless used for other routines, is a good protected place to put it), do a POKE 559,0 to disable the DL fetch instructions, then POKE it with the proper value to turn it back on afterwards. Be inventive and create your own screens with varied lines of text and graphics.

I suggest that you read *De Re Atari* and *Your Atari 400/800* for more information. The latter has a few good examples of altered display lists and tells how to create them. Two DL utilities are *The Next Step* from Online and *Tricky Tutorial #1* from Santa Cruz.

APPENDIX NINE

Numerical Conversions

If you use this map a lot, or use the Atari a lot for machine language routines, interrupts, graphics and the like, you know the need to translate between decimal and hexadecimal, even back and forth with binary, frequently. It is possible, although tedious, to do your translations by hand, using pencil and paper. The tables for doing so are below. It's not the best nor the fastest method available. I recommend you get the Texas Instruments TI Programmer calculator. It does most of this work for you, plus bit manipulation (unfortunately it does not offer binary translation). It's an indispensable tool for programmers.

There are other ways around buying the calculator: you can buy *Monkey Wrench* from Eastern House Software, which will do the hex - decimal translations for you quite nicely. Or you can buy any of the numerous disk or programming utilities which include such translation routines, such as *Disk Scan* from Micro Media. However, those who wish to do the work themselves can use a simple translator program. One such example, modified from routines that appeared separately in **COMPUTE!**, November 1981 and March 1982, is:

```
10  DIM HEX$(16),DEC$(23),NUM$(10),W$(
    4),BIN$(8),BNY$(8),TRANS(8)
15  DATA 128,64,32,16,8,4,2,1
20  FOR N=1 TO 8:READ B:TRANS(N)=B:NEX
    T N:POKE 201,14
25  PRINT CHR$(125)
30  HEX$="0123456789ABCDEF":DEC$="@ABC
    DEFGHI!!!!!!!!JKLMNO"
40  ?:?"PRESS OPTION FOR HEXADECIMAL":
    ?"(6 SPACES)SELECT FOR DECIMAL":?"
    (6 SPACES)START  FOR BINARY"
42  ?"(6 SPACES)TRANSLATIONS":A=1:MAX=
    4096
50  IF PEEK(53279)=3 THEN GOTO 100
60  IF PEEK(53279)=5 THEN GOTO 200
70  IF PEEK(53279)=6 THEN GOTO 300
80  GOTO 50
100 ? : ?"ENTER HEXADECIMAL NUMBER":?
    "$0000 TO $FFFF": INPUT NUM$:ACC=
    0:A=1:TRAP 100
120 FOR NUM=1 TO LEN(NUM$):ACC=ACC*16
    +ASC(DEC$(ASC(NUM$(NUM))-47))-64:
    NEXT NUM:T=ACC
```

```
125  IF ACC>255 THEN BYN$=".........":G
     OTO 170
130  FOR N=7 TO 0 STEP-1:BIN=2^N
135  IF INT(ACC/BIN)=1 THEN BNY$(A,A)=
     "1":ACC=ACC-BIN:GOTO 150
140  BNY$(A,A)="0"
150  A=A+1:NEXT N
170  ? :?"HEXADECIMAL","DECIMAL","BINA
     RY"
180  ? "  ";NUM$,T,BNY$
190  ? :? : GOTO 40
200  ? :? "ENTER DECIMAL NUMBER": ?"O
     TO 65535": INPUT NUM:T=NUM:Z=T:MA
     X=4096:TRAP 200
205  IF NUM>65535 THEN GOTO 200
208  IF NUM<1 THEN GOTO 200
210  FOR N=1 TO 4:BYTE=INT(NUM/MAX):W$
     (N,N)=HEX$(BYTE+1,BYTE+1):NUM=NUM
     -MAX*BYTE:MAX=MAX/16:NEXT N
220  IF T>255 THEN BNY$=".........":GOT
     O 270
230  FOR N=7 TO 0 STEP -1:BIN=2^N
235  IF INT(Z/BIN)=1 THEN BNY$(A,A)="1
     ":Z=Z-BIN:GOTO 250
240  BNY$(A,A)="0"
250  A=A+1:NEXT N
270  ?:?"DECIMAL","HEXADECIMAL","BINAR
     Y"
280  ? "  ";T,W$,BNY$
290  GOTO 40
300  ? :? "INPUT BINARY NUMBER":?"0000
     0000 TO 11111111":? :?"76543210 B
     ITS":INPUT BIN$:TRAP 300
305  IF LEN(BIN$)<>8 THEN GOTO 300
308  FOR B=1 TO 8:IF VAL(BIN$(B,B))>1
     THEN POP:GOTO 300
310  NEXT B
320  FOR B=1 TO 8:IF BIN$(B,B)="1" THE
     N TOT=TOT+TRANS(B)
325  NEXT B: Q=TOT
330  FOR L=1 TO 4:BYTE=INT(TOT/MAX):W$
     (L,L)=HEX$(BYTE+1,BYTE+1):TOT=TOT
```

```
     -MAX*BYTE:MAX=MAX/16:NEXT L
340  ?:?"BINARY","HEXADECIMAL","DECIMA
     L"
350  ?  "  ";BIN$,W$,Q
390  GOTO 40
```

This program will translate any hexadecimal, decimal, and binary number to and from the others. There are some constraints in its use: it will not translate a binary number for any hex number larger than $FF or decimal number larger than 255. It will not translate any hex number larger than $FFFF or any decimal number larger than 65535. Since about 99% of your numeric manipulations will be within these ranges, you should have no problems. You can easily remove the translation routines from the program for use in your own utility.

For a quick way to translate any number in the range of zero to 65535 ($FFFF), use the table below. It's quite simple to use: to translate hex to decimal you take the number that appears in the column that corresponds to the value in the proper row and add the values together. The total is your decimal number. For example:

```
$7AC1 = 28672   fourth column, 7
         2560    third column, A
          192  second column, C
            1    first column, 1
        31425    decimal value
```

To translate decimal into hex, you find the largest number less than the number you wish to translate and subtract it from your original number. The value in the row is the first hexadecimal value. You then do the same with the remainder until your result is zero. The values in the row are then concatenated together for a hexadecimal number. For example:

```
31425 = 31425
      - 28672 largest number, column four. first hex number = 7
         2753 remainder, minus third column
         2560 second hex number = A
          193 remainder, minus second column
          192 third hex number = C
            1 remainder and fourth hex number
Hexadecimal value = $7AC1
```

Hex number	Column				Hex number
	fourth	third	second	first	
1	4096	256	16	1	1
2	8192	512	32	2	2
3	12288	768	48	3	3

APPENDIX NINE

4	16384	1024	64	4	4
5	20480	1280	80	5	5
6	24576	1536	96	6	6
7	28672	1792	112	7	7
8	32768	2048	128	8	8
9	36864	2304	144	9	9
A	40960	2560	160	10	A
B	45056	2816	176	11	B
C	49152	3072	192	12	C
D	53248	3328	208	13	D
E	57344	3584	224	14	E
F	61440	3840	240	15	F

The next few pages are simply a listing of the decimal, hex, and binary values for the range of numbers between zero and 255. I have found this listing to be extremely useful when I couldn't enter a translator program or lay my hands on a calculator. Read the note in the introduction regarding the translation techniques for binary and hexadecimal.

Decimal	Hex	Binary	Decimal	Hex	Binary	Decimal	Hex	Binary
0	0	00000000	34	22	00100010	68	44	01000100
1	1	00000001	35	23	00100011	69	45	01000101
2	2	00000010	36	24	00100100	70	46	01000110
3	3	00000011	37	25	00100101	71	47	01000111
4	4	00000100	38	26	00100110	72	48	01001000
5	5	00000101	39	27	00100111	73	49	01001001
6	6	00000110	40	28	00101000	74	4A	01001010
7	7	00000111	41	29	00101001	75	4B	01001011
8	8	00001000	42	2A	00101010	76	4C	01001100
9	9	00001001	43	2B	00101011	77	4D	01001101
10	A	00001010	44	2C	00101100	78	4E	01001110
11	B	00001011	45	2D	00101101	79	4F	01001111
12	C	00001100	46	2E	00101110	80	50	01010000
13	D	00001101	47	2F	00101111	81	51	01010001
14	E	00001110	48	30	00110000	82	52	01010010
15	F	00001111	49	31	00110001	83	53	01010011
16	10	00010000	50	32	00110010	84	54	01010100
17	11	00010001	51	33	00110011	85	55	01010101
18	12	00010010	52	34	00110100	86	56	01010110
19	13	00010011	53	35	00110101	87	57	01010111
20	14	00010100	54	36	00110110	88	58	01011000
21	15	00010101	55	37	00110111	89	59	01011001
22	16	00010110	56	38	00111000	90	5A	01011010
23	17	00010111	57	39	00111001	91	5B	01011011
24	18	00011000	58	3A	00111010	92	5C	01011100
25	19	00011001	59	3B	00111011	93	5D	01011101
26	1A	00011010	60	3C	00111100	94	5E	01011110
27	1B	00011011	61	3D	00111101	95	5F	01011111
28	1C	00011100	62	3E	00111110	96	60	01100000
29	1D	00011101	63	3F	00111111	97	61	01100001
30	1E	00011110	64	40	01000000	98	62	01100010
31	1F	00011111	65	41	01000001	99	63	01100011
32	20	00100000	66	42	01000010	100	64	01100100
33	21	00100001	67	43	01000011	101	65	01100101

Decimal	Hex	Binary	Decimal	Hex	Binary	Decimal	Hex	Binary
102	66	01100110	163	A3	10100011	224	E0	11100000
103	67	01100111	164	A4	10100100	225	E1	11100001
104	68	01101000	165	A5	10100101	226	E2	11100010
105	69	01101001	166	A6	10100110	227	E3	11100011
106	6A	01101010	167	A7	10100111	228	E4	11100100
107	6B	01101011	168	A8	10101000	229	E5	11100101
108	6C	01101100	169	A9	10101001	230	E6	11100110
109	6D	01101101	170	AA	10101010	231	E7	11100111
110	6E	01101110	171	AB	10101011	232	E8	11101000
111	6F	01101111	172	AC	10101100	233	E9	11101001
112	70	01110000	173	AD	10101101	234	EA	11101010
113	71	01110001	174	AE	10101110	235	EB	11101011
114	72	01110010	175	AF	10101111	236	EC	11101100
115	73	01110011	176	B0	10110000	237	ED	11101101
116	74	01110100	177	B1	10110001	238	EE	11101110
117	75	01110101	178	B2	10110010	239	EF	11101111
118	76	01110110	179	B3	10110011	240	F0	11110000
119	77	01110111	180	B4	10110100	241	F1	11110001
120	78	01111000	181	B5	10110101	242	F2	11110010
121	79	01111001	182	B6	10110110	243	F3	11110011
122	7A	01111010	183	B7	10110111	244	F4	11110100
123	7B	01111011	184	B8	10111000	245	F5	11110101
124	7C	01111100	185	B9	10111001	246	F6	11110110
125	7D	01111101	186	BA	10111010	247	F7	11110111
126	7E	01111110	187	BB	10111011	248	F8	11111000
127	7F	01111111	188	BC	10111100	249	F9	11111001
128	80	10000000	189	BD	10111101	250	FA	11111010
129	81	10000001	190	BE	10111110	251	FB	11111011
130	82	10000010	191	BF	10111111	252	FC	11111100
131	83	10000011	192	C0	11000000	253	FD	11111101
132	84	10000100	193	C1	11000001	254	FE	11111110
133	85	10000101	194	C2	11000010	255	FF	11111111
134	86	10000110	195	C3	11000011			
135	87	10000111	196	C4	11000100			
136	88	10001000	197	C5	11000101			
137	89	10001001	198	C6	11000110			
138	8A	10001010	199	C7	11000111			
139	8B	10001011	200	C8	11001000			
140	8C	10001100	201	C9	11001001			
141	8D	10001101	202	CA	11001010			
142	8E	10001110	203	CB	11001011			
143	8F	10001111	204	CC	11001100			
144	90	10010000	205	CD	11001101			
145	91	10010001	206	CE	11001110			
146	92	10010010	207	CF	11001111			
147	93	10010011	208	D0	11010000			
148	94	10010100	209	D1	11010001			
149	95	10010101	210	D2	11010010			
150	96	10010110	211	D3	11010011			
151	97	10010111	212	D4	11010100			
152	98	10011000	213	D5	11010101			
153	99	10011001	214	D6	11010110			
154	9A	10011010	215	D7	11010111			
155	9B	10011011	216	D8	11011000			
156	9C	10011100	217	D9	11011001			
157	9D	10011101	218	DA	11011010			
158	9E	10011110	219	DB	11011011			
159	9F	10011111	220	DC	11011100			
160	A0	10100000	221	DD	11011101			
161	A1	10100001	222	DE	11011110			
162	A2	10100010	223	DF	11011111			

APPENDIX TEN

ATASCII And Internal Character Code Values

Character	ATASCII	Internal	Character	ATASCII	Internal
space	32	0	Z	90	58
!	33	1	[	91	59
"	34	2	\	92	60
#	35	3	]	93	61
$	36	4	^	94	62
%	37	5	_	95	63
&	38	6	CTRL — ,	0	64
'	39	7	CTRL — A	1	65
(	40	8	CTRL — B	2	66
)	41	9	CTRL — C	3	67
*	42	10	CTRL — D	4	68
+	43	11	CTRL — E	5	69
,	44	12	CTRL — F	6	70
–	45	13	CTRL — G	7	71
.	46	14	CTRL — H	8	72
/	47	15	CTRL — I	9	73
0	48	16	CTRL — J	10	74
1	49	17	CTRL — K	11	75
2	50	18	CTRL — L	12	76
3	51	19	CTRL — M	13	77
4	52	20	CTRL — N	14	78
5	53	21	CTRL — O	15	79
6	54	22	CTRL — P	16	80
7	55	23	CTRL — Q	17	81
8	56	24	CTRL — R	18	82
9	57	25	CTRL — S	19	83
:	58	26	CTRL — T	20	84
;	59	27	CTRL — U	21	85
<	60	28	CTRL — V	22	86
=	61	29	CTRL — W	23	87
>	62	30	CTRL — X	24	88
?	63	31	CTRL — Y	25	89
@	64	32	CTRL — Z	26	90
A	65	33	ESCAPE	27	91
B	66	34	UP ARROW	28	92
C	67	35	DOWN ARROW	29	93
D	68	36	LEFT ARROW	30	94
E	69	37	RIGHT ARROW	31	95
F	70	38	CTRL — .	96	96
G	71	39	a	97	97
H	72	40	b	98	98
I	73	41	c	99	99
J	74	42	d	100	100
K	75	43	e	101	101
L	76	44	f	102	102
M	77	45	g	103	103
N	78	46	h	104	104
O	79	47	i	105	105
P	80	48	j	106	106
Q	81	49	k	107	107
R	82	50	l	108	108
S	83	51	m	109	109
T	84	52	n	110	110
U	85	53	o	111	111
V	86	54	p	112	112
W	87	55	q	113	113
X	88	56	r	114	114
Y	89	57			

Character	ATASCII	Internal
s	115	115
t	116	116
u	117	117
v	118	118
w	119	119
x	120	120
y	121	121
z	122	122
CTRL — ;	123	123
|	124	124
CLEAR	125	125
DELETE	126	126
TAB	127	127

Inverse characters are the same as the characters above with 128 added to the values listed. This is done by setting the seventh bit (adding 128).

There are other codes used which are outside this range:

ATASCII	Function
155	End Of Line (Return)
156	Delete line
157	Insert line
158	CTRL — Tab
159	Shift — Tab
253	CTRL — 2 (buzzer)
254	Delete character
255	Insert character

See your *Atari Reference Manual,* pages C1 to C3 and F1. In order to print the arrow keys, clear, insert, delete, buzzer, escape key, or any of the codes listed above to the screen, you must press the ESC key before entering the keyboard character(s).

Not all of these codes can be sent to the printer. ATASCII codes zero to 31 print blank or they may send control codes to your printer, depending on the make. 96 will print a backwards apostrophe instead of a diamond, 123 will print a left bracket instead of a spade, 125 will print a right bracket instead of a clear, 126 will print a tildis instead of a backspace and 127 will print a blank instead of tab.

There is a third set of codes used by the Atari keyboard handler. These values are listed in the *OS User's Manual.*

INDEX BY LABEL

This is an index of the labels used to identify the various memory locations, registers, subroutines, and vectors in the Atari. *The references are to decimal memory locations,* not to page numbers. For an index by subject, see the next index section.

Label	Location	Label	Location
ADDCOR	782	CASSBT	75
ADRESS	100, 101	CAUX1	572
AF1	55878	CAUX2	573
AFP	55296	CBAUDL/H	750, 751
ALLPOT	53768	CCOMND	571
ANTIC	54272 - 54783	CDEVIC	570
APPMHI	14, 15	CDTMA1	550, 551
ARGOPS	128, 129	CDTMA2	552, 553
ATACHR	763	CDTMF3	554
ATAN	48759	CDTMF4	556
ATRACT	77	CDTMF5	558
AUDC1	53761	CDTMV1	536, 537
AUDC2	53763	CDTMV2	538, 539
AUDC3	53765	CDTMV3	540, 541
AUDC4	53767	CDTMV4	542, 543
AUDCTL	53768	CDTMV5	544, 545
AUDF1	53760	CFB	570 - 573
AUDF2	53762	CH	764
AUDF3	53764	CH1	754
AUDF4	53766	CHACT	755
BFENLO/HI	52, 53	CHACTL	54273
BFLAG	1792	CHAR	762
BITMSK	110	CHARSET	57344 - 58367
BIWTARR	1796, 1797	CHBAS	756
BLDADR	1794, 1795	CHBASE	54281
BLDISP	1809	CHKSNT	59
BLIM	650	CHKSUM	49
BLKBDV	58481	CHKSUN	65528
BOOT	62159	CIOINT	58534
BOOT?	9	CIOINV	58478
BOOTAD	578, 579	CIOORG	58434 - 59092
BOTSCR	703	CIOV	58454
BPTR	61	CIREAD	58729
BRCNT	1793	CIRTN	58907
BRKKEY	17	CIX	242
BRKKY	566, 567	CKEY	74
BRUN	10060	CLMJMP	6418
BSIO	1900	COLAC	114, 115
BSIOR	1906	COLBK	53274
BUFADR	21, 22	COLCRS	85, 86
BUFCNT	107	COLDST	580
BUFRFL	56	COLDSV	58487
BUFRLO/HI	50, 51	COLINC	122
BUFSTR	108, 109	COLOR 0-4	708 - 712
CART A	40960 - 49151	COLPF 0-3	53270 - 53273
CART B	32768 - 40959	COLPM 0-3	53266 - 53269
CARTRIDGES	32768 - 49151	COLRSH	79
CASBUF	1021 - 1151	COMENT	58941
CASENT	60292	COMPUT	60583
CASETV	58432	CONSOL	53279
CASFLG	783	COS	48561
CASINI	2, 3	COUNTR	126, 127
CASORG	61249 - 61666	CPYFIL	9080

182

INDEX BY LABEL

INDEX BY LABEL

INDEX BY LABEL

INDEX BY SUBJECT ▬▬▬▬

This is an index by subject. *The references are to decimal memory locations,* not to page numbers. For an index to the location and routine labels, see the previous index.

INDEX BY SUBJECT

INDEX BY SUBJECT

INDEX BY SUBJECT

If you've enjoyed the articles in this book, you'll find the same style and quality in every monthly issue of **COMPUTE!** Magazine. Use this form to order your subscription to **COMPUTE!**

For Fastest Service,
Call Our **Toll-Free** US Order Line
800-334-0868
In NC call 919-275-9809

COMPUTE!
P.O. Box 5406
Greensboro, NC 27403

My Computer Is:
☐ PET ☐ Apple ☐ Atari ☐ VIC ☐ Other _____ ☐ Don't yet have one...

☐ $20.00 One Year US Subscription
☐ $36.00 Two Year US Subscription
☐ $54.00 Three Year US Subscription
Subscription rates outside the US:
☐ $25.00 Canada   F=2
☐ $38.00 Europe/Air Delivery   FI=3
☐ $48.00 Middle East, North Africa, Central America/Air Mail   FI=5
☐ $88.00 South America, South Africa, Australasia/Air Mail   FI=7
☐ $25.00 International Surface Mail (lengthy, unreliable delivery)   FI=4,6,8

Name _____

Address _____

City _____ State _____ Zip _____

Country _____

Payment must be in US Funds drawn on a US Bank; International Money Order, or charge card.
☐ Payment Enclosed   ☐ VISA
☐ MasterCard   ☐ American Express
Acc't. No. _____ Expires _____ /_____

09-4